M000284501

Adopted into God's family

Titles in this series:

NEW STUDIES IN BIBLICAL THEOLOGY 22

Series editor: D. A. Carson

Adopted into God's family

EXPLORING A PAULINE METAPHOR

Trevor J. Burke

APOLLOS

INTERVARSITY PRESS
DOWNERS GROVE, ILLINOIS 60515

InterVarsity Press, USA
P.O. Box 1400,
Downers Grove, IL 60515-1426, USA
World Wide Web: www.ivpress.com
Email: email@ivpress.com

APOLLOS (an imprint of Inter-Varsity Press,
England) Norton Street,
Nottingham NG7 3HR, England
Website: www.ivpbooks.com
Email: ivp@ivpbooks.com

InterVarsity Press®, USA, is the book-publishing division of InterVarsity Christian Fellowship/USA® <www.intervarsity.org> and a member movement of the International Fellowship of Evangelical Students.

Inter-Varsity Press, England, is closely linked with the Universities and Colleges Christian Fellowship, a student movement connecting Christian Unions throughout Great Britain, and a member movement of the International Fellowship of Evangelical Students. Website: www.uccf.org.uk

All Scripture quotations, unless otherwise indicated, are taken from the Holy Bible, New International Version®. NIV®. Copyright © 1973, 1978, 1984 by International Bible Society. Used by permission of Zondervan Publishing House. Distributed in the U.K. by permission of Hodder and Stoughton Ltd. All rights reserved. "NIV" is a registered trademark of International Bible Society. UK trademark number 1448790.

Scripture quotations from the Revised English Bible are ©Oxford University Press and Cambridge University Press 1989.

Chapter 7 is a revision of "Adoption and the Spirit in Romans 8," Evangelical Quarterly, 70.4 (1998): 311-24, used with permission.

First published 2006

USA ISBN 978-0-8308-2623-0
UK ISBN 978-1-84474-146-5

Set in Monotype Times New Roman
Typeset in Great Britain by CRB Associates, Reepham, Norfolk

Printed in the United States of America ∞

Library of Congress Cataloging-in-Publication Data
A catalog record for this book is available from the Library of Congress.

British Library Cataloguing in Publication Data
A catalogue record for this book is available from the British Library.

P   23   22   21   20   19   18   17   16   15   14   13   12   11   10   9   8   7

Y   28   27   26   25   24   23   22   21   20   19   18   17   16   15   14

To the memory of Ken Burke
22 December 1925 – 24 October 2002
and in gratitude to Dick Dunlop
9 December 1917–

Contents

Series preface

New Studies in Biblical Theology is a series of monographs that
address key issues in the discipline of biblical theology. Contributions
to the series focus on one or more of three areas: 1. the nature and
status of biblical theology, including its relations with other disciplines
(e.g. historical theology, exegesis, systematic theology, historical
criticism, narrative theology); 2. the articulation and exposition of
the structure of thought of a particular biblical writer or corpus;
and 3. the delineation of a biblical theme across all or part of the
biblical corpora.

Above all, these monographs are creative attempts to help thinking
Christians understand their Bibles better. The series aims simultaneously to instruct and to edify, to interact with the current literature,
and to point the way ahead. In God's universe, mind and heart
should not be divorced: in this series we shall try not to separate what
God has joined. While the notes interact with the best of scholarly
literature, the text is uncluttered with untransliterated Greek and
Hebrew, and tries to avoid too much technical jargon. The volumes
are written within the framework of confessional evangelicalism, but
there is always an attempt at thoughtful engagement with the sweep
of the relevant literature.

While some of the volumes in this series have offered fresh insight
into biblical themes commonly studied in almost every generation,
this contribution from Dr Burke offers a fresh and probing look at a
strand often overlooked and sometimes misunderstood. Christians
who read the writings of Paul soon become familiar with terms such as
justification, sanctification, reconciliation, redemption, and election.
They soon learn, too, that they are children of God – or 'sons of God',
as a more pedantic rendering puts it. But what additional theological
weight is carried by the five passages where Paul tells believers that
they have been *adopted* as sons? Or even, as one passage puts it,
that they *will* be adopted as sons at the last day? Such questions must
be addressed not only by understanding the sociolegal customs of

11

Paul's day (in other words, the questions have an historical dimension), but also by examining in some detail how this adoption terminology is carefully integrated into a variety of theological categories. Not only the importance of God's family but also the enormous privilege of belonging to it are powerfully underscored by Paul's understanding of what it means to be the adopted sons of God. With such themes in view, a wide array of pastoral implications soon springs to light. In other words, this volume not only probes a neglected theme – it also edifies.

D. A. Carson
Trinity Evangelical Divinity School

Author's preface

This book was written on the move. I started to write it while teaching in the South Pacific, and completed it when I moved to a new post in North America. The bulk of the book, however, was written while on sabbatical in Belfast, Northern Ireland, during the academic year of 2003–4.

My fascination with Paul's family terms in general and adoption in particular began in Nigeria,West Africa, where I was a missionary lecturer in New Testament in a theological seminary. Because my students did not have many theological books (a Bible, one-volume commentary and theological book were their only library), I sought to have my lecture notes printed for them to use. One of my first handouts, 'Doctrines in Romans Simply Explained', featured adoption.

Teaching a class on Romans exegesis also coincided with one of the highlights of our married life: the birth of our first son, Luke, and my awakening to the joys (and rather early starts!) of fatherhood, which sharpened my interest and study of adoption.

I owe a huge debt to many people who have helped in one way or another in the writing of this book. I am especially grateful to Professor D. A. Carson for the invitation and privilege of contributing to this series. I owe a huge debt to him for his interest in the project, his many insightful comments and support, all of which have been a huge stimulus in completing the book. I am grateful too to Dr Philip Duce and the staff at Inter-Varsity Press for their fine editorial skills.

Moreover, I wish to thank students and faculty in the institutions where I have had the privilege of teaching and who have interacted with this material: Peter Achimugu College of Theology, Ankpa, Nigeria; Samuel Bill Theological College, Abak, Nigeria; The Evangelical Theological College of Wales, Bridgend; The Pacific Theological College, Suva, Fiji Islands; and now, Moody Bible Institute, Chicago, where I teach. My present colleagues' interest in how this book was progressing has been a great encouragement.

I am also deeply grateful to my MPhil supervisor, Dr Margaret E. Thrall, University College of North Wales (Bangor), who supervised the original thesis 'Adoptive Sonship (HUIOTHESIA) in the Pauline Corpus', of which this book is a revision, and to Dr (now Prof.) Loveday C. A. Alexander, University of Sheffield, for examining the work and providing ways to improve it. I also wish to thank many individuals who have read early drafts of this work, including Professors I. Howard Marshall (Aberdeen), John M. G. Barclay (now of Durham), and Revd Dr Christopher J. H. Wright, Langham Partnership, who read and commented on parts of the book in an earlier format. My present colleague Dr Gerald W. Peterman also kindly read and commented on part of the book.

Books, of course, are written in the midst of daily living and this one is no different, except for the nature of the circumstances pertaining to our family. During one of the most difficult periods of our family life, we had to take our older son, Luke, back to Methodist College, Belfast, to board while we remained 12,000 miles way in the South Pacific, Fiji Islands. Our year apart proved to be a testing and difficult time. Having settled our son into school, I returned to Fiji only to receive the news one week later that my father, Ken Burke, had been taken seriously ill and had died. I immediately made the same journey back to Northern Ireland, this time with an even heavier heart, for my father's funeral. It was during this time that I was grateful to my father-in-law, Dick Dunlop, for once again providing much support and as always an open house to stay on the farm. It is to these two fathers that I dedicate this book. During this second visit, I was very grateful too to Dr Bruce Winter for the opportunity to stay at Tyndale House for two weeks to enable me not only to reflect on the above traumatic events but also to write further on this book. Thanks are also due to Dr Elizabeth Magba, Tyndale House Library, for acquiring a number of articles.

I also wish to express my sincere appreciation to Revd Harold Boyce and Margaret Galbraith in my native Belfast, who read parts of this book in an earlier format. Thanks too to my teaching assistants at Moody Bible Institute, Ashish Varma and my son Simeon Burke, for compiling the indexes.

This book would also have been completed earlier were it not for a period of illness when I was about to take up my new appointment at Moody Bible Institute. On nearing completion, the acquisition of important bibliographical material by Joe Cataio, Librarian at Moody Bible Institute, was not only timely but spurred the process along to completion. I am very grateful to my employer for awarding me the 2006 Faculty Writing Grant, which was a great help and encouragement in the latter stages of writing.

My greatest debt, however, is to my wife, Yvonne, and our two sons, Luke and Simeon, the former having read and commented on much of the material, the latter two having listened to many discussions of Paul. Their understanding, support and encouragement as I retreated repeatedly to my study are deeply appreciated. Our children continue to be one of the greatest sources of delight to us as parents.

Trevor J. Burke
Chicago, June 2006

Abbreviations

1Q3S	*Stories about the Tribes of Israel* (Dead Sea Scrolls)
1QS	*Rule of the Community* (Dead Sea Scrolls)
2 Macc.	2 Maccabees
4Q372	*Apocrypha of Joseph^b* (Dead Sea Scrolls)
4Qflor	*Florilegium* (Dead Sea Scrolls)
AB	Anchor Bible
AGJU	Arbeiten zur Geschichte des antiken Judentums und des Urchristentums
A. J.	*Antiquitates judaicae*
AnBib	Analecta biblica
ANRW	*Aufstieg und Niedergang der romischen Welt*
Apoc. Bar.	*Apocalypse of Barnabas*
AV	Authorized Version
BBMS	Baker Biblical Monograph Series
BDAG	Bauer, W., F. W. Danker, W. F. Arndt and W. F. Gingrich (2000), *A Greek–English Lexicon of the New Testament and Other Early Christian Literature*, 3rd ed., Chicago: University of Chicago Press
BECNT	Baker Exegetical Commentary on the New Testament
Bib	*Biblica*
BJRL	*Bulletin of the John Rylands University Library of Manchester*
BJS	Brown Judaic Studies
BNTC	Black's New Testament Commentaries
b. Pes.	*Babylonian Talmud, Pesaḥim*
b. Šab.	*Babylonian Talmud, Šabbat*
BST	The Bible Speaks Today
b. Ta'an.	*Bablynonian Talmud Ta'anit*
BTB	*Biblical Theology Bulletin*

17

BTCL	Biblical and Theological Collection Library
c.	circa
CBQ	*Catholic Biblical Quarterly*
CIL	*Corpus Inscriptionum Latinarium*
CR:BS	*Currents in Research: Biblical Studies*
Dig.	*Digesta*
Diod. Sic.	Diodorus Siculus
Dom.	*De domo suo*
ESV	English Standard Version
EvQ	*Evangelical Quarterly*
ExpTim	*Expository Times*
Fin.	de Finibus
Gk	Greek
Haer.	*Adversus haereses*
IBS	*Irish Biblical Studies*
ICC	International Critical Commentary
Instit.	John Calvin, *Institutes of the Christian Religion*
Inst.	*Institutiones* (Gaius)
Int	*Interpretation*
JB	Jerusalem Bible
JBL	*Journal of Biblical Literature*
JETS	*Journal of the Evangelical Theological Society*
JRS	*Journal of Romans Studies*
JSNT	*Journal for the Study of the New Testament*
JSNTSup	Journal for the Study of the New Testament Supplement
JTS	*Journal of Theological Studies*
Jub.	*Jubilees*
LCL	Loeb Christian Library
LD	Lectio divina
LEC	Library of Early Christianity
lit.	literally
LXX	Septuagint
N. A.	*Noctes Atticae*
NAC	New American Commentary
NCB	New Century Bible
NEB	New English Bible
Neot	*Neotestamentica*
NIBCNT	New International Biblical Commentary on the New Testament

NICNT	New International Commentary on the New Testament
NIGTC	New International Greek Testament Commentary
NIV	New International Version
NIVAC	New International Version Application Commentary
NovT	*Novum Testamentum*
NovTSup	Novum Testamentum Supplements
NRSV	New Revised Standard Version
NSBT	New Studies in Biblical Theology
NT	New Testament
NTS	*New Testament Studies*
Off.	*De officiis*
OT	Old Testament
pl.	plural
PLip	L. Mitteis (1906), *Griechische Urkunden der Papyrussammlung zu Leipzig*, Leipzig (no publisher)
Poet.	*Poetica*
POxy	*The Oxyrhynchus Papyri*
Prov.	*De providentia*
PSB	*Princeton Seminary Bulletin*
Quaest. Amphil.	*Quaestiones Amphilochiis*
RB	*Revue biblique*
REB	Revised English Bible
RSV	Revised Standard Version
SBET	*Scottish Bulletin of Evangelical Theology*
SBLDS	Society of Biblical Literature Dissertation Series
Sir.	Sirach
SJT	*Scottish Journal of Theology*
SJTOP	Scottish Journal of Theology Occasional Papers
SNTSMS	Society for New Testament Studies Monograph Series
Sobr.	*De sobrietate*
SP	Sacra pagina
TDNT	*Theological Dictionary of the New Testament*
Them	*Themelios*
T. Jud.	*Testament of Judah*
T. Levi	*Testament of Levi*
T. Reub.	*Testament of Reuben*
TynBul	*Tyndale Bulletin*

UBS	United Bible Societies
Vir. ill.	*De viris illustribus*
WBC	Word Biblical Commentary
WEC	Wycliffe Exegetical Commentary
Wis.	Wisdom of Solomon
WTJ	*Westminster Theological Journal*
WUNT	Wissenschaftliche Untersuchungen zum Neuen Testament
ZNW	*Zeitschrift für die neutestamentliche Wissenschaft und die Kunde der älteren Kirche*

Chapter One

Adoption:
A misinterpreted metaphor?

Introduction

The relationship between God and his people has been variously
described and understood by Old and New Testament authors. Of all
the biblical writers it is arguably the apostle Paul who employs the
richest vocabulary in describing how a person relates to God. For
example, he speaks of election (Eph. 1:4), justification (Rom. 3:24),
redemption (Gal. 3:14) and reconciliation (2 Cor. 5:19) to name a few
forms of relationship. These weighty biblical expressions are rich in
the social setting in which Paul lived and moved and deepen our
appreciation of the saving significance of Christ and the Christian's
relationship to God.

In addition to the above theological terms, another Pauline
expression has attracted less attention, the word *huiothesia*, 'adoption'.[1] The expression *huiothesia* comprises two Greek words: *huios*,
'son',[2] and *thesis*, 'placing', and etymologically denotes either the

---

[1] Dunn (1998: 469) has rightly stated concerning adoption that its 'presence is noted
but [its] significance ... is too little reflected on'.

[2] In the ancient Graeco-Roman world both sons and daughters could be adopted,
although the latter was less common, as daughters could not continue the line. Thus
when I use 'sons' I am not excluding daughters, and this is perhaps reflected in Paul's
movement in Rom. 8 from 'sons' (*huioi*, v. 14) to 'children' (*tekna*, v. 16). At the
same time, Paul's preference for the term 'sons' in the adoption texts makes us aware
that he lived in patriarchal society. His use of 'sons' in this context makes it clear that
sons were not only the usual subjects for adoption but that they also stand as
representatives of females. The NRSV translation of the Greek word *huioi* (v. 14)
as 'children' muddies the waters and obscures this issue. This is because Paul wishes
to make the point that our adoption as sons is dependent on Jesus as Son of God, and
Rom. 8:12–17 is deliberately sandwiched between two references to Jesus as the
Son of God (cf. Rom. 8:3, 29). Our adoption as God's sons is inextricably tied to
God's Son; hence to translate *huioi* (sons) as 'children' in v. 14 blurs this important
point.

process or act of being placed or 'adopted as son(s)'.[3] *Huiothesia* is unique to the writings of the apostle Paul, occurring five times in three of his letters (Rom. 8:15, 23; 9:4; Gal. 4:5; Eph. 1:5). No other author in the New Testament employs this expression. Further, *huiothesia* and the verbal form *huiotheteō* are not found in the Old Testament (including the received text of the LXX), and *huiothesia* is also conspicuously absent from the corpus of classical Greek writers and from other Jewish literature of the period (e.g. Philo and Josephus). The earliest known occurrences of the term in the Greek world are found in funerary inscriptions of the second century BC at Adelphi and Crete. The first known literary appearances, however, are found in the writings of the two Hellenistic historians Diodorus Siculus and Nicolaus Damascenus. Diodorus, who to a large extent paraphrases Polybius, uses the 'adoption' term in the story of Aemilius and Scipio. He writes, 'when Aemilius, his real father, died and left his property to him and to Fabius, the sons he had given in *adoption* (*huiothesian*), Scipio performed a noble act, which deserves to be put on record' (Diod. Sic. 31.27.5; my emphasis). Diodorus also employs the expression in the Greek myth of Zeus, who persuaded his wife Hera to adopt Heracles (Diod. Sic. 39.2).

When we turn to the writings of the apostle Paul, the word 'adoption' is always employed metaphorically (never literally), and has no equal or parallel in the New Testament. Adoption graphically and intimately describes the family character of Pauline Christianity,[4] and is a basic description for Paul of what it means to be a Christian. *Huiothesia* is a theological metaphor Paul 'particularly cherished' (Dunn 2003: 435) and is used to denote the blessing of God's people by their heavenly Father. In short, 'for ... Paul ... *adoption* into the family of God *is a key metaphor* for the new status believers have obtained' (Yarbrough 1995: 140; my emphasis).[5]

---

[3] Scott (1992: 13–57) has carried out one of the most exhaustive computer analyses of the semantic range of *huiothesia* and concludes that it has a Hellenistic *meaning* (not background) and denotes 'adoption as son'. It has to be said that Scott's conclusion was one Lightfoot (1975: 168) had arrived at well over a century earlier. Others, for example Byrne (1979), prefer the more general translation 'sonship' on the basis that *huiothesia* does not exclusively refer to an *act* (of adoption) but to *status* (sonship) as well; see also Schweitzer 1993: 397.

[4] Interestingly, Stanton (2003: 183) describes the *central themes* of Paul's gospel and concludes his essay with the following summary of that good news: 'Paul's gospel is the good news of God's once for all disclosure of Jesus Christ as his Son, sent for our salvation so that "we might receive the adoption as God's children" (Gal. 4:4–5).'

[5] Atkins (1991: 187) states regarding the significance of *huiothesia* for Paul, 'Paul's use of adoption terminology is both structurally and functionally a centerpiece of his understanding of what it is to be a follower of Christ.'

Theological misunderstandings of adoption

During my study of adoption, which began when I was teaching an exegesis class on Romans in a theological seminary in West Africa, I was struck by two main points: first, throughout the history of the church, adoption has (at times) been misunderstood; and second, popular and scholarly interests in this expression have been too narrowly focused. Regarding the former, adoption has been mis-interpreted by systematicians and 'has ... been more often in the dark than in the light' (Westhead 1995: 102). For example, adoption has been mistakenly viewed as the positive side of justification.

This confusion was evident at times during the sixteenth and seventeenth centuries, when Reformed theologians sought to situate adoption within the *ordo salutis* (scheme or plan of salvation) (see Garner 2002: 3).[6] Francis Turretin, one of the most influ-ential Reformed theologians of his time, discusses the relationship between adoption and justification and poses the question 'What is the adoption which is given us in justification?' To which he replies, 'Adoption is included in justification as a part' (Ferguson 1986: 83).[7] By conflating adoption and justification Turretin eradicates the distinctiveness of adoption, thereby diminishing the theological importance of this Pauline term. Others, such as the post-Reformation theologian John Leith, have understood 'adoption [as] a synonym for justification' (Leith 1973: 99), a view shared by R. L. Dabney during the nineteenth century who described adoption in the following manner: 'Adoption cannot be said to be a different act of grace for justification ... [Adoption] *performs the same act* for us ... which justification does' (1996: 627; my emphasis).

On other occasions, systematic theologians have misconceived this term, misconceptions that persisted into the twentieth century, as is evident in the writings of L. Berkhof. Berkof (1981: 515) repeats the mistake of earlier systematicians by viewing adoption as a subsection of justification: 'there is also a positive element in justification ...

---

[6] Garner states the doctrine of adoption has received 'minimal attention by the church fathers'. Notably Irenaeus discusses adoption, and Origen and Augustine also mention it. During the Reformation Luther did not make much of adoption, whereas Calvin's theology is undergirded by an understanding of this term and has even been described as a 'Gospel of adoption' (Gerrish 1993: 89). For a discussion of Calvin's appreciation of adoption see Ferguson 1986: 81–88; Trumper 2002; Griffith 2001: 135–154; Westhead 1995: 102–115.

[7] According to Ferguson (1986: 83), Turretin's conclusions contributed to the demise of adoption in English-speaking Reformed theology.

justification is more than mere pardon ... believers are children of God by adoption'.[8] The table below depicts the views of Kuyper, Berkhof and Murray in regard to their understanding of adoption and its relationship to other theological terms. Kuyper and Berkhof mistakenly view adoption as a subset of regeneration and justification respectively, whereas John Murray rightly regards adoption as distinct but also related to justification and regeneration in the *ordo salutis*:

Abraham Kuyper	Regeneration/adoption–faith–justification–sanctification–glorification
Louis Berkhof	Regeneration–faith–justification/adoption–sanctification–glorification
John Murray	Regeneration–faith–justification–adoption–sanctification–glorification

Table 1.1

These misunderstandings still continue today, as evidenced in the remarks of Anthony Hoekema (1994: 185; my emphasis):

two *positive benefits of justification* that we mentioned earlier [are] first our adoption as children of God. By this I do not mean the spiritual rebirth whereby we become children of God through regeneration ... I mean adoption in the legal sense: our being placed in the status of sons ... of God.

The subsuming of adoption under justification allots a secondary role to the former, which has resulted in the theological integrity of adoption being compromised and the expression being relegated to a secondary position. The consequences of this have meant that 'adoption was treated as a minor aspect of the way of salvation' (Theron 1956: 8), with adoption becoming the Cinderella of Pauline theology. To be sure, adoption is related to justification and is incomplete without it; hence any treatment of the former must include the latter. Nevertheless, adoption ought not to be subsumed under justification or mistaken as a synonym for justification. Undoubtedly, justification is the primary (Packer 1988: 231; Carson 1994: 1114) blessing of salvation upon which all the other saving benefits depend. But even though adoption is related to justification,

[8] Other systematicians devote minimal attention to this term: e.g. Hodge (1979: 184), who in his massive three-volume *Systematic Theology* (2,000 pages!) mentions 'adoption' only once.

it is nevertheless an act of God's grace *different, distinct* from and *additional* to justification' (Murray 1961: 132; my emphasis).[9] J. L. Girardeau (1986: 479) rightly draws the distinction between the two concepts when he states:

> The Scriptures make a difference between [justification and adoption]. They treat adoption as something over and beyond justification ... justification ... introduces the ... sinner into the society of (the) righteous ... adoption ... introduces the sinner into the society of God's family.

Adoption and justification are not the same – adoption emphasizes aspects of the believer's relationship to God that are not present in justification.[10] To be declared righteous at the bar of God is one thing; it is, however, quite another to be adopted into God's family and able to call him '*Abba*, Father' (Gal. 4:6; Rom. 8:15). Put another way,

---

[9] See also Buchanan (1962: 276), who states, 'According to the Scriptures, pardon, acceptance, and adoption, are distinct privileges ... while the first two properly belong to the (sinner's) justification, as being both found on the same relation ... the third is radically distinct from them, as being founded on a nearer, more tender, and more endearing relation.'

[10] Since the 1980s, the traditional interpretation of justification and Paul's understanding of the Law have been challenged. According to the conventional understanding of justification and the Law, Paul endeavoured to earn God's favour by trying to keep the Law, something he found impossible to do. It was only with his conversion that Paul was liberated from enslavement to a legalistic religion. In response to this view, Sanders (1977) followed by others (e.g. Dunn) has advanced the so-called 'new perspective', in which it is argued that first-century Judaism was never regarded as a works-based religion. According to this view, Jews of Paul's day did not keep the Law to merit God's favour; rather, God gave the Law in order to regulate an already existing covenantal relationship. Put differently, keeping the Law did not 'get one in' but was a means of 'keeping one in' a covenantal relationship with God. Thus, in Sanders' view, the phrase 'covenantal nomism' sums up the fact that God first established a covenant with Israel, and the Law was given as a means of maintaining this covenantal relationship with himself.

There are various weaknesses with Sanders' views. For example, Sanders has a minimalist view of 'sin' and 'justification' as not exclusively forensic but forensic and transformative. Also, regarding the Law, some ancient Jewish texts, as Sanders admits (e.g. *4 Ezra*; *2 Apoc. Bar.*), actually view good works as meritorious for salvation. Thus we are prompted to ask that if such evidence exists, which Sanders has overlooked, might there not be other evidence that has yet to come to light? Again, it needs to be properly appreciated that ancient texts often have more to do with the setting forth of ideals or aspirations than with practice. So while the texts might inspire first-century Jews to regard the Law as maintaining their relationship with God, it is conceivable that the outworkings of this were very different, and could easily degenerate into a situation where behaviour or 'works' were regarded as earning favour with God. For the most recent interaction with the new perspective see the two volumes edited by Carson, O'Brien and Seifrid 2001 and 2004.

God does not only justify people and then leave them destitute with nowhere to go – he adopts them into the warmth and security of his household. Because of this, James I. Packer (1988: 230) rightly insists that 'adoption is ... *the highest privilege that the gospel offers*; higher even than justification' (emphasis in original) owing to the *'richer relationship* with God it involves' (Buchanan 1962: 277; my emphasis).[11] In short, adoption is the pinnacle of Pauline theology or, as John Murray (1976: 233) succinctly puts it, 'adoption is ... the apex of redemptive grace and privilege'.[12]

Not only has adoption been misunderstood for justification but it has also been confused with regeneration, a term Paul rarely uses – probably because the mystery religions used the latter expression and the apostle wanted to avoid it.

We find similar confusion in R. Peterson's (2001: 52) popular treatment of the term: in an effort to present or preserve a familial theme, and in the interests of theological unity, he understands John 1:12–13 and 1 John 3:1–3 as instances of adoption.[13] In his exegesis of John 1:12–13 Peterson concludes, 'to grant the right to become children of God is equivalent to adoption' (2001: 85). Peterson is of the view that the Greek term *exousian* (authority) in John 1:12 carries a judicial tone similar to that found in Paul's adoption term. This judicial tone of John 1:12 gives way to the new birth in John 1:13, a theme to which John returns later in his Gospel (John 3).

But it is unlikely that the evangelist would mix his familial metaphors in such a short space. Indeed, the context suggests that John's main point is that believers are *born* from above and that this is unattainable by human means, a point he repeatedly emphasizes in John 1:13b: 'children *born* not of natural descent, nor of human decision or a husband's will, but *born* (*egennēthēsan*) of God' (my emphasis).[14]

---

[11] It is worth mentioning that Dr Packer in a personal correspondence to me when I first began to research this metaphor was of the view 'that the theme (of adoption) is unduly neglected'.

[12] With regard to the importance of adoption, Ridderbos (1977: 199) states, 'Undoubtedly the adoption as sons can be put on a level and mentioned in one breath with justification.'

[13] Other proponents of this view are Candlish 1869: 146; Murray 1976: 277; Ferguson 1981: 83; Beasley-Murray 1987: 13. Stibbe (1991: 152) in relation to another text in John's Gospel writes, 'Both ideas, that of succession and that of *adoption*, are present in 19.25–7' (my emphasis).

[14] Carson (1991: 126) distinguishes between the Johannine and Pauline use of family language here: 'The language is *unlike* that of Paul, who describes ... the believer as "son" of God but believers are "sons" only by adoption' (my emphasis).

Again, in relation to 1 John. 3:1–3, a passage Peterson entitles 'The Source of Adoption – God's Love', he says, '[to] "be called children of God" by God the Father is to be adopted by him' (2001: 53). Once again, in 1 John 3:1–3 the issue to the fore is the amazing grace of God in our becoming his sons, which comes about when we are *born* (*gegennēmenos*, 3:9) into the family of God. Thus regeneration, a Johannine term, delineates the imagery of *natural birth*, which the author uses to emphasize the fact that Christian sonship is not our native condition: a person needs to become a son of God by *spiritual* rebirth.

Adoption, on the other hand, is a forensic term (more on this later) and denotes a legal act[15] or *transfer*[16] from an alien family (cf. Eph. 2:2, lit. 'sons of disobedience') into the family of God.[17] 'Not birth but adoption is Paul's analogy for the manner in which childhood begins in the believer' (Schlatter 1995: 181). Moreover, as we have already noted, *huiothesia* is an expression peculiar to the Pauline corpus and is not employed by any other New Testament author, including the writer of the Fourth Gospel. Thus Paul and John use two very different metaphors to express ways by which the Christian becomes a member of God's family. Berkhof (1981: 516) therefore is right when he sounds the caveat 'sonship by adoption should be carefully *distinguished* from ... sonship by regeneration' (my emphasis).

As Jeanette Stevenson-Moessner (2003: 99) rightly points out, the differences between these two expressions have not been appreciated:

> To read Scripture and highlight passages on adoption is to read it through a different lens ... The fact that we always assume the

[15] Whaling (1923: 228) states, 'Regeneration ... is a creative act, while adoption is a legal and forensic [*sic*].' Peterson (2001: 109) puts it nicely: 'Adoption is a legal action, taking place outside of us, whereby God the Father gives us a new status in his family. Regeneration is a renewal of our nature, occurring within us, in which the Father imparts spiritual life to us.' Of course, within the *ordo salutis* adoption always presupposes regeneration. Interestingly, the Christian church – especially in evangelical circles in the United States and in parts of the United Kingdom – has long emphasized the theological concept of regeneration but has unfortunately overlooked the Pauline theme of adoption. Sermons have been preached from pulpits on the theme of regeneration, and Sunday school curriculae and theological college syllabi demonstrate a greater familiarity with this theological expression than with Paul's adoption metaphor.

[16] Whereas justification emphasizes the penal aspect of salvation, redemption emphasizes deliverance, and propitiation emphasizes the cultic, Paul's adoption term underscores the notion of transference from one family to another.

[17] See further Garner 2002: 126–156. It needs to be noted that Paul like John also uses the expression 'sons of God'; however, in this study I am more concerned with the narrower focus of what it means to be an adopted son, an expression John does not employ.

family is biologically knit reveals our prejudice in favor of biological 'seed' and our elevation of physical progeny. It is to miss the family of faith.[18]

And, we might add, to miss Paul's unique emphasis that believers become members of this divine household by adoption.

To summarize this brief discussion so far, it should be noted that Paul's adoption term is not only related to, but is also distinct from, other theological terms and merits a more significant place in Pauline Christianity. Adoption describes aspects not found in any other of the above soteriological terms Paul uses. With this in view, my thesis in this monograph is as follows: if adoption is important and distinct enough from other soteriological terms in the thinking and theology of Paul, then it is worthy of greater consideration. Rather than adoption being regarded as on the periphery of Paul's theological agenda, it should occupy a more vital role in our theological reflection and understanding.

In the light of the above misunderstandings a fresh inquiry and *theological* appraisal of this important metaphor is long overdue. Despite being mentioned only five times by the apostle (four of which occur in Paul's capital epistles), adoption, as I hope to demonstrate here, possesses an importance far exceeding the number of references to it in the Pauline letters.[19] Moreover, according to Ryken et al. (1998: 15), the 'significance [of adoption] is great because of its conceptual and emotive power and its relationship to many other familial ideas' (e.g. 'father', Gal. 4:6; Rom. 8:15; 'sons', Gal. 4:6–7; Rom. 8:14; 'slave', Gal. 4:7; Rom. 8:15; 'heir(s)', Gal. 4:7; Rom. 8:17). And, most important to this investigation, while many agree that adoption is a legal term, this juridical perspective alone truncates our understanding of the expression and isolates it from its full theological scope. This scope is wide-ranging and includes other branches of theology, including eschatology, Christology, pneumatology and

---

[18] The title of her book, *The Spirit of Adoption: At Home in God's Family*, might lead one to think that it deals primarily with the genitival construction *pneuma huiothesias*, 'Spirit of adoption' (Rom. 8:15, NIV margin). However, the author's generally stated aim is to 'support families in adoption and to formulate a theology of adoption that is applicable to Christian churches' (2003: 8). Stevenson-Moessner's book is both stimulating and pastorally sensitive, and includes an informative chapter entitled 'A Theology of Adoption'.

[19] It is worth recording that 'adoption' (*huiothesia*) is in fact mentioned more times in the New Testament than 'regeneration' (*palingenesia*; cf. John 3:3; Titus 3:4–6), yet the former description comes much more readily to the minds of Christians when asked to describe the meaning of 'salvation'.

ethics/morality,[20] all of which impinge directly upon Paul's adoption term. The theological importance of adoption has been rightly stressed by James I. Cook (1978: 139–40):

> huiothesia is for Paul ... a *theological* confession. All too frequently overlooked is the fact that ... he always uses it to describe what may be termed theological adoption, that is, the placing of persons into sonship to God!

In the light of Cook's observations and the considerable theological confusion surrounding Paul's adoption term in the past, this book will mainly focus on addressing the theological importance of the adoption metaphor within the context of our exegesis of the relevant texts (Rom. 8:12–17, 18–23; 9:4; Gal. 4:1–7; Eph. 1:1–6).

Interests in adoption have been too narrowly focused

In recent years there have been some green shoots of recovery (Westhead 1995: 102) as far as interest in Paul's adoption term is concerned: unfortunately, scholarly research had been too one-sided, focusing mainly on the background. Most notable is the important monograph *Adoption as Sons of God: An Investigation into the Background of HUIOTHESIA*, by James M. Scott (1994b), who addresses the most likely milieu, Graeco-Roman or Jewish, from which Paul was drawing in order to give theological expression to this term. Scott is not only of the view that there are bona fide cases of adoption in Israelite society (e.g. Exod. 2:10; Esth. 2:7; Gen. 48:5–6),[21] but he also attempts to situate the background of *huiothesia* against a *single* Old Testament text, 2 Samuel 7:14 (see discussion in chapter 3). Other New Testament scholars such as Alan Mawhinney (1982), however, have arrived at a different conclusion and, along with the majority of scholars today (including Lyall 1969: 456–468), posits a Graeco-Roman background.[22]

The debate about background needs some re-evaluation and is one

---

[20] For a brief summary of how adoption elucidates these theological themes see Burke 1995: 64–65.

[21] See the appendix for a discussion of some alleged cases of adoption.

[22] I tend to side with Lyall and Mawhinney; see Burke 1995: 62–74; 1998: 311–324; but also see the Old Testament background against Israel's and the Israelites' relationship with God as son(s). See chapter 3.

to which we shall return in the course of our inquiry. But it cannot be separated from the complexity of Paul's own background, which is a rich tapestry of Jewish, Roman and Greek cultures. To try to separate these in the quest to determine which one Paul was most likely to have used for his adoption metaphor is difficult and should not be simplistically reduced to an 'either or' conclusion. In order to resolve the issue of background to Paul's adoption term we need to consider carefully the various cultures prevalent in the ancient world and how, if at all, these influenced Paul and manifested themselves in the relevant texts.[23]

One of the consequences of this narrow agenda is that the majority of Pauline *commentators* confine their remarks on the adoption pericopae to the issue of background and little else, as if this were the only matter relevant to adoption. Undoubtedly, background is important, but other vital and fascinating aspects of adoption remain largely untapped and overlooked (e.g. the relationship between adoption and the Spirit, Rom. 8:15). What is required, and is still largely unexplored, is a *full-orbed* approach to this metaphor, a view shared by Norman R. Petersen (1985: 275 n. 25): 'commentators usually observe that this ... term is used "religiously" but I know of no study that has dealt with adoption in terms of its full role in Paul's thought'.[24]

One of the main aims of this study on adoption is to attempt to widen the discussion and open up fresh areas of debate. For example, in view of the new and exciting insights classical historians have given us into the family in the ancient world, Pauline scholars are awakening to the usefulness of such insights in throwing fresh light on the New Testament text, especially Paul's use of an array of kinship terms, including adoption.[25] For example, given that honour in the ancient world was accorded to a son adopted into a new family, what can this tell us about those whom God has adopted as members of his household? Also, if adoption is another family expression Paul employs in his letters, what if anything can this tell us about his understanding of the nature of the church or community of believers?

---

[23] Witherington (1998: 52–88) argues for a tricultural approach to the apostle's background.

[24] Whaling (1923: 235) also lamented as long ago as 1923 that 'a complete and well-rounded, and systematic presentation of the biblical meaning of *huiothesia*, or of *the theological significance of adoption is still a desideratum*' (my emphasis). See also Burke 1995: 62–74; 2001: 119–134.

[25] A fictive kinship term is one that describes the familial relationship that exists between people who are not necessarily related by blood. See Burke 2003a.

In the next chapter we begin our investigation with a brief discussion of metaphor and metaphor theory. Here it is worth reflecting on the fact that if the apostle Paul (or any other biblical author for that matter) had not employed metaphors as a vehicle of communication, then our understanding of God and the theological message of the Scriptures would be greatly impoverished as a result. Chapter 3 explores what is perhaps the most debated question in respect of adoption; namely, the most appropriate background(s) to this metaphor. In the light of the fact that God's very nature is relational and expressed in family terms as Father, Son and Holy Spirit,[26] the trinitarian implications of adoption are profound and thoroughgoing, as chapters 4 to 7 demonstrate. In chapter 4 we consider the role of God as Father ('*Abba*, Father', Gal. 4:6; Rom. 8:15) in adopting believers into 'this new "family of God"' (Meeks 1986: 129). This is followed in chapter 5 by a treatment of Jesus as God's Son and the Christological and Christocentric importance this has for the believer's adoption as son. Chapter 6 discusses the crucial role and relationship between the Spirit and adoption (*pneuma huiothesias*, Rom. 8:15) and the ensuing moral implications this brings. In chapter 7, and in the light of the fact that *adoption* is a family expression and that *honour* was a foundational value in ancient family life, we examine the interrelationship between adoption and honour. In chapter 8 we explore the eschatological tension between the 'now' (8:15) and the 'not yet' (8:23), and the consequences for God's adopted children who live in the intervening period between the present and the future.

But first we begin our inquiry with a brief discussion of metaphor theory.

[26] See chapter 4 for a discussion of the 'personal/familial' characteristic and function of the Holy Spirit.

Chapter Two

Adoption:
Another soteriological
metaphor for Paul

Introduction

So far I have employed the word 'metaphor'[1] and the phrase 'Paul's adoption term' without any explanation. It is therefore important for us at this juncture to define what we mean by the term 'metaphor' and determine how an understanding of its use and function can assist us in this study.

Metaphorical language forms an important part of every culture; indeed, metaphors are so much part and parcel of our daily communication that we often use them without thinking. Metaphor is sometimes thought of as an ornamental or decorative way of speaking; but this is to overlook its real function, which is essentially didactic – metaphor is a powerful means of communication, enabling us to grasp or see things in new and fascinating ways.

But how was the expression *huiothesia* first *heard* and understood by the early Christians to whom Paul wrote? This is an important question, not least because we do not want to read our twenty-first-century, Western understanding of adoption into a first-century practice, and, as we shall see later, there are important differences between the two.

A working definition of metaphor

Metaphor can be defined in various ways.[2] Aristotle's (*Poet.* 21.7)

---

[1] Sometimes Paul's adoption term has been described as a 'motif', 'image' or 'picture' (e.g. Garner 2002: 127, 137, 150), as if these were more or less equivalent terms or reductionist in meaning. For reasons adduced in the main text, 'adoption' is a metaphor and this is the term I shall employ during the course of this book.

[2] For more on the theoretical basis of the study of metaphor see Burke 2003a: 18–28.

classical definition is representative of many when he focuses on the level of *terminology*:

> metaphor is the transference (*epiphora*) of a name from the object to which it has a natural application: this transference can take place from genus (*genos*) to species (*eidos*) or species to genus or from species to species or by analogy (*analogia*).[3]

Somewhat similar is the working definition and the one most helpful for our purposes advanced by two leading linguists, Lakoff and Johnson (1980: 154), who argue that the main function of metaphor is to 'provid[e] a partial understanding of *one kind of experience in terms of another kind of experience*' (my emphasis).[4] On the basis of this definition, we could say that Paul's use of family terms in general and his adoption term in particular is clearly metaphorical: that is, he applies a family expression to a field to which it 'originally' did not belong and understands Christian relations in terms of family relations, by way of some kind of analogy.[5]

However, it is possible the analogy between the 'one kind of thing' and 'another' may be so weak as to be unviable as a basis for a metaphor. In other words, if Paul's use of his adoption metaphor reflects only a common usage, then the connection on the cognitive level with its original context (the family in the ancient world) would be weak and its impact lessened. In such instances Paul's use of his adoption metaphor would be only a mere convention and its usefulness to our investigation would therefore be limited. We shall see, however, that Paul's adoption metaphor is suffused with meaning drawn from the family in the ancient world.

The characteristics and function of metaphor

Metaphorical language forms an important part of everyday communication, so much so that reality cannot be understood apart from metaphor. Metaphors shape our way of thinking. It is not just language that is metaphorical but our conceptual system is too

---

[3] See also the lucid discussion in Soskice 1985: 3–10.

[4] See also Caird (1980: 17), who states that metaphor in its 'simplest form is the transfer of a name from its original referent to another'; Williams 1999: 4 n. 1.

[5] There is a lively debate among linguists concerning the cognitive content of metaphor. Arguments for and against the cognitive view are presented by Kittay (1987: 316–324) and Davidson (1978: 29–46) respectively.

(Lakoff & Johnson 1980: 3–6). As a result, it is sometimes difficult to tease out reality without metaphors.

In accordance with Lakoff and Johnson's definition of metaphor (an understanding/experience transferred from one realm to another), linguists employ different terms: the *source* domain or *donor* field and *target* domain or *recipient* field.[6] Thus the family in the ancient world, or more specifically the father-to-adopted-son relation, serves as the *source* domain or *donor* field, whereas the Christian's relationship to God is the *target* domain or *recipient* field. This can be represented diagrammatically:

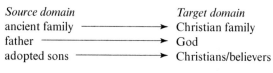

Figure 2.1

A related issue and an important question all this raises is, 'How do metaphors function?' Stephen Fowl (1990: 471) comments in this regard, 'metaphors work by linking two or more things together that do not conventionally go together, thus inviting a hearer or reader to allow the conventional associations of each object to interact with each other'.

In the case of Paul's adoption metaphor a human–divine relationship (God as 'Father' and Christians as 'adopted sons') is described, which triggers in our twenty-first-century minds a common set of associations regarding this relationship. We need, however, to uncover the 'system of associated commonplaces' (Black 1962: 41) related to the social practice of adoption in the first century AD. For example, in the ancient world it was commonly expected that adopted sons were to honour and obey their fathers, and that fathers should exercise authority and demonstrate affection towards their adopted sons. Thus when Paul's adoption term was first heard, a process of selection and screening occurred, where some aspects of the source domain were hidden, while others were highlighted.

This process is one with which the modern-day hearer of Paul's family expressions must grapple; moreover, the selection and screening (and even distortion!) are likely to be more severe the more temporally removed we are from the culture in which the expressions

---

[6] Linguists employ other terms, such as *tenor* and *vehicle*. *Tenor* refers to a word in the literal frame, while *vehicle* refers to the figurative or metaphorical word.

were first coined.[7] This means that only some elements will be relevant, which depends primarily on two main factors: first, the *literary* context (sometimes called the 'cotext') or the textual surroundings of the word or statements used; and second, the *social* or *cultural* context (the perceptions of fathers and adopted sons in that particular culture). We shall briefly consider these two aspects of a metaphor.

The literary context

The immediate literary context plays an important role in helping us determine whether or not an author is speaking metaphorically. If we consider the phrase 'my Father is the gardener' (John 15:1) in the Johannine literary context, we can see that it is clearly being used as a metaphor.[8] John is not literally speaking about horticultural methods. However, in a different context the same expression 'my Father is the gardener' would be a literal statement. What is important to note is that the metaphor functions as metaphor only within its context. The surrounding literary context or cotext (Cotterell & Turner 1989: 16) helps us determine whether or not this is so. Now clearly, when Paul for instance speaks of the Galatian (Gal. 4:5) or Roman (Rom. 8:15, 23) Christians as *God's* 'adopted sons', the context determines that we understand this metaphorically rather than literally,[9] as the apostle is describing the *believer's* relationship to God. This is clear from what Paul writes in Ephesians 1:3–5 to remind his readers of the very nature of their adoption: 'Praise be to the God and Father of our Lord Jesus Christ, who has blessed us in the heavenly realms with every *spiritual blessing* (*pneumatikē eulogia*) in Christ' (v. 3; my emphasis), one of which was the blessing of *huiothesia* (v. 5).

---

[7] Caird (1980: 49) provides an excellent discussion of the verbal, situational, traditional and cultural contexts at work in understanding metaphor. Caird proffers an everyday example of how important culture is in understanding what a speaker means. For example, a Frenchman attempting to translate the sentence 'I'm mad about my flat' needs to know whether the speaker is an Englishman enthusiastic about his living quarters or an American furious about her punctured tyre.

[8] See Carson (1991: 511–518) and his discussion of John 15:1–8, the 'vine', which he understands as a 'metaphor'.

[9] Yarbrough (1995: 126) comments, '*Most of the references* (i.e., to parents and children) *are in fact metaphorical*, serving the purpose to define the relationship between God and believers on the one hand and between Paul and his coworkers and churches on the other' (my emphasis).

The social context

Paul is a master of metaphors and draws from a wide range of social contexts in his use of them. For instance, he borrows from the spheres of the military (2 Tim. 2:3–4), athletics (Phil. 3:12–14; 2 Tim. 2:5) and agriculture (1 Cor. 3:6–8; 2 Tim. 2:6), to name but a few. Paul's most frequent use of metaphors, however, are those pertaining to family life, and adoption falls within this general category.[10] Moreover, it is interesting to note how New Testament scholars have often used the analogies of the body, temple and so on to describe and understand the church. But on statistical grounds, not to mention the sheer range of vocabulary the apostle employs, the family is not only one of the most important metaphors but is also the most pervasive he uses to describe his communities. In this respect Robert Banks (1994: 53) is right when he comments, 'the comparison of the Christian community with a "family" must be regarded as the most significant metaphorical usage of all ... More than any other image utilized by Paul, it reveals *the essence of his thinking about community*' (my emphasis).

What is important for our purposes is that these family 'metaphors open a window on the world of those who use them' (Williams 1999: 2) and, most importantly, are 'semantically embedded in a socio-cultural framework' (van der Watt 1999: 142) of Paul's day.

Paul's letters are addressed to real communities in real historical situations and, as Abraham J. Malherbe has rightly pointed out, 'Paul's theology was inextricably related to social reality' (1995: 53–66). The role the ancient social context plays in the shaping of Paul's theology should not be overlooked or downplayed. Indeed, increasingly New Testament scholars are recognizing the value of placing Paul in his ancient sociohistorical context and how this can help us interpret his writings better. Jan van der Watt (1999: 12; my emphasis) helpfully underscores the significance of the social context when he remarks:

> the *socio-historical framework* within which a metaphor was originally created plays an important role in the continued cognitive and emotive functioning of metaphor. When reading ancient texts, it is even more critical that one should assimilate socio-historic data when interpreting metaphors. In order to

---

[10] For more on this see Banks 1994 and his ch. 5, which he has entitled 'The Church as a Loving Family'.

understand the intensity, intent and meaning of a metaphor in an ancient text, it is necessary to understand the socio-historical context in which it was originally used.

The apostle Paul's *huiothesia* expression was an integral part of the family matrix in antiquity. Moreover, if adoption was not a known practice of the ancient social world, his hearers would not have understood it and it would therefore have lost its communicative power. But adoption is not just a metaphor; it is a 'sociological metaphor' (Petersen 1985: 157) rooted, as I shall show in the next chapter, in the Roman sociolegal practice of the ancient world.[11] 'Roman history provides many examples of adoption' (Williams 1999: 64) and *huiothesia* would have been a term pregnant with meaning for Paul's readers.[12]

Adoption as another soteriological metaphor

Traditionally, New Testament scholars have understood expressions such as justification (Rom. 5:1), redemption (Gal. 3:13) and propitiation (Rom. 3:25) as important salvation metaphors for the apostle Paul. *Justification* is a penal metaphor and connotes the drama of the law court, *redemption* draws from the realm of the slave market, and *propitiation* is a cultic metaphor stemming from Jewish sacrificial practice.[13] As stated earlier, Pauline scholars often emphasize one of the above soteriological terms to the extent of marginalizing the others. But to insist on and isolate any one of the above terms as the *sum total or description* of Paul's understanding and teaching on salvation is 'an error of some magnitude' (Ferguson 1986: 86). This is because Paul's understanding of what God in Jesus Christ has done for sinful humanity is so rich, diverse and kaleidoscopic that it ought not to be reduced to a single expression.

It will be immediately obvious that Paul's adoption metaphor is a noticeable absentee from the above list. In recent years, however, there has been an increasing awareness and appreciation among

[11] Yarbrough (1995: 140–141) also notes that Paul's family metaphors were 'rooted in the day to day lives of the people to whom he proclaimed his gospel'; Frilingos (2000: 97) states, 'Paul draws on the network of meanings when he introduces family metaphors into his epistles'.

[12] Lassen (1997: 104) states in this regard, 'Based on ideals of the Roman family, *metaphors* of the family were created; they were used outside the Roman family, in the religious, social and political sphere' (emphasis in original).

[13] For a discussion of each of these metaphors see Morris 1983.

systematicians and New Testament scholars that *huiothesia* is another soteriological metaphorical expression for the apostle Paul. James D. G. Dunn (1999: 296) rightfully insists that there is a '*diversity of metaphors that Paul uses in his talk of salvation* for example, sowing and watering (1 Cor. 3:6–8), grafting and harvest (Rom. 11:17–24), first instalment and first fruits (Rom. 8:23), birth (1 Cor. 4:15), *adoption* (Rom. 8:15)' (my emphasis).

Similarly, Alister McGrath refers to adoption under the rubric of what he calls the 'Pauline Images of Salvation' (McGrath 2001a: 431),[14] and Gordon Fee includes *huiothesia* under the general title of 'The Pauline Soteriological Metaphors'. Adoption, Fee concludes, is one of a number of 'metaphors that emphasize the believer's salvation' (Fee 1994: 855; Trumper 1997: 98).

'Salvation' for the apostle Paul is an umbrella term under which all of the above expressions fall, a point summed up by C. A. Anderson Scott (1961: 17–18; my emphasis)[15] when he comments:

> Christianity according to St. Paul is best studied under the aspect of salvation, inasmuch as 'Salvation' is really the most comprehensive term for what the Apostle found in Christ. It includes ... all the chief factors in Christianity ... and embraces all the great topics with which we are familiar – Redemption, Justification, Reconciliation, *Adoption*, Sanctification ...

The appearance of adoption here alongside other soteriological terms invites further reflection and clarification concerning the relationship and distinctiveness of this metaphor to these other soteriological terms. First, I am not saying that adoption is the most significant of other Pauline soteriological metaphors,[16] nor that the frequency of occurrence of a metaphor is indicative of its importance. The number of times an expression occurs in the letters of Paul, or elsewhere in the New Testament, is not a sufficient yardstick by itself to enable us to conclude that one expression is more important than another. In the

[14] See also Rollins (1987: 108), who includes a discussion of adoption as another metaphor for salvation; Turner (1980: 3) also writes, '*Huiothesia* is a distinctively Pauline term, defining the nature of *God's salvation*' (my emphasis); Snodgrass (1996: 49) states, '*Adoption* is family imagery used to explain the salvation experience, both present and future' (emphasis in original).

[15] Also see Ryken (1998: 754), where we read, 'To be *saved* is to be incorporated or adopted into the family of God ... One is not a child of God by nature; the image of adoption thus emphasizes the graciousness of *salvation*' (my emphasis).

[16] See Martin (1990), who argues that 'reconciliation' is at the centre of Paul's theology.

final analysis, the determining factor regarding the importance of soteriological metaphors is the way in which these metaphors relate to others (where this happens) and where each is tied, or not tied, to major themes in biblical theology. Thus, to take the examples of substitutionary penal atonement and propitiation (Rom. 3:25), these metaphors (often regarded as unfashionable, out-of-date expressions to explain the work of Christ) are necessarily tied to massive structures regarding the wrath of God, the sacrificial system in the Old Testament and so on.[17]

However, some scholars (e.g. Green & Baker 2000: 148) suggest that the above metaphors (e.g. propitiation) are not only culturally binding to the first century but are equally unintelligible to twenty-first-century people.[18] According to Green and Baker, the meaning of Christ's death 'in the end cannot be captured by language or images' and we must therefore 'cast about for metaphors and models that speak of this mystery to the people around us' (111). Green and Baker overlook the importance of the double witness of Scripture and the tradition of the church and discard penal substitution as a model. Why? Because, they conclude, 'the theological and missionary task [is] not that we mimic their words and repeat their metaphors' (114).

But if 'the Church has always seen the need to use the very words, metaphors, and models that are handed down to us by the biblical witness [then] [i]t is necessary to do this in order to safeguard the tradition that has been entrusted to the Church' (Boersma 2004: 110). Rather than discarding what Scripture and the church have preserved, we should, instead, 'treasure our metaphors, particularly those which have, over the centuries, commended themselves as especially illuminating' (110, citing Gunton). On the one hand, the metaphor 'propitiation' emphasizes the *objective* or Godward side of soteriology – that is, how a God who stands against us in wrath now stands with his justice completely satisfied.[19] Such metaphors should

---

[17] For a discussion of these soteriological themes see Morris 1983; see also Trueman's (2002: 1–2) insightful editorial.

[18] I owe some of what follows to Boersma's (2004) discussion.

[19] For Green and Baker (2000: 54) the doctrines of substitutionary atonement and propitiation are relativized, indeed marginalized, by being dismissed as merely selected metaphors, and rather infrequent ones at that. They suggest e.g. that the anger of God is a metaphor and does not speak of reality. Green and Baker comment, 'Perhaps we attribute "anger" to God only because we have no other human language with which to comprehend God.' But as Boersma (2004: 48) contends, 'The biblical use of metaphors to describe the meaning of the cross does not somehow make them less valuable or less real. They are not *just* metaphors' (emphasis in original). Boersma goes on to cite Colin Gunton: 'linguistic usages which demand a new way of thinking about living in the

have pride of place in any treatment and understanding of Paul's soteriology.

But if certain metaphors, such as propitiation, underscore the objective side of salvation, other metaphors, including *huiothesia*, tend to focus more on what happens to us – that is, they look at salvation from the *subjective* or experiential side and focus more on the result of what is achieved for the people of God.[20] Whichever way we look at it, salvation, according to the apostle Paul, is profound and many sided. Stated differently, just as a ray of white light breaks up into the colours of the rainbow when refracted through a prism, so Paul's understanding of salvation is rich and multifaceted. Each of the above metaphors describes aspects of the saving significance of what God in Christ has done for sinful humanity. Moreover, *huiothesia* adds nuances of meaning vis-à-vis Paul's soteriology that are absent from other salvation metaphors.

As already noted, different connotations are associated with the different salvation terms Paul employs; for example, justification uses the language of the law court, and adoption aids our understanding because it draws from the realm of the household. Primarily, adoption is a *family* term that in the ancient social world of Paul's day denoted many things, but above everything else it signified the *transfer* of a son (usually an adult) as he is taken out of one family and placed in another with all its attending privileges and responsibilities. This aspect of *transference* encapsulates and has been captured nicely by Francis Lyall (1984: 83) as he describes the Roman sociolegal practice of adoption and the implications of what has taken place:

> the profound truth of Roman adoption was that the adoptee was taken out of his previous state and was placed in a new relationship of son to his new father, his new *paterfamilias*. All his old debts were cancelled, and in effect the adoptee started a new life as part of his new family.

---

world. Here is *real* sacrifice, victory and justice, so that what we thought the words meant is shown to be inadequate and in need of reshaping by that to which the language refers.' Boersma (49) concludes, 'It is the same when we speak about God's wrath. Here is "real" wrath that in turn forges the way in which we understand "wrath" in our everyday lives.'

[20] McIntyre (1992: 26–52) has argued that although adoption is not a subordinate metaphor to other terms Paul uses, it is a soteriological metaphor of 'second order'. McIntyre goes on to qualify this by saying, 'a second order metaphor is not necessarily of "secondary import" or "importance" ... it is of primary importance in certain references'.

Again, in the words of John Murray, 'Adoption, as the term clearly implies, is an act of *transfer* from an alien family into the family of God himself' (1961: 134; my emphasis).

Adoption as an organizing soteriological metaphor for Paul

Not only is adoption a sociological metaphor; it is seldom if ever appreciated that 'adoption serves as an organizing' (Garner 2002: 242) metaphor for salvation.[21] Sinclair Ferguson has argued that adoption, in keeping with other important soteriological metaphors in Paul's writings, shares the necessary biblical criteria for it to be recognized as an organizing metaphor for the doctrine of salvation.[22] Thus, for example, *huiothesia* (1) centres in the person and work of Jesus Christ, the Son of God; (2) it shares a moral focus evident in other soteriological expressions in Paul's writings; and (3) it is eschatological in nature (i.e. it expresses the 'already/not yet' tension characteristic of the New Testament's view of present Christian existence). I discuss these only briefly here, since we return to them in greater detail later.

Adoption is centred in the person and work of God's Son, Jesus Christ

When Paul speaks of adoption in his letters, it is crucial to note that he follows a pattern; that is, in Galatians 4:5 and Romans 8:15, for example, he first relates adoption to Jesus Christ, God's Son (Gal. 4:4; Rom. 8:3). By so doing, Paul's understanding of *huiothesia* is both Christocentrically and Christologically grounded in the *person* and *work* of Jesus Christ, God's Son. As regards the first of these, Paul employs a double purpose clause in Galatians 4:4–5, the second of which demonstrates how adoption is rooted in the revelation of the Son of God in the last days: 'when the fullness of time had come, *God sent his Son ... in order that we might receive the adoption as sons*' (*exapesteilen ho theos ton huion autou ... hina tēn huiothesian apolabōmen*) (my emphasis). In Paul's view there is a clear link between the appearing of God's Son in the human condition and our

---

[21] My point here is not that adoption is *the* 'organizing metaphor' under which all other important soteriological expressions in Paul fall. Rather, *huiothesia* is merely one expression tied to but also distinct from these theological themes.

[22] I am indebted to Ferguson's stimulating essay (1986: 86–87), although I have amended his criteria in what follows.

huiothesia, so that Herman Ridderbos rightly concludes, 'The sonship of believers is ... closely bound up with the fact that Christ is the Son of God. When God reveals his Son, the adoption as sons takes place' (1977: 199).

But Paul also strikes an important Christological and soteriological note in the first purpose clause in Galatians 4:5, when he states that God's Son was revealed '*in order to redeem* (*hina tous ... exagorasē*) ... that we might receive the adoption as sons' (my trans.). Ultimately, Paul *grounds* our adoption in the *work* of God's Son on the cross. Paul's thinking here in Galatians (and in the other relevant passages) demonstrates a triad of interconnected metaphors – slavery, redemption and adoption – and in describing his readers as being in '*slavery* to the basic principles of the world' (Gal. 4:3; cf. Rom. 8:15) he moves from their need of *freedom* (redemption, Gal. 4:5) to that of receiving the *adoption as sons* (Gal. 4:6; Rom. 8:15). The point Paul does not want his readers to miss is that when one is adopted into the family of God, it is uniquely and exclusively 'through Jesus Christ' (Eph. 1:5) and 'at infinite cost to him' (Ferguson 1989: 31). In short, it is through God's Son that we are adopted as sons of God, and if we take Paul's *huiothesia* metaphor 'out of its *Christological context* we shall misinterpret and misunderstand it' (Smail 1980: 147; my emphasis).

Adoption demands an appropriate ethical response

In keeping with the scope of his other soteriological metaphors,[23] Paul also discusses the moral implications of adoption. Indeed, this ethical perspective of *huiothesia* is an important one for the apostle and has often been overlooked by commentators and scholars in the past. Burke (1995: 64) says, 'the *ethical* responsibility for God's sons to live circumspectly pervades Paul's thesis of adoption', and nowhere is this better delineated than in the apostle's discussion in Ephesians 1:5–6 (cf. Rom. 8:12–17; 8:29).[24]

An important feature of the introit to Paul's letters is the way in which he traces the manifold blessings of the Christian back to God

[23] McGrath (1988: 115–128) discusses 'The Ethical Dimension' of justification.

[24] Pauline authorship of Ephesians was not challenged until the late eighteenth and early nineteenth century. Prior to that time Ephesians was universally recognized as Pauline. Today, however, this is not the case – the majority of New Testament scholars are of the view that Paul did not write Ephesians. Reasonable arguments, however, have been advanced for Pauline authorship (van Roon 1992; O'Brien 1999; Hoehner 2002). Another related issue is that of the opening phrase 'in Ephesus' (1:1), which most scholars believe to be textually uncertain and as a consequence think that this was a circular letter for all of the churches in Asia Minor, circulated, perhaps, at the same time that Colossians and Philemon were sent to specific addresses.

the Father (e.g. Gal. 1:3, 4; Phil. 1:2; 1 Thess. 1:3). Ephesians 1:2, 4–5 is no exception in this respect; and the fact that the apostle Paul begins his letters in this way is no accident or mere repetition, for every time his remarks are tailored to the needs of each Christian community. In the case of his letter to the Ephesian believers, Paul's introduction underscores that having God as our Father is the source of Paul's ethical exhortation for adopted sons to behave in a manner befitting those who claim to belong to God's new family.[25]

Thus in Ephesians 1:3–5 Paul at the outset strikes a theocentric note by extolling God the Father, 'who has blessed us in the heavenly realms with every spiritual blessing in Christ' (v. 3). He then informs his Ephesian readers that this same Father has also elected and predestined us unto the adoption as sons by Jesus Christ with the supreme purpose that we should be holy and without blame before him. As Allen Mawhinney (1988: 188) rightly states of Ephesians 1:4–5, 'Paul expresses the Christian's holiness and blamelessness as the goal or purpose of his election and predestination to sonship.'

It is noteworthy here how Paul anchors adoption in the divine purposes of God the Father, which he then uses as a basis to link *huiothesia* with sanctification without ever blurring the distinction between these two. Paul wishes to stress that our adoption as sons is not an end in itself; rather, God the Father has a goal in view for his adopted sons and there is also an obligation upon the latter to honour the former by seeking to live in such a way as to attain that goal. In this respect the social reality and practice of adoption in antiquity is most enlightening for what Paul has to say about the believer's responsibility as an adopted son. Just as in the ancient world all sons, including those who had been adopted, were expected to behave in a manner that would not discredit their father or besmirch the family name, so it is the responsibility for spiritually adopted sons belonging to the divine household to live scrupulously and blamelessly by bringing glory to their holy, heavenly Father.

Adoption expresses the eschatological tension between the 'now' and the 'not yet'

When Paul discusses different soteriological metaphors in his writings, there is a tension struck between what believers have in the present (the 'now') and what has yet to be consummated in the future

---

[25] DeSilva (2000: 207, 211) writes, 'Having God as Father becomes a source of ethical exhortation throughout the New Testament.'

(the 'not yet'). In other words, there is an eschatological stress between what has already happened in the event of individuals coming to faith and the work of God in reclaiming individuals for himself, which still lies in the future. In fact, such an 'eschatological viewpoint underlies the whole of Pauline theology' (Kreitzer 1994: 253–269).[26]

This eschatological tension can be seen, for instance, in Paul's principal soteriological metaphor, justification, when he informs the Roman Christians that they 'have [already] been justified' (Rom. 5:1) but that they can still look forward to being acquitted at the final judgment: 'by faith we eagerly await through the Spirit the righteousness for which we hope' (Gal. 5:5). Similarly, we read that redemption is 'now', 'the redemption that came by Christ Jesus' (Rom. 3:24), but that 'the redemption of our bodies' (Rom. 8:23) still awaits. This dialectic is admirably stated within the few verses on adoption in Romans 8. The alpha point, the already, is the present reality of the 'Spirit of *huiothesia*' (Rom. 8:15), which believers now have; but the omega point, its completion, still lies ahead: 'as we wait eagerly for our adoption as sons' (Rom. 8:23).[27] In sum, adoption has 'a retrospective and a prospective dimension' (Ferguson 1986: 87) ('what we now have is real, but it is not the whole' [Morris 1988: 324]), and, in keeping with other soteriological metaphors in Paul's

---

[26] The ancient perception of the overlap between the present and the future was much more real and tangible than ours in the twenty-first century, as Philip Esler (2003: 261) remarks: 'The commonplace expression in New Testament studies "now and not yet" is indelibly stamped' on us and 'we are accustomed to envisaging precise moments or events in future, possibly a long way off, that may have no real connection with the present experience, for example, the first manned space flight to Mars.' And according to Malina (1996: 195), what distinguishes 'the forthcoming' (i.e. the Mediterranean sense of the future) from the future in twenty-first-century society 'is the degree of immediate and direct organic connection with some presently experienced person, event or process. When exactly that potentiality might be realized is not at issue as it would be for us. Rather the item at issue is the inevitability of the outcomes rather than how many and when.'

[27] Some New Testament scholars have difficulty with the 'not yet' dimension pertaining to our adoption as sons (Rom. 8:23). On the basis of Rom. 8:14–15 they argue that if adoption is fully received, how then can an already adopted son be adopted at a later stage? See Fitzmyer 1993: 510. Fitzmyer partly reaches this conclusion on the basis that *huiothesia* in Rom. 8:23 is not authentic. He tries to argue that it is an intrusion into the text and therefore does not fit the context of what was stated previously in v. 15. But if the presence of *huiothesia* in v. 23 is a case of *lectio difficilior* (the more difficult reading), then according to the principles of textual criticism it is a better attested reading and should be accepted. Hence there is here a dialectic between the fact of our adoption as sons that we already possess and the fuller sense of that adoption that will be displayed when we are set free from the bodily limitations in the future.

writings, delineates what has already been accomplished but also points forward to a glorious consummation of what is yet to be.

Summary

It is time to draw together some of the threads of the discussion in this chapter. We have established that *huiothesia* is always employed metaphorically by the apostle in his letters. Further, it is likely that adoption was a term Paul took from his own social context (although we shall test this hypothesis in the next chapter) and applied to his understanding of Christian relations. It is important (in chapter 3) to understand this term against its sociohistorical context in order to understand the metaphor properly; only then can we appreciate the impact of its meaning on Paul's hearers.

We have also seen how Paul employs metaphors drawn from many walks of life to describe the saving grace of God. Thus, to argue that 'justification' is the only term to describe salvation, as opposed to terms such as 'adoption' or 'redemption', seems from this perspective to miss the rich, metaphorical language the apostle Paul had at his disposal (Badcock 1997: 105). Paul employs a variety of expressions in his understanding of salvation, and 'adoption' is another important term. *Huiothesia* also satisfies the criteria for consideration as another organizing soteriological term for the apostle. Indeed, adoption adds nuances of meaning absent from other salvation terms and is indisputably the most intimate of Paul's metaphors because it is taken from the realm of the family in the ancient world.[28]

---

[28] Some might argue that a father in antiquity was an authority figure, which is true, but a 'new consensus' among classicists is emerging; namely, that a father's authority was also benign (Saller 1994: 96).

Chapter Three

The origin and background of Paul's adoption metaphor

Where does Paul's *huiothesia* term originate? What were the sources of his theology, and if we can identify them, how, if at all, have they influenced his use of the adoption metaphor? Such questions invariably open up one of the most contentious issues in respect of Paul's adoption term; namely, the *background* he employed when giving theological expression to his metaphor.

In response to these questions, scholars have usually couched the issue in the following manner: when Paul used his adoption term, was he drawing from an Old Testament background? Or did he have in mind the Greek or Roman sociolegal practices prevalent in the non-Jewish Mediterranean civilization of his day?[1] Stating the question in this way unfortunately betrays a false 'either or' antithesis that not only pre-empts any objective presentation and discussion of the available evidence but also assumes a dichotomy between the Jewish and Graeco-Roman cultural traditions and backgrounds.[2] This last

[1] During the twentieth century, Greek, Jewish and Roman legal backgrounds were posited, with the balance of weight coming down in favour of the Roman (Calder 1930: 372–374; Theron 1956: 6–14; Lyall 1984: 67–99 respectively).

[2] We cannot neatly compartmentalize ancient society into 'Jewish' and 'Graeco-Roman' worlds, since these cultural backgrounds were inextricably woven together prior to the time of the apostle Paul. We know that Judaism was progressively Hellenized during the third and second centuries BC and that Palestine was a part of this Hellenization process. Indeed, Jerusalem itself was remade into a Greek city between 175 and 167 BC, until the Torah was restored as the law of the land by the house of Judas Maccabaeus.

Furthermore, the interplay of these cultural influences is clearly evident in ancient literary writings contemporaneous with Paul. Examples of Jewish works that have been infiltrated, to a greater or lesser degree, by the Hellenistic world are 4 Maccabees, the Philonic corpus and Pseudo-Phoclyides. For more on this see the decisive work of Hengel (1977) and the more recent collection of essays edited by Engberg-Pedersen (2001). Engberg-Pedersen (2000: 3) asserts, 'Scholars must attempt to shed all unacknowledged, ideological, and historically unfounded presuppositions in addressing Paul in his context, by giving up altogether using any form of the Judaism/Hellenism divide as an interpretative lens. Instead, one must look entirely open-mindedly at the facts.'

point is important not least because since the 1980s there has been a greater appreciation and understanding of the interplay between the broad cultural backgrounds in the ancient world that have impacted the New Testament writings in general and the Pauline corpus in particular. Consequently, scholars are much less prone to think of Hellenism/Judaism(s) in such a disjunctive manner as illustrated above.

Very much related to this question of the background(s) that may have impacted Paul's *huiothesia* term is another important factor: Paul's own diverse cultural background, a rich blend of milieus. Paul was a Jew, 'a Hebrew of Hebrews, ... a Pharisee' (Phil. 3:5), linguistically he was fluent in Greek and Aramaic (cf. Acts 21:40; 22:2), and if we accept that he was also a Roman citizen[3] (Acts 22:27), we begin to appreciate not only the richness but also the diversity and complexity of his heritage. To be sure, this does not automatically include or exclude any of the above backgrounds that may be associated with Paul's adoption metaphor; clearly, we need to test these by carefully scrutinizing the evidence before coming to an informed conclusion. It is to this evidence that we now turn.

The Old Testament background

As noted earlier, there are no biblical laws in the Old Testament governing the practice of *huiothesia*.[4] This lack of formal legal adoption in the Old Testament Scriptures, however, has not prevented scholars attempting to root Paul's *huiothesia* expression

---

[3] The biblical case for Paul's Roman citizenship rests on three texts in Acts (16:37–39; 22:25–29; 25:7–12). According to the first, Paul's mention of his Roman citizenship ensures his release from jail after having been flogged. This text has proved problematic, since Roman citizens were exempt from public floggings, and one reason why Paul does not mention his citizenship is so that he can follow in the sufferings of Jesus (e.g. Phil. 3:10–11; 2 Cor. 4:7–10; 6:4–10). In Acts 22:25–29 Paul's citizenship is invoked and proves useful in securing protection by the Roman garrison from an angry crowd. In Acts 25:7–12 Paul appears in Caesarea before Festus, who offers to conduct a full trial back in Jerusalem. But Paul refuses on the basis of his Roman citizenship. How Paul acquired his Roman citizenship is a matter of some debate. According to traditions preserved in Jerome (Philemon commentary; *Vir.* 5) and Photius (*Quaest. Amphil.* 116), Paul's parents were carried off as prisoners of war from the Judean town of Gischala to Tarsus. Presumably, enslaved to a Roman, they were freed and granted citizenship. As a result, Paul was 'born' a Roman citizen, which is one possible rendering of the phrase *egō de kai gegennēmai* in Acts 22:28. Stegemann (1978: 200–229) argues against Paul's Roman citizenship, arguments strongly rebutted by Hengel (1991).

[4] See appendix for discussion of some alleged cases of adoption.

in particular Old Testament texts.[5] We shall examine two main examples; namely, the relationship of the nation of Israel and the king of Israel to Yahweh as instances of 'adoption'.

The nation of Israel: God's 'adopted son'?

We deal with the nation of Israel first, since Paul employs the term *huiothesia* in respect of Israel in Romans 9:4 and since James Cook (1978: 137) insists that this text 'remains the logical place to *begin* an exegetical inquiry into the *origin* and content of the Pauline notion of adoption' (see also Byrne 1979: 81). Romans 9:4 reads, 'Theirs is the adoption as sons (lit. *huiothesia*), theirs the divine glory, the covenants,[6] the receiving of the law, the temple worship and the promises.' Here Paul locates adoption within a formal list of historical privileges the nation of Israel enjoyed.[7] According to Paul, adoption heads the list of honourable blessings bestowed upon the people of God. In the apostle's mind, at least, God had taken Israel, one of the most insignificant groups of people in the Ancient Near Eastern world, to be his adopted son. For Paul, *huiothesia* was a privilege that adhered to Israel as a whole, setting this nation apart from the surrounding nations for blessing and service.[8] Some biblical scholars have sought to link Romans 9:4 with different Old Testament texts, one of which is Exodus 4:22–23, which reads, 'This is what the LORD says [to Pharaoh]: Israel is my firstborn son ... "Let my son go, so that he may worship me."' This text has been understood by commentators in terms of Yahweh's adoption of the nation of Israel, and has drawn the following comment from George A. F. Knight (1998: 160): 'Here we are told that God the Father called out of Egypt this peculiar people and that ... he had adopted his Son ... and that he had done so for no other reason than ... that he loved the Son.'

James Cook (1978: 138) is even more convinced of the precise nature of this filial relationship and argues forcefully in respect of

---

[5] Ziesler (1992: 58) is representative of many when he assumes that 'despite the absence of the word from the LXX, in the OT the idea that Israel had been chosen (adopted?) by God as his child is clearly present, e.g., Ex. 4:22, Hos. 11:1'.

[6] The singular 'covenant' is the preferred reading in the Nestlé apparatus. For a defence of this reading and a discussion of the Exodus allusions in respect of the terms 'glory', 'receiving the law' etc. in Rom. 9:4, see Christianen 1997: 220–224.

[7] Byrne (1979: 83) analyses the form and construction of the six expressions in Rom. 9:4 and concludes that the list of privileges pre-exists (in 'Hellenistic Judaism') Paul's usage. However, the passages he advances (2 Macc. 2:17; *4 Ezra* 5:23ff.) do not share the same terms, especially *huiothesia*.

[8] Moo 1996: 562; Theron 1956: 14.

Exodus 4:22 that '[this] adoptive relationship between Yahweh and his people ... is foundational to the Old Testament'. Given that Israel had no myth of descent from the gods, as found in the prevailing cultures of that time, adoption, it is alleged, was an appropriate term to describe the nation's relationship to God (Davids 2001: 13). Similar arguments have also been made regarding another Old Testament scripture in the prophecy of Hosea, where, despite Israel's disobedience and subsequent captivity into exile, the author describes the restoration of Yahweh's relationship with the nation thus:

> When Israel was a child, I loved him,
> and out of Egypt I called my son.
>
> (Hos. 11:1)

Many assume this text depicts Israel's relationship to God in terms of adoption, the upshot of which has prompted C. E. B. Cranfield (1975: 397) to conclude, 'when Paul used the word *huiothesia* in Romans 9:4 he had Old Testament material in mind', because the notion of 'adoption is implied in Yahweh's relation to Israel, his "son"' (Bruce 1982: 197).[9] Thus those subscribing to this viewpoint conclude that Paul's contribution to our understanding of his adoption expression does not consist in him coining a new metaphor (Atkins 1991: 179), but rather in his extending a traditional way of speaking about the privilege of Israel in the Old Testament and applying it to the Christian community.[10]

Before we consider other more important evidence in relation to sonship in the Old Testament, we shall signal some reservations of the above view at this stage. First, *Paul* is working on the *assumption* that Israel's relationship to Yahweh is an adoptive one. What Paul states about Israel's adoption in Romans 9:4 points retrospectively to the Old Testament Scriptures, where we would expect to find all the related historical links and connections to which he refers. In particular, we would anticipate finding some clear textual and linguistic evidence to support Israel's relationship to God as an

---

[9] See also Rees (1977: 55), who is also of the view that 'in some sense He [God] bestowed ... adoption upon Israel'.

[10] Atkins (1991: 179), drawing on the insights of Adolf von Harnack, points out that 'Adoption terminology in the New Testament may be an application to every individual of an older, Jewish understanding of God's relationship with God's people. In this manner, a theological understanding with Jewish roots may have been used by Paul to describe the relationship of Christians to God.'

adopted son. However, when we look to the Old Testament Scriptures for such support, it is absent. As we have already seen, the term 'adoption' is not found in the LXX. Moreover, it should be noted in respect of Exodus 4:22 and Hosea 11:1 how 'in the historical tradition, the assertion that Israel is Yahweh's son *precedes* the Exodus, a fact of which Hosea was aware' (C. J. H. Wright 1990: 17; my emphasis).

Much more important on the horizon of the Old Testament authors is the more general language of sonship, not adoption. Indeed, the theme of *sonship* has a remarkable and powerful trajectory, not only in the Old Testament (see below) but also throughout the whole canon of Scripture (e.g. Matt. 5:9; Luke 6:35; John 1:12; 11:52; 2 Cor. 6:18; Gal. 3:26; Rom. 8:14; Heb. 2:10; 12:5–8), and is more dominant than many have realized. Sonship in the Hebrew Bible has a broad spectrum of meanings[11] and denotes the more usual filial relationship (Gen. 3:16; Exod. 21:5). This designation of 'son(s)' also extends to a wider range of relationships (Gen. 49:8; Judg. 8:19), including membership of a family or tribe (e.g. Deut. 2:4, 12, 22). Angels too are described as 'sons of God' (Gen. 6:2, 4), as are human rulers and judges (Ps. 82:6). The pagan king Nebuchadnezzar (Dan. 3:25) employs this expression to describe the mysterious fourth person in the fiery furnace. Even Satan (Job 1:6; 2:1) is identified as a 'son of God'.[12]

With this aspect of sonship in view, it is also important to take cognizance of the way in which Old Testament writers make the important distinction between Israel, the nation, as 'son' (in the singular) and individual Israelites who are described as 'sons' or 'children' (in the plural). We shall now consider these in turn.

The nation of Israel as son of God

The father–son relationship between God and Israel is but a mirror of the real relationship and expectations between parents and children in ancient Israelite society as a whole. Notably, the nation of Israel's relationship of son to God does not come about because of any action on the part of the former; rather, it is a consequence of divine initiative. Jeremiah 31:9 especially emphasizes this aspect of God's sovereignty: 'I am Israel's father, / and Ephraim is my firstborn son'

[11] Here I am relying on Ninan 1994.

[12] For more on the background and common expectations of the father–son relationship in Israelite society see C. J. H. Wright 1992: 119–121. I am drawing heavily on Chris Wright's fine study for some of my discussion here.

(cf. Exod. 4:22; Deut. 32:6; Hos. 11:1; Isa. 63:15–16; 64:8). Out of all the nations of the then known world Yahweh set his covenant love upon Israel for no other reason than that he loved them (Deut. 7:7). The 'glue' that held this relationship together was love, Yahweh's love for his children, which not only denoted real affection but also expected obedience and faithfulness. In fact as mentioned above, this filial relationship was founded upon Yahweh's covenant love for his people, an intimacy seen most graphically in Hosea, where God is described as a father who teaches Israel his infant son to take the first faltering steps:

> It was I who taught Ephraim to walk,
> taking them by the arms.
>
> (Hos. 11:3)

Yahweh too is described as Israel's provider in times of trouble when protection was needed. This is especially evident when Yahweh fought and cared for the nation during forty years of wandering in the wilderness: 'The LORD your God ... will fight for you ... in the desert ... you saw how the LORD your God carried you, as a father carries his son' (Deut. 1:29–31). Closely connected to this father–son relationship in regard to Yahweh and Israel is the whole issue of the land and Israel's inheritance, which 'is another way of expressing and reinforcing the point that Israel is Yahweh's son, for it is the firstborn who inherits' (C. J. H. Wright 1992: 123). The land was an unconditional gift by Yahweh and not a result of anything Israel as son could possibly earn or merit. It is significant how, as Leo Perdue points out, the land was not given to 'Israel's and Judah's kings or even to their temple and priests but rather to the children of Israel in general and in particular to their households from the very beginning of the nation' (Perdue 1997: 237).

It is also important to note how in Exodus 4:22 the nation is described as Yahweh's 'firstborn son', where the word *firstborn* implies that other sons will follow (C. J. H. Wright 1992: 130).[13] We have observed already how Israel's filial relationship to Yahweh was unique (e.g. Deut. 7:7), the inference being that Yahweh was *not* the

---

[13] This is the meaning conveyed in the agricultural expression 'first fruits', indicating that more of the same would follow. Christ is also described by Paul as the 'firstborn among many brothers' (Rom. 8:29), meaning that his resurrection sets him apart as the head of the family and that Christians will share in the status of sonship as they are added to the family.

father of other nations of the world. Having said this, the notion of Israel being Yahweh's firstborn son looks forward to a time when other nations will enter into the blessing of sonship (C. J. H. Wright 1992: 130; contra Ninan 1994: 26).

In order that this might be brought about, Israel was to play an instrumental role, since inextricably linked with the nation's distinguished filial privileged position was the responsibility to be a beacon and witness to the surrounding nations. Thus bound up with Israel's distinct relationship of son was an important 'missionary' and evangelistic thrust. 'From this point of view, the sonship of Israel can be understood as a "missionary" concept' (C. J. H. Wright 1992: 130). If the expectation of other nations to become 'sons' was to be realized, it was imperative for Israel to exercise its own filial duties and responsibilities as 'son', which included fidelity and obedience to Yahweh and his covenant. This is no small point, as sonship language in the Old Testament has an important bearing on a whole raft of issues, including ethics, likeness, obedience and so on. As a result of Israel's privileged relationship to Yahweh, the nation is a holy nation and this sanctified status and subsequent manner of living was not an optional extra for the Jewish people but a call by God to filial fidelity and obedience.

Israel, however, failed to live in accordance with God's expectations and, while on the one hand the Old Testament presents us with a tender picture of God the Father lovingly caring for and bringing up this wayward son, Israel on the other hand proved to be rebellious and seditious. As a consequence, Yahweh was required to take the necessary punitive action to curb the nation's waywardness. God's judgment of Israel, his son, was especially apparent during the nation's wilderness wanderings, which were a 'schooling period' (Ninan 1994: 25), and the eventual loss of nationhood and political exile; indeed, it seemed the more that Yahweh called this son to himself 'the more recalcitrantly he ran the other way' (Knight 1998: 160), to the extent that Israel 'deserted the Rock, who fathered' them (Deut. 32:18).

Despite Israel's reckless behaviour in the pre-exilic era (see below), however, the familial relationship with Yahweh did not fracture completely: 'The father–son relationship between God and Israel ... contained within itself an element of permanence ... the Father could not ultimately disown his son' (C. J. H. Wright 1992: 127). Indeed, it is important to note that the original declaration of Israel's sonship (Exod. 4:22) was appealed to as the foundation of a restored relationship in the post-exilic era (Isa. 63:16; 64:8). Israel's relationship of son to Yahweh in the pre-exilic era (Exod. 4:22) was restored after the nation had been subjected to captivity, as Chris Wright (1992: 126; my emphasis) points out:

> The father–son relationship between Yahweh and Israel was a ground for hope and permanence, even when Israel stood among the wreckage of a broken covenant – a covenant, that is, broken by their own disobedience. *The sonship relationship was something that survived the greatest disaster.*

In spite of *all* that had happened to Israel and *all* that the nation had come through, Hosea 11:1 specifically reminds us that Israel's sonship was still intact, demonstrated by the way in which Yahweh rescues his son from the embers of the exile with the reminder of his unbroken covenant love:

> When Israel was a child, I loved him,
> and out of Egypt I called my son.

Allied to this is the promise and the prospect of a brighter future for Israel, God's son. This filial relationship between Yahweh and Israel, as we have seen, is a seam that runs deep in the Old Testament, bridging both pre- and postexilic eras. But in the postexilic era in particular we see Yahweh desiring a new father–son relationship between himself and Israel, restated and again based upon the principle of reciprocity: Yahweh would provide the gift of an inheritance, while Israel would be expected this time to respond in obedience.

His poignant invitation is recorded by the prophet in the first-person singular:

> How gladly would *I* treat you like sons
> and give you a desirable land,
> the most beautiful inheritance of any nation.
> *I* thought you would call me 'Father'
> and not run away from following me.
>   (Jer. 3:19; my emphasis)

In Jeremiah 4 the 'missionary' thrust and blessing that will ensue is repeated and laid before Israel, God's son, with the proviso that the nation obeys this time:

> If you put your detestable idols out of my sight
> and no longer go astray,
> and if in a truthful, just and righteous way
> you swear, 'As surely as the LORD lives,'
> *then the nations will be blessed by him*
> and in him they will glory.'
>
> (Jer. 4:1–2; my emphasis)

The prospect is held out before Israel once more to respond positively and grasp the opportunity to live honourably as Yahweh expected and intended his son to live. Only *then* would the promise of blessing to other nations as sons become a real possibility. In all this we see the special and unique relationship between Yahweh and Israel; moreover, the relationship was permanent and enduring, and because there was a future for his son, there would also be a future for the rest of the world (C. J. H. Wright 1992: 130). Yahweh could not and would not abandon his son; more positively, he was inextricably connected to Israel forever.

But not only are there occasions when Israel as a nation is referred to as God's son, there are also times when the plural is used to describe Israelites as 'sons' or 'children'. It is worth noting these before we proceed.

Israelites as sons/children of God

Closely allied to the notion of Israel as a son (in the singular) are those occasions in the Old Testament when the Israelites are referred to in the plural as 'sons' of Yahweh (C. J. H. Wright 1992: 123). For example, Isaiah, the evangelical prophet, cries:

> Hear, O heavens! Listen, O earth!
> For the LORD has spoken:
> 'I reared children and brought them up...'
>
> (Isa. 1:2; cf. 30:9; Jer. 3:22)

We also read in Deuteronomy 14:1–2, 'You are the children of the LORD your God ... you are a people holy to the LORD your God. Out of all the peoples on the face of the earth, the LORD has chosen you to be his treasured possession.'

Particularly striking here is the fact that Deuteronomy 14:1–2 'invokes the father–son relationship as the basis for exhortation to holiness' (Wright 1997: 18). 'Just as Israel, as a result of its relationship with Yahweh, is a holy nation, so these sons of Yahweh must be also' (Lagrange 1908: 483). On different occasions sonship language is used to remind the Israelites of how far they have fallen from God's standards by rebelling against his ways. For example, whereas Isaiah describes the Israelites as 'rebellious children' (30:9) because they have turned their backs on their father, Jeremiah, the so-called weeping prophet (3:21), describes them as 'faithless sons' (3:22) 'because they have perverted their ways / and have forgotten the LORD their God'.

In accordance with father–son relations in the ancient Near East, the expectation was for a son to obey his father (C. J. H. Wright 1992: 121) and to honour him at all times, an expectation unrealized at national (Israel) and individual (Israelites) levels. Malachi laments this fact concerning God's people, a people swiftly losing touch with the living God, when he states, ' "A son honours his father, and a servant his master. If I am a father, where is the honour due to me? If I am a master, where is the respect due to me?" says the LORD Almighty' (Mal. 1:6).[14] What we find, then, in these prophetic references to the Israelites as sons of God in the plural form is that on the majority of occasions God's people are on the receiving end of Yahweh's anger and rebuke. The reason is obvious: the Israelites are 'failing in their duty as sons to live in ethical obedience to God' (C. J. H. Wright 1992: 123).

Before we conclude our survey of the Old Testament evidence, there is one final aspect of sonship that has been posited as the background to Paul's adoption term; namely, the king's relationship to God as 'adopted son'.

King David: God's adopted son? (2 Sam. 7:11–16)

In recent years one Old Testament text that has been the focus of scholarly attention as far as the study of the background to Paul's adoption expression is concerned is 2 Samuel 7:11–16. Here we read of Nathan speaking a timely and prophetic word to king David:

> The LORD declares to you that the LORD himself will establish a house for you: When your days are over and you rest with your fathers, I will raise up your offspring to succeed you, who will come from your own body, and I will establish his kingdom. He is the one who will build a house for my Name, and I will establish

---

[14] For more on the relationship between adoption and honour see chapter 7. See also Burke 2003a: 53–55, 67–68, 77, 90, where honour is discussed as one of a raft of stock meanings of the father–son relationship in the first-century era.

the throne of his kingdom for ever. I will be his father, and he shall be my son ... Your house and your kingdom shall endure for ever before me; your throne shall be established for ever.

In the early 1990s James Scott endeavoured to argue the case for considering 2 Samuel 7:11–16 (cf. Ps. 2:7) as an instance of an 'Adoption formula' (Scott 1992: 100). As well as finding a number of instances of adoption in the Old Testament, the most important being that of Moses (e.g. Exod. 2:10; Esth. 2:7, 15; Gen. 48:5–6), Scott regards the throne oracle to David in 2 Samuel 7:14 as a genuine case of divine adoption. God enters into a unique covenant relationship with an individual, King David, out of which he promises him a royal dynasty. This covenant, the Davidic, is the third mentioned in the Old Testament, and in keeping with patrilineage (the kingship system traced through the father) a covenant relating to the monarchy was expressed in a dynastic succession from father to son.

Scott's understanding of the promise in 2 Samuel 7:14 is subsumed under the wider context of God's covenant with Israel, which allows for the participation of the whole people in the adoption privilege of the king. Scott (1992: 100) insists that the relationship between the king (David) and the people of God (the Israelites) in 2 Samuel 7 includes 'national adoption'. The phrase 'I will be his father, and he shall be my son' (v. 14) is a promise that Yahweh would make an eternal dynasty with the house of David or 'the Davidide'.[15] 'Specifically, the 2 Sam. 7:14 tradition expects, that at the advent of the Messiah, God would redeem his people from exile in a Second Exodus; he would restore them to a covenant relationship; and he would adopt them with the Messiah, as his sons' (Scott 1992: 268). All these aspects, argues the author, converge in later Jewish texts (*Jub.* 1:24; 4QFlor 1:1; *T. Jud.* 24:3) and are ultimately fulfilled in the New Testament (Gal. 4:1–7).

Scott's thesis invites a number of responses. First, can we equate kingship with adoption? For, as De Boer (1974: 22) argues, 'the right of adoption brings us into an entirely different realm of ideas than that of kingship'. De Boer (22) further asserts:

Adoption has to do with the rights of children in a family and such rights are often stipulations concerning inheritance. It is quite clear

---

[15] Scott uses lexical evidence to link this adoption formula to the alleged adoption of Moses (Exod. 2:10), Esther (Esth. 2:7) and Ephraim and Manasseh (cf. Gen. 48:5). But it is very unlikely that these are genuine instances of adoption. See appendix.

that such an adoption is not relevant when the king at his coronation is elevated to the status of a son of God.

Second, and more importantly, if 2 Samuel 7:11–16 is an example of an adoption formula,[16] can we conclude on the basis of this text alone that (Byrne 1994: 290; my emphasis)

> Paul's singular use of the Hellenistic term for 'adoption' ... reflects a conscious appropriation of a Jewish tradition which saw 2 Sam. 7:14 understood as adoption, fulfilled or to be fulfilled in the messianic age? It would be far easier to believe that this was the case had the Jewish tradition prior to Paul, at least in its Greek form, used the word *huiothesia* in this respect. But the word nowhere occurs. Nor in this context do the more customary Greek periphrases for adoption (on Philo, *Sobr.* 56). We have only certain texts reiterating the language of the 2 Sam. 7:14 oracle. This may have been understood 'adoptively', but *in the absence of more precise language, we remain on the level of surmise.*[17]

In the light of 'this lack of intervening evidence' we cannot be completely sure that Paul was alluding to 2 Samuel 7:11–16; moreover, to situate the entire background of Paul's adoption term against a *single* text, as Scott endeavours to do, is much like a one-legged stool that will not stand. As we have seen, this text needs to be considered within the wider and much more important aspect of sonship in the Old Testament and the importance of sonship within the intertestamental literature, especially the book Wisdom of Solomon (cf. 2:13, 16, 18; 5:5; 9:7; 22:7, 20; 16:10; 18:13; 19:6).[18] The pervasiveness of the general idea of sonship is where Paul's

---

[16] It should also be noted that the king is never referred to as a 'son of God' in 2 Sam. 7:12–14.

[17] As we shall see when we turn to the 'adoption' text, there are also fundamental flaws with Scott's exegesis of Gal. 4:1–7. Here he couches everything in terms of Egyptian typology, where Israel's redemption from slavery (vv. 1–2) is a type of eschatological redemption effected by Christ (vv. 3–7), whom he regards as a second Moses. In addition to his structuring of 4:1–7, the major difficulty is that Paul in his letters is not the slightest bit concerned with the *Egyptian* period of bondage but with the period *after* Israel's emancipation from captivity. Sampley (2003: 42–76) also questions Scott's conclusions: 'Scott's separation of the Hellenistic meaning from the Jewish background is problematic. Even if Paul sought to evoke Jewish expectations based on 2 Sam. 7:14, he could not have removed himself from the Greco-Roman world. Rather, as a Jew at home in the urban centers of the Greek East, Paul's usage would have been informed by his (and his readers') Greco-Roman context.'

[18] See Byrne (1979) for a discussion of the intertestamental literature.

understanding of *huiothesia* is rooted in the Old Testament. Before I summarize these findings we need to consider two other backgrounds, the Greek and Roman contexts.

The Greek background

The case for a Greek legal background to Paul's adoption metaphor has not been without its advocates. David Moore-Crispin (1989: 216), for instance, on the basis of two manuscripts from Graeco-Egypt (*POxy* 1206; *PLip* 28) states, 'The external evidence favouring Hellenistic law generally as the source of Paul's legal metaphors is particularly strong with respect to adoption.' There is no doubt that Greek law would both have been known and have been available to the apostle Paul. Though Tarsus, Paul's place of birth, was a Roman colony, many of its inhabitants were not Roman citizens and local Greek laws would have been in operation. Greek law also ruled in many of the cities through which Paul travelled on his missionary journeys and was present in areas close to Judea; for example, the Greek cities of the Decapolis, immediately across from the Sea of Tiberius. It is possible that this is the origin of Paul's knowledge of Greek law. But did Paul consciously draw from this source in using his adoption term?

Perhaps the first point that should be made is that most of the Greek data are drawn from the fourth century BC, which is early and remote from the time of the apostle Paul. In view of this, we ought to exercise caution in regard to the weight we place on this evidence. Under Greek law, and by the time of Isaeus, adoption could occur in one of three ways.

First, the civic Code of Gortyn in Crete, the source for the earliest reference to adoption in Greece, describes how adoption could take place *inter vivos* (during the life of). In this case, the adoption procedure was executed through a formal ceremony during the lifetime of the adopter, who would register the adoptee with the latter's consent in the *dēmos* (the local government constituency) and the *phratria* (a social grouping of families) to which the adopting family belonged. There were, however, limitations with this transaction in that while the adoptive son was allowed some rights of inheritance, 'these were not as great as those of a son by birth' (Smith 1970: 9).

A second adoption procedure was adoption by will or testament, which took effect only upon the death of a testator. Here the adoptee had then to claim his inheritance relying on that will. A son adopted by will was legally bound to marry the testator's legitimate daughter; otherwise the will and the adoption became invalid, and the door was opened for the next of kin to claim both the daughter and the estate.

A third possibility was 'posthumous adoption'. In this instance, if a man died without legitimate issue and without having adopted a son, the next of kin succeeded the estate, or his issue was adopted into the family of the deceased as his son.

Greek law, as we shall see below, shares many similarities with its Roman counterpart. For instance, only a person without any legitimate surviving offspring could adopt. Also, adoption quite often occurred late in a person's life, and strict regulations were in place to ensure the mental fitness of the adopter. Again, Greek and Roman law share the normal social expectation that all offspring, including adopted sons, were to look after their parents in later life and give them a decent burial (Goody 1969: 62).[19]

However, there were also clear differences between Greek and Roman legal procedures, for there are Roman 'regulations concerning adoption, which find ... no parallel in Greece' (Woodhouse 1908: 111). For example, the absolute nature of adoption, so much a part of the Roman legal practice, was conspicuously absent in Hellenistic law, in that an adoptee did not sever completely his relationships with his old family when entering the 'new' family. Thus an adopted son may have stepped from the family of his natural father into the family of his adoptive father but 'he did not lose his relationship to his mother' (109). More importantly, in Greek law the family cultus was to be guarded lest it become extinct. While adoption may have begun as a device to ensure continuity of the family cult, it increasingly became more popular as a means of ensuring that an estate continued within the family. As Woodhouse (108) states, 'The Athenian of the days of Isaeus adopted a son, in very many cases at least, primarily in order to leave him *property*' (my emphasis). In other words, succession became the dominating influence for adoption in Greek law, and this was carried out by transmitting the estate down the line to a blood relative.

Finally, there was no such thing as a coherent body of Greek law that could be consulted, because Greek civilization consisted of a number of city states, each with its own legal system and organization. Such fragmentation meant that there was no one single body of

---

[19] Interestingly, Jesus relativizes or subordinates the family obligation of children to bury their parents to the more pressing need of following him (Luke 9:59); for more on this theme see Barton 1994.

legalized adoption procedure in Greek law (Lyall 1984: 98).[20] The cumulative weight of these differences is significant and leads us to conclude that although Greek law does not provide a meaningless background against which to understand Paul's metaphor of adoption, Roman law as we shall now see is more sharply defined and is 'a better source ... being richer and more thoroughgoing' (98).

The Roman background

As we examine the case for a Roman sociolegal milieu, we return again to the views of James Scott, who is especially critical of any Roman legal background to Paul's adoption expression.[21] Scott takes little cognizance of the fact that adoption was a family metaphor stemming from the ancient social world of Paul's day and was an expression that would have resonated immediately with his first hearers. More specifically, the important work recently carried out by such classicists as Rawson (1986: 1–57) on the ancient family (including the many sociological studies on the New Testament today) has provided many insights that New Testament scholars now employ to throw fresh light on key biblical texts.[22] This includes not only well-known passages such as the *Haustafeln*, 'household codes' (e.g. Eph. 5:21 – 6:9; Col. 3:18 – 4:1), which deal with real family relations, but also the many passages in the Pauline letters where family terms such as 'fathers', 'children' (e.g. 1 Thess. 2:10–12; 1 Cor. 4:14–21)[23] and 'siblings' (cf. 1 Thess. 1:4; 2:1, 9, 14, 17; 3:2, 7; 4:1, 6, 10 [twice], 13; 5:1, 4, 12, 14, 25, 26, 27) are employed metaphorically.[24]

The key question many scholars are rightly asking today is the extent to which Paul's familial metaphors – of which adoption is an integral part – are based upon or borrow from an understanding of the social realities of families in the ancient world? Paul seems to be

---

[20] There were other differences as well, including the fact that, unlike Roman practice, the authority of the father over his son was reduced when the latter reached puberty (when the adolescent came of age). Also, where the adoption was by will or posthumous, there was no relationship between adoptive father and heir.

[21] Scott (1992: 267) draws the distinction between Paul's *huiothesia* term having a Hellenistic *meaning* as opposed to a Hellenistic background.

[22] Some excellent work has also been carried out on aspects of the Jewish family, but more still needs to be done (see e.g. the collections of essays in Cohen 1993 and Moxnes 1997).

[23] See e.g. Burke 2003a: 36–97, 130–162; and Balla 2002.

[24] Note how from beginning to end 1 Thessalonians breathes brotherly language. See Burke 2003a: 163–249.

tapping into these stereotypical family attitudes and norms in order to describe his understanding of the church as a family. Adoption is an ancient family expression; it is not just a legal but a *socio*legal term; hence an understanding of the social dynamics of ancient Roman family life is germane to any proper understanding and interpretation of Paul's *huiothesia* term. Jeanne Stevenson-Moessner (2003: 111) is therefore right to point out that

> adoption was an accepted and high-profile method of perpetuating a lineage [and] Paul would have been keenly aware of the role of adoption in the Roman-world at the time of his writings and missionary travels, and he used this widely understood cultural process to illustrate the formation of a spiritual family.[25]

At the outset of our consideration of Roman law we ought to note a number of important reasons why an understanding of this background is useful for our study of Paul's metaphor of adoption.

First, it is striking that Paul uses his *huiothesia* metaphor only in letters to communities directly under the rule of Roman law (Gal. 4:5; Rom. 8:15, 23; 9:4; Eph. 1:5). Ephesus, situated on the west coast of Asia Minor, was the leading city (outside Rome) of the Roman Empire. Galatia (if we accept that Paul was writing to Derbe, Lystra and Iconium, the so-called south Galatian theory) by the time of Paul would have had a significant Roman presence.[26] And Rome itself, of course, would have been familiar with Roman law; indeed, it is not without significance that Paul's adoption expression occurs most frequently in his capital epistle to the church at Rome.[27]

---

[25] Stevenson-Moessner's (2003: xi) stated aim in her volume 'is to address the issues surrounding adoption of children, heavily weighted toward theology'. Thus she makes many pastorally sensitive comments in respect of the practice of adoption, which are set within a biblical framework, and has an excellent chapter, 'A Theology of Adoption', which demonstrates an understanding of the cultural context of adoption in the ancient world of Paul's day.

[26] The case for a Roman presence is even stronger if we accept the North Galatian theory. Those holding to this theory take Acts 16:6 ('the region of Phrygia and Galatia') and Acts 18:23 ('the region of Galatia and Phrygia') as references to Paul's trips to 'North Galatia'.

[27] Some have argued that the church members in Rome may have been largely composed of people more familiar with Greek law than Roman law. But although the Roman congregation comprised immigrants who would have been familiar with Greek ideas and concepts, most retained only the memory rather than the practice of the law of their cities of origin. All this obviously presupposes there were no Roman citizens in the congregation. Additionally, it is difficult to believe that the new influx of outsiders into the church was averse to learning and practising the (Roman) laws that governed the community in which they resided.

Second, Roman law was the law of Paul's own citizenship and would have been the law governing the apostle's family life, and in particular his relationship with his parents.[28] Wherever Roman citizens travelled within the empire, they were entitled to all the rights and privileges Roman citizenship provided (Sherwin-White 1978: 57).

Third, and more generally, adoption in its Roman form was becoming more widespread even in other areas throughout the empire, particularly among Roman emperors. Adoption was a means by which succession to power was brought about; from the late first century to the middle of the second century AD and later, successive Roman emperors adopted men not related to them by blood with the intention that an adoptee should succeed the emperor in the principate. Adoption became crucial to the continuation of the line of the Julio-Claudian emperors, as illustrated below:

Octavian (Augustus)	27 BC – AD 14
Tiberius	AD 14–37
Gaius (Caligula)	AD 37–41
Claudius	AD 41–54
Nero	AD 54–68

In each of the above cases adoption ensured the continuation of the Julio-Claudian line. Thus Julius Caesar adopted Octavian (who issued the decree at the time of Jesus' birth that the Roman world should be registered, Luke 2:1) as his son in 44 BC. Octavian in turn adopted a son named Tiberius, who adopted Gaius Caligula. Gaius' uncle, Claudius, subsequently adopted Nero, who so devastatingly interrogated and persecuted the Christians.

Most interesting among all of these imperial adoptions is Claudius' adoption of Nero, just four years before Paul wrote his letter to the church at Rome. What is particularly significant about this case is that the emperor already had a daughter, Octavia, who was in no sense a blood relation of Nero, but because of the adoption of the latter they were brother and sister in the eyes of the law. When Octavia and the adopted son Nero desired to marry, special legislation had to be passed in order to allow Nero to marry a girl who was legally his own sister! This example illustrates the absolute nature of the adoption of Nero and that he, because of his adoption, was legally in every way considered the same as a natural born son (Bowen 1978: 218).

[28] See n. 3 above.

Gaius' comment well illustrates this: 'Adoptive sons in their adoptive family are in the same legal position as real sons' (*Inst.* 2.136). This legal status is reflected in the following adoptive formulae (Gellius, *N. A.* 5.19.9):

> May it be your will and command that L. Valerius may be to L. Titius in right and in law his son, just as if he were born from him as *pater* and from his *materfamilias* and that he [Titius] may have in relation to him [Valerius] the power of life and death, as there is to a father in the case of a son.[29]

The above sequence of adoptions in the Roman Empire, as Stevenson-Moessner (2003: 30) states, shows how

> during Christ's lifetime and after his death, the legal and political acceptance and ramifications of adoption were played out at the highest level of Roman government, as emperors who had no biological sons chose heirs to ensure the continuation of the Julio-Claudian family tree. For Christians this becomes extremely significant because the three New Testament books that mention adoption – Galatians (ca 55 C.E.), Ephesians (ca 58–63 C.E.), and Romans (54–58 C.E.) – were written at a time when adoption secured the lineage of the ruling family in Rome. The writer of these books ... Paul ... would have been aware ... of the process.

Roman family life

What did adoption mean in law and practice, and hence metaphorically? Adoption was essentially a family term and, according to the Roman orator and writer Cicero, the most specific expression of human identity was found in the Roman family.[30] The family was the fundamental bedrock of ancient Roman society and regarded as the primary context of social, religious, political and economic

---

[29] I owe this quotation to Walters 2003: 53. See also Scott 1992: 11–13.

[30] See Cicero, *Off.* 1.53–54; Gardner & Wiedemann 1991: 2. It should be noted that neither ancient Greek nor Hebrew nor Latin had words that directly translate the English word 'family' or 'house'. The Greek *oikos, oikia*, Hebrew *bayit* and Latin *domus* can all refer to the physical building, but can also mean 'household', including the material goods and slaves. In the English-speaking world 'house' can also have an extended meaning, like 'House of Windsor', so the term can be employed in different ways; see further Moxnes 1997: 21.

security and fulfilment.[31] Family life in antiquity, including the Roman family, was hierarchically organized and structured with the *paterfamilias* situated at the apex of the pyramid (Jeffers 1991: 147). This hierarchical arrangement ensured that individuals had responsibilities and obligations commensurate with their place and role within the household. The importance of this, as James Jeffers points out, is that 'the household could only survive as long as all members knew their place in the hierarchy and performed those tasks and obligations relative to their status' (48).

As the head of the household the *paterfamilias* was the one primarily responsible for maintaining peace and concord within his own family. In all matters the *paterfamilias*'s authority (*potestas*) was absolute;[32] indeed, the authority of the household head institutionalized in the *potestas* and exercised by the *paterfamilias* was so binding in the *domus* that it was not until he had died that married children were free to form a household of their own. Stephen Joubert (1995: 215) states in regard to the father's influence in the family, 'The *paterfamilias*' lifelong power over his slaves, adopted children and biological children formed the backbone of Roman society; it was a palladium of Romanism.' The hierarchical structure of the *familia*, however, does not mean that ancient fathers were incapable of demonstrating affection towards their offspring.

Clearly, parents in ancient society loved their children, even though the manner in which fathers and mothers manifested such affection was different, as Seneca (*De prov.* 2.5)[33] the Roman statesman and contemporary of the apostle Paul points out:

> Do you not see how fathers show their love in one way, and mothers in another? The father orders his children to be aroused

[31] See Judge 1960: 30–32 for a discussion of how ancient society was a delicate balance of religion, occupation, civic affairs, politics and the family; to upset any one of these would bring changes to all the others.

[32] Theoretically, a father had the power of life and death (*ius vitae necisque*) over his own children, but he was restrained from abusing his authority by custom and public opinion (Gardner 1998: 2). Eyben (1991: 115) states, 'the *paterfamilias* had the right to expose his child, to scourge him, to sell him, to pawn him, to imprison him, and, *in extremis*, even to kill him'.

[33] Seneca's sentiments, perhaps more than any other classical philosopher, come closest to Christian teaching. It is worth noting and often overlooked that John Calvin wrote a commentary on Seneca's *De clementia*. And Lightfoot (1976: 270–333) has compiled an exhaustive list of parallels in thought and language between Seneca and Paul, as well as an assessment of their basic differences.

from sleep in order that they may start early upon their pursuits, even on holidays he does not permit them to be idle.[34]

Although there is no mention of adoption in this example, doubtless adopted sons would have received the same fatherly affection as biological sons, and would have been treated no differently.

Generally speaking, the Roman *familia* comprised a husband, wife and their dependents (natural children, slaves [freedmen, freedwomen]) and their offspring. Thus the Roman *familia* was much bigger and wider than our twenty-first-century Western understanding of the term 'family' (the nuclear family).[35] Additionally, the *familia* embraced those who were sons by reason of having been adopted.[36] As we have observed, the family was of fundamental importance to Roman society, so much so that when it was under threat of extinction, adoption was a lifeline for a 'family in danger of dying out' (Crook 1967: 135). This was usually due to the *paterfamilias*'s inability to have offspring of his own or because his own children had failed to live to adulthood; and so that he might have an heir, recourse was made to adopting a son from another family.

Adoption was a well-known practice in the ancient world and was not only of great importance in Roman law and society but was also a 'treasured status' (Finger 1993: 48). This is because adoption was not only a safeguard against the demise of a family but also provided new

[34] The old view of an austere and overly authoritarian father has been replaced by a 'new consensus' that views him as an affectionate figure. In connection with this, Castelli (1991:109) rightly situates Paul's understanding of the father metaphor in its ancient Graeco-Roman setting, where fathers exercised authority over their offspring. But she misses the point when she goes on to state in regard to Paul, 'the paternal metaphor does not necessarily evoke a sense of kindness or love'. There is clear evidence from a broad, eclectic range of primary sources (Jewish and non-Jewish, literary and non-literary) that fathers in antiquity were expected to demonstrate love for their children and that such affection is also clearly seen in Paul's letters when he refers to God and himself in paternal terms (Balla 2002: 59–81; Burke 2003: 47–50, 65–66, 71–75, 85–87).

[35] Scholarly debate in relation to the structure of the ancient family is unresolved. Saller (1994: 336–355) argues that the nuclear family, 'the mother–father–children triad', was the 'dominant family type' in the ancient world. Martin (1996: 58), however, not only questions Saller's methodology but also concludes on the basis of epigraphic evidence, 'The Romans had no name for the "nuclear family" as differentiated from the *familia* or *domus* not because the nuclear family did not exist in the sociological or biological sense (that is, in certain modernist discourses), nor because it was not important as a series of relationships, but because it was not important to them to distinguish those relations firmly from other, less intimate, family relations.'

[36] In the case of adoption by *adrogatio* (see below for definition of this term) the fusion of two families further complicates what we mean by the expression 'family' (see later).

opportunities for the adoptee that would otherwise not have existed. Unlike twenty-first-century Western society, where children are the subjects of adoption, in ancient Roman society the subjects of adoption were already adults, by which time, according to Beryl Rawson, 'the chances of survival were greater and the adopting father could see what he was getting as a son and heir' (1986: 12; Williams 1999: 82 n. 130). Again in contrast to contemporary society, where childlessness is one of the main reasons for embarking on such a course, the Roman conception of adoption was rooted in the old religious basis of the Roman family, where each family had its own cult or *sacra* (sacred things).[37] Of paramount importance to every Roman household was family worship; indeed, the ancient Roman world was awash with gods and each god was venerated in accordance with ancestral customs. Some gods were regarded as providers for the family: gods of the hearth (*Vesta*) and of the larder (*Penates*) were responsible for guarding the storehouse and guaranteeing the supply of food respectively. Other gods were deemed responsible for giving protection to the household (Barclay 1997: 67).

The *genius* or *numen* of the family, a kind of spiritualization of the family itself, was also the focus of domestic worship and referred to as 'its procreative force, and especially the living spirit of the *paterfamilias*' (Orr 1978: 1595).[38] The *paterfamilias* was the embodiment of the family that continued from one generation to the next in the father and the son. In fact, the continuation of the cult in the Roman family was so crucial that if it was under threat due to a lack of male offspring to carry it on, adoption was seen as the solution.[39] Two methods of adoption were practised in ancient Rome: *adrogatio* and *adoptio*.[40] In both instances the role of the *paterfamilias* is vital in instigating the process.

---

[37] Cicero (*Dom.* 35) provides three reasons for adoption: the maintenance of *nomen* (name), *pecunia* (property) and *sacrum* (religious rites).

[38] Gardner and Wiedemann (1991: 33) cite the inscription *CIL* VI, 259, which underscores the power of the *paterfamilias* and about which they comment, 'All the dependents of the master of the household owed their existence to his Genius, i.e., power to generate or sustain life. *This applied to adoptive children as much as to biological children...*' (my emphasis).

[39] Williams (1999: 83 n. 137) states, 'adopted sons were obligated to perpetuate ... the *sacrum* of the new family'.

[40] Mawhinney (1992: 29) succinctly states the distinction between the two procedures: 'If the person to be adopted was under the authority of a *paterfamilias* the act was called *adoptio*. If the person to be adopted was himself the *paterfamilias* of his family it was called *adrogatio*.'

Adrogatio

Adrogatio, the older adoption procedure, applied in the case of a man (never a woman), and denoted the adoption of a person who was *sui iuris*: namely, not under the legal power or authority (*potestas*) of his father. Given this, a preliminary investigation was carried out by the official priests of the state to ensure the suitability of the interested families and the security of the family about to lose a member. The initial search considered a range of issues, including the motives of the two parties involved, the character of the adopter, and most importantly the effect the *adrogation* would have on the two families. The latter was crucial because the person *adrogated* (the *adrogatus*) was not the only one affected by what would eventually take place – all those under his paternal authority (*potestas*) also passed under the power of the new *paterfamilias*. The resulting effects of *adrogatio* to the families involved were very serious, as they brought about the fusion of two families. On the one hand, it ensured the perpetuation of one household while on the other, it signified the demise of the other *familia* (including the possibility of its *sacra*). Essentially, the person adopted lost *patria potestas* over his own children, and both he and his offspring came under the *potestas* of the adoptive father. Hence, strict regulations governed this practice of adoption, as the orator and politician Cicero makes clear – only a man who had no offspring could undertake *adrogatio*:

> 'What, gentlemen,' he asked, 'is the law relating to adoption? Clearly, that the adoption of children should be permitted to those who are no longer capable of begetting children, and who, when they were in their prime, put their capacity for parenthood to the test.'[41]

For many years (until the time of Diocletian, c. AD 284–305) the practice of *adrogatio* as a form of adoption was *restricted to Rome* itself, the only venue where the *comitia curiata*, 'council' (later, by the time of Cicero, before thirty *lictors* and still later, for provincials, the emperor),[42] could meet to consider the matter. In the light of this

---

[41] Cited in Goody (1969: 60). Cicero goes on to attack the adoption of Clodius, which had political implications and was against sacerdotal law because the adopter already had a son.

[42] Lictors were members of a special class of Roman civil servants, with special tasks of attending magistrates.

severe geographical restraint, it is unlikely that the apostle Paul had the procedure of *adrogatio* in mind when he used his *huiothesia* term.[43]

Adoptio

A much more important and acceptable adoption procedure was that known as *adoptio*.[44] This involved the adoption of a male *alieni iuris* (one under the legal power and authority of another), which was much more satisfactory socially and sacrally than adoption of a male *sui iurius*, because it meant that no family or its religious cult was being wiped out (Watson 1975: 41). According to this form of adoption, one came under the authority of the *patria potestas* of the adopting father through a fictitious purchase. The whole procedure involved, in the first instance, the severing of the old *potestas* followed by the establishing of the paternal authority of the new father. This was carried out by the *pater-familias* selling off his offspring into civil bondage (*in mancipio*), thereby making him a slave. On the release of his son the latter was still the property of the father and could by right be sold into bondage by him again and again. In order to avoid the son becoming a kind of familial football, a law was laid down in the Twelve Tables[45] (established by the second Decemvirate, c. 450 BC), which stated that when a son was sold three times by his father, the latter ceased to have any authority over him (cf. Cicero, Fin. 1.7.24). It was from this law that the *adoptio* procedure was derived. Such was the completeness and permanent nature of the act, for both the giver as well as the receiver, that adoption was a procedure not entered into lightly (Goody 1969: 60).

The actual act of adoption was overseen by several witnesses and, according to A. N. Sherwin-White, the ancient historian, the certification of any matter in Roman law required seven witnesses, a rule we can assume applied in the Roman legal practice of adoption. Sherwin-White (1978: 149) goes on to point out the significance of this: 'these documents ... were guaranteed by the signatures of the seven witnesses required by Roman law in the certification of all

[43] See further Buckland 1963: 124–128; Atkins 1991: 177.

[44] Hollingshead (1998: 125) states, 'In the case of *adoptio*, the individual adopted, alone as an individual, entered a new family line ... his ... kinship ties were terminated in both directions ... It is likely that Paul constructed his metaphor around the Roman practice of *adoptio*.'

[45] For more on this see ch. 1 of Watson 1975.

documents. If your certificate is challenged, you produce your witnesses.'[46]

Thus in cases where there was a query over whether an adoption had indeed taken place, this could be verified by those who were present. Generally speaking, adoption changed hereditary succession, and the adoptee's legal position and privileges were the same as that of a legitimate biological son. Adoption in the Roman world brought changes to every area of the adoptee's life. Principally, adoption constituted on the one hand a break with the old family and on the other a commitment to the new family, along with all its attending privileges and responsibilities. According to Berger and Nicholas (1970: 9) the resulting effect of *adoption*

> was to place the adopted person for all legal purposes in the same position as if he had been a natural child in the *potestas* of the adopter. The adopted son took his adoptive father's name and rank. He acquired rights of succession on death in his new family and lost all such rights as he had in his old family.

Given this background and if, as James D. G. Dunn (1993: 217) has stated, 'almost certainly Paul had in mind the legal act of adoption, by which a Roman ... entered another family and came under the *patria potestas* of its head', then there ought to be a number of analogies with Roman law that are useful for understanding Paul's adoption expression. We need to be especially alert to this when exegeting the Pauline passages. Also we should note one other important point.

Although there may be aspects from the Roman sociolegal milieu helpful for understanding Paul's adoption term, these do not fully exhaust the meaning of *adoptio*. James Hester perhaps overstates his case when he comments, '*all* the elements present in the Roman form of adoption are present in Paul's adoption metaphor' (1968: 60–62; my emphasis). But we must not automatically assume a simplistic one-to-one correspondence between the ancient social practice of adoption and Paul's metaphorical usage of the term – no overlap is

---

[46] See also Hester 1968: 60–62. Atkins (1991: 177) on the other hand cites the necessity of having five witnesses verify that an adoption has taken place. In any case, the point is that the Roman legal procedure of adoption required a plurality of witnesses – one was insufficient; contra Scott 1993: 15–18. Crook (1984: 106) cites the *Digesta* in respect of divorce, which like adoption required a plurality of public witnesses: 'No divorce is valid unless made in the presence of seven adult Roman citizens' (*Dig.* 24.2.9).

complete and there will always be discontinuities where the analogy breaks down.

There are occasions when Paul employs his adoption metaphor where there is no antecedent in either the ancient legal backgrounds we have considered or in the Old Testament Scriptures themselves (Ryken et al. 1998:15). For instance, there was no role for an intermediary or a go-between in the Roman sociolegal practice of adoption. In the New Testament, however, spiritual adoption always and only takes place through God's own Son, to whom the believer has been united by faith (Eph. 1:5).[47] Also, there is nothing in any of the backgrounds we have considered that corresponds to the eschatological aspect between the 'now' and the 'not yet' in adoption according to Paul.

Furthermore, while the issue of the background is important and has dominated the discussion since the early twentieth century, a strictly legal approach to Paul's adoption term truncates our understanding of the expression and severs it from its full theological scope.[48] Adoption is a theological or, better, eschatological expression, which will be the primary focus of my exegesis in succeeding chapters.

Summary

The background to Paul's adoption metaphor has both in the past and the present attracted much discussion. Paul expressly employs the term *huiothesia* of the nation of Israel in Romans 9:4. According to this text and to Paul's way of thinking, Israel is clearly God's son by adoption. When we trace this back into the Old Testament, however, the lingistic evidence is lacking and it is difficult to identify one specific text, even though many scholars understand texts such as Exodus 4:22 and Hosea 11:10 in adoptive terms. The 'subject of adoption is very hazy in the Old Testament' (Wright 1997: 17) and it is 'impossible to trace adoption to Jewish law' (Hester 1968: 58). 'Nowhere does the OT speak of Israelites being adopted ... into God's family as other Pauline references portray ... [T]he institution

---

[47] Best (1998: 125) draws attention to the following areas where the analogy breaks down. Roman adoption arose out of a need of a father to have an heir; God has no need of an heir. Roman adoption generally occurred within similar social classes; God's adoption brings the son to an incomparably better status.

[48] Cook (1978: 139) states in this regard, 'He (Paul) always uses it (i.e., adoption) to describe what may be termed theological adoption, that is, the placing of persons into sonship to God.'

of adoption of individuals into a family is not portrayed in the OT' (Hoehner 2002: 195). What is more, when the Old Testament authors speak of Israel's relationship to God as son, they prefer to couch this relationship in *redemptive* (Isa. 63:16) and *elective* (Deut. 7:7) terms rather than in terms of adoption.

A much more important theme on the landscape of the Old Testament (and the intertestamental literature; e.g. Wis. 12:7, 21; 16:10; Sir. 36:17), which permeates the entire canon of Scripture, is the *general notion of sonship*, and if there is any Old Testament background to Paul's adoption term, it is more likely to be found here. The theme of sonship is the larger, more important one in the biblical corpus of which the distinctively Pauline doctrine of adoption is a part.

Adoption needs to be understood within the general social framework of the ancient family: adoption, for example, was an initiative undertaken by the *paterfamilias* not only as a safeguard against the family dying out but also for the purpose of continuing the sacral cult. The procedure was usually carried out in the context of witnesses, with the result that adopted sons shared the same privileges as natural-born sons. It is also likely in view of recent research into the Roman family that a *paterfamilias* would show affection towards a newly adopted son.

We have also observed the relevance of the Roman procedure of adoption over that of the Greek: whereas in the former the adoptee's severance from his family is absolute, in the latter it is not. Additionally, Paul's Roman citizenship and the fact that he uses adoption only in letters written to churches under direct Roman rule add further weight to the case for a Roman background.

What remains to be seen is whether the points elucidated above have influenced or shaped Paul's *huiothesia* terminology, and whether there is any concrete evidence to show that Paul is relying on a Roman sociolegal background. Moreover, even if there are occasions where there are parallels between the practice of adoption in antiquity and Paul's use of this in his letters, there may well be times when this is not the case. It may be that here we are in touch with aspects of Paul's own unique and creative thinking on adoption, where he provides novel insights to serve his own theological purposes.

Chapter Four

'*Abba*, Father' and his family of adopted sons

Introduction

Having considered the question of the background to Paul's *huiothesia* metaphor, I begin my first chapter of exegesis. As stated earlier, my approach will be theological, but theology must be understood within the exegetical context of the Pauline letters themselves. A cursory reading of the main texts on *huiothesia* reveals a theological thrust essentially trinitarian in nature, where each member – Father, Son and Holy Spirit – has a unique and vital part to play in a person's being adopted into the family of God. This trinitarian pattern is, for example, immediately obvious in Galatians 4:4–6, where Paul informs his readers of the climactic moment in the redemptive-historical purposes of God: 'But when the time had fully come, *God* [the Father] sent his *Son* . . . that we might receive the full rights [adoption] of sons . . . Because you are sons, God sent the *Spirit* of his Son into our hearts, the Spirit who calls out, "*Abba*, Father"' (my emphasis).

There are good reasons for specifically focusing on the role of God as Father in this chapter.[1] The first and most important reason is that the Christian's 'adoption is concerned with the Fatherhood of God in relation to the redeemed' (Murray 1976: 223); indeed, 'our adoption as sons is one of the Father's best blessings' (Stibbe 1999: 48).[2] The second reason for addressing the matter of God as Father in relation

---

[1] Balla (2002: 190) thinks that a complete monograph could easily be given to a study of the use 'Father' in the New Testament. It is interesting how Tom Smail (1980), writing against an overemphasis on the Spirit by the charismatic movement in the 1970s in the United Kingdom, sought to redress this imbalance. The title of his book is *The Forgotten Father: Rediscovering the Heart of the Christian Gospel*, where the back cover describes 'the Christian gospel . . . [as] . . . essentially a *Father* movement' (my emphasis).

[2] Stibbe (1999: 48) also states, 'It [adoption] is a great gift of the *Trinity*' (my emphasis). He goes on to write, 'Paul makes it clear that the whole of the Godhead was committed to the task of adopting us . . . All three persons of the Godhead are involved in our adoption as sons.'

to adoption is that some feminists argue that the term 'Father' should be complemented with other terms such as 'mother'.[3] Others go as far as to suggest that the term 'father' should be discarded altogether and replaced by terms such as 'lover', 'companion', 'friend' or 'liberator' (McFague 1987). These are issues that need to be addressed, but we need to first consider how the author of Ephesians uses this expression in relation to adoption.

The Father's plan: Elected and predestined unto adoption (Eph. 1)

Introduction

If adoption is about anything it is about belonging, a belonging where God as 'Father' occupies centre stage in his 'family'. One locus where Paul particularly emphasizes the Father's role in respect of our *huiothesia* is Ephesians 1.[4] Moreover, if we wish to gain a rich and deep understanding of the image of the fatherhood of God, then we can do no better than contemplate the first chapter of Paul's letter to the Ephesians – no other Pauline letter celebrates the notion of God as Father as this one. Schnackenburg states (1991: 74) in this regard, 'The idea of the Father ... comes so strongly to the fore in Ephesians' (see also Patzia 1995: 149). There are eight references to 'Father' in this letter out of a total of forty in the whole Pauline corpus, which, according to Hoehner (2002: 107), 'is more ... than any other letter' (1:2, 3, 17; 2:18; 3:14–15; 4:6; 5:20; 6:23) (see also Thompson 2000: 121–122). It is worth tracing some of these references in a little detail to grasp Paul's understanding of the fatherhood of God and how he

[3] Castelli (1994: 291) writes, 'while woman could indeed function as heirs to property according to Roman law, there is no evidence that women were ever adopted in order to ensure their access to inheritance'. She goes on to lament the fact that 'the exclusion of women, results in a gender imbalance requiring women to "become male" before they can become heirs'. Castelli also relies on Kathleen Corley, who admits, 'Paul may not intend to exclude women from the ranks of the sons of God.' Moreover, Corley recognizes the difficulty of others who try to render *huiothesia* in Rom. 8:23–24 with 'adoption as children'. To do so, she concludes, is 'to deal with the problematic language by introducing a new metaphor ... The question is whether or not it is a faithful rendering of Paul's metaphor, which seems to have been gender specific' ('Women's Inheritance Rights in Antiquity and Paul's Metaphor of Adoption', unpublished paper). This is precisely the point I raised in chapter 1 n. 2; namely, to use the phrase 'adopted as son' more faithfully reflects the cultural context of the first-century world of Paul. One cannot have it both ways.

[4] Scott (1992: 175) mentions adoption in Ephesians only briefly in passing, but does not discuss it.

links this to his adoption metaphor. We should also note in relation to his adoption metaphor that although 'adoption in Ephesians has not been in the forefront of discussion', it is in this letter perhaps more than in any other that the apostle provides one of the fullest scriptural treatments of the term and where 'the doctrine of adoption is ... extensively developed' (Stevenson-Moessner 2003: 111–112).[5]

Paul begins this letter with the greeting 'Grace and peace to you from *God the Father* and the Lord Jesus Christ' (v. 2; my emphasis) after which he bursts into a eulogy of thanks and praise 'to the *God and Father* of our Lord Jesus Christ, who has blessed us in the heavenly realms with every spiritual blessing in Christ' (v. 3; my emphasis). He then delineates a catalogue of blessings including 'election' (v. 5), 'predestination' (v. 5), 'redemption' (v. 7) and the 'forgiveness of sins' (v. 7), all of which hinge upon and can be directly traced back to the divine Father. As John Stott (1979: 33) points out, 'God the Father is the source or origin of every blessing we enjoy. His initiative is set forth plainly, for he is himself the subject of almost every verb in these verses.'

Another benefit that also comes about as a direct result of the Father's action on our behalf, and that sits like a jewel in the crown of this passage, is 'adoption'. Paul states, 'Praise be to the God and *Father* ... For ... *he* predestined us to be *adopted as his sons*' (*huiothesia*, vv. 3–5; my emphasis). Given this, it is little wonder that the apostle goes on later in this chapter to describe this God in doxological terms as a '*glorious* Father' (1:17; my emphasis).

We have already observed how Paul's presentation of adoption is both a present reality, the 'now', Romans 8:15, as well as the future 'not yet' (Rom. 8:23). In addition to these aspects, Paul in Ephesians 1 discusses another, namely the *past*, as he reminds his readers how God '*predestined* us to be adopted as his sons' (Eph. 1:5). Ephesians 1:3–14 in the original language constitutes one long, majestic sentence comprising 202 words in total, which breaks down into three parts. It is in essence 'a profound example of "declarative praise"' (O'Brien 1994: 69) with verses 3–6 essentially describing the work of the Father, verses 7–12 the Son, and verses 13–14 the work of the Holy Spirit.

Given that we are chiefly interested at this point in the Father's role, we shall focus on verses 3–6, which read:

---

[5] This is in part due to the fact that many New Testament scholars today doubt that Paul wrote Ephesians. See chapter 2 n. 24 and the literature cited there.

Praise be to the God and Father of our Lord Jesus Christ, who has blessed us in the heavenly realms with every spiritual blessing in Christ. For he chose us in him before the creation of the world to be holy and blameless in his sight. In love he predestined us to be adopted (*huiothesian*) as his sons through Jesus Christ, in accordance with his pleasure and will – to the praise of his glorious grace...

At the outset of this passage Paul stresses that the life of God's family of adopted sons is grounded solely in the action of the Father's electing individuals: 'praise be to the God and *Father* ... he *chose* us ... to be adopted as his sons' (vv. 3–4; my emphasis). Just as we noted earlier the language of election is used in respect of God's choosing the nation of Israel to be his son (cf. Deut. 7:7), so Paul brings the same language into service to describe the believer's adoption as a son. Simply and briefly, God elected individuals to adoption: his 'adopting grace' (Stibbe 1999: 44). Election here is one of a number of divine gifts that 'must be understood as coming to believers personally and individually [since] ... God has chosen a people for himself, and this includes members of that people' (O' Brien 1999: 99).[6] Equally, God had it in mind to form these individuals into a community, a family of Christians, who are related to one another within the body of Christ; hence there is also an important corporate dimension (see later in this chapter) (Klein 1990: 179–180).

The New Testament understanding of the verb 'elected' (*exelexatō*) has primarily to do with choice, and this choice, Paul informs us, is the sole prerogative of our Father-God. Adoption is thus a gift of God's free grace and excludes all human merit; it is absolutely *sola gratia* and an awareness of this should alert us to the fact that it 'rule[s] out all the boasting of man with his natural or acquired qualities' (Schweizer 1993: 399). This undeserving favour is what undergirds Paul's theology, and we therefore miss the very essence of what is involved in *huiothesia* when we fail to recognize that it is all of the grace of God, as David deSilva (2001: 6; my emphasis) comments:

An important facet of God's favour is *adoption* into God's people, even *into God's own family*, bringing one into relation with a body of people toward whom one has obligations of close kin (and from

---

[6] Atkins (1991: 183) also makes the point 'Salvation is expressed in individual terms by faith alone. The function of adoption is to explain this concern for the *individual*' (my emphasis).

whom one can hope for the love and support characteristic of close-knit families).[7]

All filial relations in the ancient world – including individuals who had been adopted – were governed by the principle of reciprocity, and it is because of the amazing grace that God has bestowed upon his children that we owe an incalculable debt to God and his Son. In addition, this requires all who have been adopted into 'God's household, to *serve* the members of God's family as God has directed' (deSilva 2001: 67; my emphasis). Believers have been adopted into the most venerable of all families, God's very own household; however, there is no room for pride or conceit, but humility issued forth in gratitude to the Father and in service to our brothers and sisters in Christ.

Careful note should be taken of how Paul stresses that this divine selection is pretemporal, in that it took place in eternity and prior to the existence of the cosmos and everything in it ('before the creation of the world', v. 4). Lincoln (1990: 23) points out in this regard, 'To say that election in Christ took place before the foundation of the world is to underline that it was provoked not by historical contingency or human merit, but solely by God's sovereign grace.' This Father's choice is for a purpose – which is to say that 'election is not merely *from* . . . or election *by* means of . . . [but election] *for* which God has designated' (Barth 1974: 106), the reason and goal of which will become clearer immediately below.

Closely allied with and followed by the term 'election' is the expression 'predestined' (*proorisas*, v. 4) (AV, 'foreordain'), a verb that among New Testament writers is employed explicitly only by the apostle Paul (e.g. Rom 8:29, 30; 1 Cor. 2:7). The term 'predestine' does not connote a cold, calculated act of God whereby he arbitrarily decided to pick out some and cast aside others. Quite the opposite, because Paul here qualifies 'predestine' with the prepositional phrase 'in love' (*en agapē*)[8] to underscore the Father's deep affection in

---

[7] It is also worth noting, and is indeed often overlooked, that the term 'grace' (*charis*), like other expressions employed by the apostle Paul (e.g. *ekklēsia*), was not coined by him but was in use in the secular world of the first century. DeSilva (2001: 7) notes that the word 'grace', for example, was 'the language of the exchange of favors, of the giving of assistance and the returning of gratitude'.

[8] The position of the prepositional phrase 'in love' has been a matter of some scholarly debate. If it is to be taken with what precedes (cf. UBS Greek text and the AV, REB, NEB translations), it should be read, 'For he chose us in him before the creation of the world to be holy and blameless in love'. Alternatively, we can link the phrase with what follows, as I have done (cf. NIV, RSV), giving the following translation: 'In love he

'marking us out' as his adopted sons.[9] The importance of this prepositional phrase serves to emphasize the fact that God 'adopts because he *loves* those he adopts' (Best 1998: 125; my emphasis);[10] and this is the reason why love should be central in God's church and among God's children, because the church, the 'community [is] a loving family' (Banks 1994: 47–57).[11] Indeed, God the Father loves and binds himself to believers in his Son as surely as a Roman father bound himself to his adopted sons. Such affection is not merely confined to this side of the great divide, but there is an even greater and more glorious 'prospect before the adopted sons of God in an eternity of love' (Packer 1988: 241). Something of the undeserving love of the Father in predestining and choosing to include us in his family of adopted sons and daughters is well stated by James I. Packer (1988: 241):

> God adopts us out of his free love, not because our character and record shows us worthy to bear his name, but despite the fact that they show the opposite. We are not fit for a place in God's family; the idea of His loving and exalting us sinners as He loves and has exalted the Lord Jesus sound ludicrous and wild – yet that, and nothing less than that, is what our adoption means.

The decision to take the phrase 'in love' with verse 5 is substantiated by the use of the verb 'predestine', which is always employed positively and, like election, denotes that God has a purpose or a specific goal in view. Moreover, the term 'predestine' 'always requires a complement' (Berkhof 1981: 112), which means 'we are not merely predestined but predestined *for* or *to* something' (Liefeld 1997: 38; my emphasis). Paul, within the context of this passage, spells out the soteriological significance of what that 'something' is; namely,

---

predestined us to be adopted as his sons.' This means that the phrase 'in love' stands emphatically at the beginning of the Greek sentence and verse. Schnackenburg (1991: 54) writes, 'God's *loving* predestination has as its goal our ... (*huiothesia*)' (my emphasis). Schnackenburg (53) also makes the point that predestination as used by Paul is always to do with God the Father and 'is never connected with the thought that we are ... predestined "in Christ"'.

[9] Klein (1990: 187) comments in relation to this, 'Predestination is not capricious, arbitrary, or accidental; rather it is purposeful and pleasurable. God has marked out or predetermined a goal for ones chosen in Christ. He purposed to mark out for them the most desirable of all gifts: adoption into his family as his children.'

[10] Packer (1988: 229) also remarks, 'As God loved His only begotten Son, so he loves His adopted sons.'

[11] This is the title of chapter 5 of Banks's excellent book, which has been seminal in the thinking of many students of Paul's communities.

'predestination ... to a *relationship* with God the Father ... described in v. 5 under the imagery of *adoption*' (O'Brien 1999: 99; my emphasis).[12] Viewed from God the Father's perspective,[13] then, the believer's adoption as son is not an afterthought; still less is it a filial disposition that came about by chance or mere accident. On the contrary, the motive and impulse for this new family of adopted sons and daughters finds its spring and origin in the eternal and loving purposes of this Father-God who always had in mind to enter into a relationship with us. Understood in this light, adoption is an astonishing privilege and is one of the most intimate, personal and relational terms employed by the apostle Paul to describe our association with this *Abba*-God.

Adopted in accordance with the Father's pleasure and will

Paul proceeds to inform his readers that God not only has an eternal purpose in adopting us but also takes great delight in bringing us into his household: 'he ... adopted [us] as his sons ... in accordance with his *pleasure* and *will*' (v. 5; my emphasis). The apostle's use of the preposition *kata*, 'according to', emphasizes that such an action was the 'norm' or 'standard', while Paul uses the term 'pleasure' (*eudokia*) elsewhere in relation to his passionate concern for his own people, Israel (Rom. 10:1), which connotes the warmth and joy with which the Father executed this plan in making us his adopted sons and daughters. Stibbe (1999: 53) captures the essence of God's action when he says:

> It pleased him to enfold us in the eternal family of faith. It brought him joy and thrilled his heart. Even though this adoption would not be cost-free, God did not undertake this task by gritting his teeth and clenching his fists. No, it was his pleasure as well as his will.[14]

---

[12] This is also made clear by the use of the preposition *eis*, which denotes direction or appointment; namely, predestined 'to' adoption.

[13] Lincoln (1990: 25) observes how the theocentric emphasis of vv. 5 and 6 is demonstrated in another way by Paul's use of the prepositional phrase *eis auton*, 'to himself' (i.e. God the Father) in v. 5a. This phrase refers back to the subject of *proorisas*, of which he states (25), 'The sonship therefore has God as its goal, "toward him," and this emphasis is suggested in the translation by adding "his own" to the notion of adoption as sons.' Lincoln (9) concludes, 'Believers bless God the Father, because his choice of them is intended to bring them into a relationship with himself.'

[14] Interestingly, Mark Stibbe writes, often quite movingly, from first-hand experience of having been adopted himself.

Adoption is also in accordance with God's will, an important theme that recurs more frequently here than in any other Pauline letter (i.e. 1:5, 9, 11; 5:17) (Snodgrass 1996: 37). The emphasis here is that what God had purposed in eternity (our adoption as sons) cannot be thwarted, changed or overturned. God planned and purposed the believer's adoption in the past and his will was sovereignly brought to pass in time. Included also in the word 'will' is the fact that we do not find God but that God has found us and 'willed' or wanted us to be included as members of his family.

God's new family of adopted sons and daughters

A second important point to note in these early verses of Ephesians 1 is the clear progression in the apostle's thought. After linking the twin notions of God as 'Father' and our *huiothesia* (Eph. 1:3–4), Paul goes on to present an 'ecclesiological focus', that is familial in nature.[15] Recognizing this development, Jeanne Stevenson-Moessner (2003: 112) also rightly points out that

> although some scholars have connected the theme of adoption to Christology, the study of the person and work of Christ, ... the doctrine of adoption as it impacts *ecclesiology*, the study of the life of the church's practices of faith has been completely overlooked.

Having reminded the Ephesian believers of their adoptive sonship relationship to the Father (Eph. 1:5) 'the realisation of ... adoption becomes the *groundwork* for theological discussion of what it means to be family or household of God (17; my emphasis; see also Trumper 2005: 67).

This note is picked up in Ephesians 2:19 by Paul, where he calls upon the Ephesians to reflect on what they once were, compared to their present position in Christ. Paul does this by the juxtaposition of family and non-family language and by a deliberate play on words, clearly evident in the original Greek: 'you are no longer foreigners and *aliens* (*paroikos*) but ... members of God's *family/household* (*oikos*, 2:19; my emphasis).[16] This is amazing when we consider the

---

[15] O'Brien (1999: 99) writes, 'We have already seen that throughout the paragraph the recipients of "every spiritual blessing" are mentioned again and again (vv. 3, 4, 5, 6, 7, 8, 9, 11, 12, 14) in what has been called an "ecclesiological focus".'

[16] The phrase *oikeioi tou theou* is best understood as a possessive genitive giving the translation 'members of God's household' (Horrell 2001: 305). Horrell argues that the sibling language in the Pastoral Letters gives way to a more hierarchical structured household. See Burke 2003a: 225–249, where it is argued that even in (one of) the

deep-seated hostility, even hatred, that existed between Jew and Gentile (2:16), but it is only by the power of God that the believer has been incorporated into the church or household of God, which not only removes the dissension and divisions but also brings a solidarity and accompanying sense of belonging.[17]

How can this transformation in relations come about? Only because, as Paul had stated earlier at the outset of the letter, God had chosen and predestined Jews and Gentiles for adoption as sons (Eph. 1:5). Mawhinney (1993: 82) sums up the seismic change in relations that has taken place: 'the fact that God has chosen to adopt them and make them members of his one family strips away every reason for pride that could lead to dissension'.[18] The result is that those who once were not a people, the Gentiles, have now been united with Jews, who were *the* people, and both have been adopted *'into a single family under a shared Father'* (deSilva 2000: 206; my emphasis).[19] Adoption is a unifying metaphor and the razing of the barriers of hostility between Jew and Gentile now means that *'both* have access to the Father by the one Spirit' (2:18) (deSilva 2000: 206; my emphasis). In all this we can see how Paul's *huiothesia* expression functions inclusively, because 'adoption stands at the heart of what makes us kin to one another' (deSilva 2000: 206).

Crucially, *huiothesia*, as employed by Paul, is a theological metaphor that 'performs ... [an] integrative function by incorporating both groups (Jews and Gentiles) into one new community,

---

earliest Christian communities (e.g. 1 Thess. 5:12–15) distinctions existed between siblings (as they did between real sibling relations in the ancient world) and that some form of hierarchy prevailed among the first communities. Rather than thinking, as is often argued, that the first Christian churches started out egalitarian in nature only to be replaced by more hierarchically structured communities, some form of structure and organization based on the household was there right from the inception of the earliest churches.

[17] No less relevant or amazing are some modern-day examples: Croatians and Serbs, Irish Catholics and Ulster Protestants (the latter of which I am acutely aware), Tutsi and Hutu in Rwanda, black and white South Africans and Americans who, because of their adoption through faith into the *familia Dei* (family of God), have removed the hatred, suspicions and divisions between them. I have witnessed such unity in Nigeria, where I once worked, between Christians from the Igala and Igbo tribes, and most recently in the postcoup era of 2000 between Fijian and Indo-Fijian in the South Pacific where I have been teaching.

[18] Packer (1988: 231) states the matter perfectly: 'adoption is a *family* idea, conceived in terms of *love*, and viewing God as *father*. In adoption, God takes us into his family and fellowship, and establishes us as his children and heirs' (my emphasis).

[19] White (1992a: 289) states similarly of the Galatians, 'Paul uses the image of adoption to accentuate the unnatural and spiritual character of his *gentile converts'* election and sonship' (my emphasis).

a family of adopted sons' (Atkins 1991: 187).[20] If the church is the family of God's adopted sons and daughters, then it is they more than all people on earth who ought to reflect and mirror the unity of the family before the eyes of a watching world. Paul strikes a similar note elsewhere in his letters when he calls upon the Galatian Christians to 'do good to all people, especially to those who belong to the *household of faith*' (*oikeious tēs pisteōs*, Gal. 6:10; my emphasis),[21] which, notes Victor Furnish (1978: 204), 'defines only the minimum of love's response, not its farthest extent'. It is worth noting that a father (*paterfamilias*) in the ancient world was primarily responsible for ensuring harmony and agreement among the household members, but equally all offspring, including adopted sons, were responsible for ensuring that they did not do anything that would cause discord or bring the family name into disrepute.

A related point here is how Paul in Ephesians 3:14–15 goes on to build upon the role of God as Father adopting us as his sons and daughters into a united family. Indeed, just as adoption is a metaphor rooted in the social world of the apostle Paul so also is the image of the church as a 'household'. This historical context is crucial in understanding these verses. Ephesus, as we observed earlier, was a Roman city and when this letter was written, Roman subjects where expected to demonstrate their allegiance by bowing before the Divine Father of the Roman Empire, the emperor.[22] Here, however, Paul develops another subtle form of subjection to God as Divine Father, which supersedes the power of both the Roman Empire and the male parent as the head of the Roman household. There is a shift from any earthly allegiance to '*God* who acts as a proper-well-to-do *paterfamilias*' (Meeks

---

[20] Smail (1980: 146) also sounds an important ecclesiological note when he states, '*The church* is not God's incarnate Son ... but the *family of his adopted sons*' (my emphasis). White (1992a: 289) writes also, 'Paul uses the image of adoption to accentuate the unnatural and spiritual character of his gentile converts.'

[21] Martyn (1997: 391) states in this regard, 'We are not liberated from slavery to live on our own ... We are taken by God into his own family.' On this note, New Testament scholars have applied various models to describe the church, such as voluntary associations and synagogue, but the closest parallel is that of the family. Moreover, the household in my mind is not just a model, but the early Christian communities were caught up in the social realities of the household to the extent that they were structured in accordance with ancient households.

[22] I am indebted to Stevenson-Moessner (2003: 112) for some of the points that follow. Stevenson-Moessner (2003: 123 n. 31) states, 'the adoptive family constituted in Ephesians is contrasted to the royal family in the Holy Roman Empire'.

1993: 170):[23] 'I kneel before the Father, from whom his whole family in heaven and on earth derives its name' (vv. 14–15).[24] The believer's ultimate loyalty was not to the Divine Father of the Roman Empire or to an earthly father of a household, but to God as the Father of his family secured through adoption.[25]

In the light of this ecclesiological context in Ephesians 'adoption has an important corporate dimension' (Mawhinney 1993: 83.). *Huiothesia*, as stated earlier, is 'an individualistic act which is fully explained in terms of personal piety' (Mawhinney 1993: 83), whereby we are chosen by God the Father to become his children. Equally important is the corporate dimension and the ecclesiological ramifications at work here – the adopted son is not an only son who stands in isolation from others within the local or universal church family. Rather, God the Father has not only created us but has also called us into community by adoption into his family. Moreover, 'Ephesians is relentlessly relational' (Snodgrass 1996: 19) and the believer is vitally connected and united by faith to others within the household of believers, and therefore has a responsibility to be concerned for their welfare and to look out for the needs of their own 'kith and kin'. In all this God's new family is neither a human *organization* nor a secular club to which a person signs up;[26] rather, something much more profound and far reaching is involved, in that we have been marked out, chosen and adopted by God to become members of a vibrant, dynamic *organism*, the household of God, with the very life and

[23] Hollingshead (1998: 137) also states, 'It should be no surprise that ... the Christians he [Paul] encountered swear allegiance to Caesar, the *paterfamilias* of the Empire. Early Christians would swear no such allegiance, because, like Paul, they had encountered another *paterfamilias* in God.'

[24] There is a deliberate play on words in the Greek: *patēr*, 'father', and *patria*, 'family'. Thus some English translations (e.g. JB, NIV margin) have tried to preserve this by rendering the phrase 'the father from whom all fatherhood ... derives its name'. Taken this way Paul is using God's fatherhood as the archetype for all families. Yet *patria* does not usually have the meaning 'fatherhood', but rather 'family', and it is better to understand this verse as meaning the 'family' of the church militant on earth and the church triumphant in heaven as two aspects of the one family of God. This also fits in with the universal aspect of the church, which the author portrays throughout the letter (cf. 1:22; 3:10, 21; 5:22–23, 27, 29, 32).

[25] Paul's language of the household would also have resonated in another important way with his Gentile readers, because in the Roman world of his day to be a 'member of a household meant refuge and protection, at least as much as the master was able to provide. It also meant identity and gave the security that comes with a sense of belonging' (Towner 1993: 418).

[26] This is not to say that Paul's communities did not have some form of structure right from their inception. Clearly they did, as Eph. 2:20 and 1 Thess. 5:12–15 demonstrate. This is a central thesis in my monograph (Burke 2003a: 225–249).

energy of the 'Spirit of adoption' (*pneuma huiothesias*, Rom. 8:15) flowing through and at work within.[27]

God as a sovereign *paterfamilias* (Gal. 4:1–7)

What Paul has to say about God's role as 'Father' and our adoption as sons is not restricted to the letter of Ephesians; these twin notions are also integrally linked in other adoption passages. Paul, for instance, specifically writes to the Galatian Christians, '*God sent his Son ... that we might receive the full right [adoption] of sons*. Because you are sons, God sent the Spirit of his Son into our hearts, the Spirit who calls out, "*Abba*, Father"' (Gal. 4:4–6; my emphasis; cf. Rom. 8:15).[28] The importance of this paternal language and its relationship to *huiothesia* in Galatians is evident by the way in which the term *patēr* recurs twice in the passage on adoption (vv. 2, 6) to which we shall return in a moment. It should also be noted that Paul's references to God as 'Father' here are not mere custom, nor are they solely limited to the above adoption passages alone. In fact, they are in evidence much earlier in Galatians and, given the Aramaic term *abba* also stands behind the expression 'Father' (Stanton 2002: 9),[29] their significance merits further consideration.

Paul begins his letter to the Galatians with the familial or fatherly designation for God, *patēr*: 'Paul, an apostle – sent not from men nor

[27] See p. 140 for how this view fits in with my understanding of the phrase *pneuma huiothesias*.

[28] Barnett (1999: 95–96) draws some useful parallels between Luke 1 and Gal. 4:4 to argue the case that Paul knew of the underlying tradition about Jesus' birth. Compare the following: Luke 1:68–70, 'God ... has come and has redeemed his people ... as he said through his holy prophets' and 'the time had fully come ... to redeem' (Gal. 4:4–5); Luke 1:32, 'He will be ... called the Son of the Most High' and 'God sent his Son' (Gal. 4:4); Luke 1:26–38 and the conception of a son and Luke 3:23, 'Jesus ... the son, so it was thought, of Joseph' and 'born of a woman' (Gal. 4:4); Luke 2:27, 41–42, and the presentation of Jesus in accordance with 'the custom of the Law' and Paul's comment 'born under law' (Gal. 4:4).

[29] There is good reason for considering Paul's use of the term 'Father' not just in the adoption passages where it occurs, but particularly at the beginning of his letters. James D. G. Dunn (1993: 619) states, in the light of Gal. 4:6–7 and Rom. 8:14–17, that there is a connection between the two and that 'underlying the Greek *patēr*, "Father," was the Aramaic *abba*' (see also Jeremias 1971: 65). Martyn (1997: 84) also advances contextual reasons why there is a proliferation of paternal language in Paul's letter to the Galatians: 'Paul gives special emphasis to this expression in Galatians (1:1, 3, 4; 4:2, 6), and no doubt the reason is his concern to develop the notion that the Galatians are liberated children of the God who is the gracious Father. That concern may have arisen in his mind partly because he has learned that the Teachers are preaching sermons about father Abraham and about the need of the Gentiles to become genuine children of Abraham.' See chapter 7 for further discussion.

by man, but by Jesus Christ and God the Father' (1:1).[30] This is immediately followed by the more intimate double description of *'our father'* in verses 3 and 4: 'Grace and peace to you from God *our* father and the Lord Jesus Christ, who gave himself for our sins to rescue us from the present evil age, according to the will of *our* God and Father' (my emphasis). These paternal references at the outset of the letter might appear at first sight conventional, but the description 'Father' (*patēr*) is not routine, as evidenced by the way in which this same family expression comes full circle and converges twice (cf. vv. 2, 6). Most significant for our purposes is the way in which 'father' combines with *huiothesia* in verses 4–6: 'God sent his Son ... that we might receive the full right of sons (*huiothesia*) ... Because you are sons, God sent the Spirit of his Son into our hearts, the Spirit who calls out, "*Abba*, Father"' (Gal. 4:4–6). In Paul's view this Father God has not only sovereignly initiated our salvation (Gal. 1:1, 3, 4), but the cry '*Abba*, Father!' emitted by the adopted son echoes back an awareness of the reality of this filial disposition as it strikes 'home' (4:6).

The importance of these opening references to God as Father in Galatians (1:1, 3, 4) is often overlooked, but it is important to note that the view Paul presents here is consonant with ancient Graeco-Roman culture and not that of twenty-first-century Western society (Esler 2000: 168).[31] David deSilva rightly underscores the connection and significance of these early paternal citations when he states, 'Paul uses references to God as the Father of believers at the start of many of his letters, showing the prominence and almost "givenness" of this *new household* and its *paterfamilias* within Christian culture' (2000: 207; my emphasis).

Paul uses paternal terminology in different ways and for different purposes, but the way he employs the expression 'Father' early on in his letter to the Galatians and then combines it with his adoption metaphor underscores the fact that God as adoptive Father is the sole initiative and authority in salvation. This important aspect of God's

---

[30] Witherington and Ice (2002: 33) make the following point in regard to Paul's use of paternal language: 'One of the interesting facets of Paul's use of Father language is that he almost never allows the term to stand alone. For example, when Paul refers to "our Father" it is always coupled with the term "God", either "God, our Father" or "Our God and Father". What this coupling suggests is that the term "Father" is not simply an equivalent for the term *theos* but a specification of the role God plays in relationship to believers ... he is "our Father"' (my emphasis).

[31] Balla (2002: 190) states in relation to adoption language, 'All this implies that the relationship between the Christians and God is explained by Paul using a language belonging to the realm of the household.'

fatherly authority as it applies to his role as *paterfamilias* is perhaps most strikingly demonstrated in Galatians 4:1–7, a passage that invites further reflection and exploration.[32]

An illustration: The human father (4:1–2)

Most scholars and commentators (e. g. Dunn, Martyn) are of the view that Paul in Galatians 4:1–2 provides a legal illustration, which he then goes on to develop and apply in verses 3–7.[33] But what is most important to note in these verses is the overarching way in which the apostle uses 'language related to the image of the *paterfamilias*' (Balla 2002: 189) in the ancient world (vv. 1–2), which he then 'applies . . . to God' (Balla 2002: 189) in verses 3–7 in respect of adoption. Additionally, there is a linguistic link straddling both the illustration (vv. 1–2) and the application (vv. 3–7), where the term *patēr* (vv. 2, 6) connects both sections.[34]

Contextually, Paul in chapter 4 is still speaking about the law, a subject he deals with in some detail in chapter 3, where he likens the law to a prison warden (*ephroupoumetha synkleiomenoi*, v. 23) and a

---

[32] Thompson (2000: 126) rightly comments, 'Galatians 4:6 is the *locus classicus* for understanding the Fatherhood of God in Paul.'

[33] Thus James Scott is very much in the minority when he sets this passage within the framework of Egyptian typology. Instead of viewing vv. 1–2 as illustration and vv. 3–5 as application, Scott contends that these verses allude to Israel's subjection to 430 years of Egyptian bondage and subsequent exodus and adoption to sonship (cf. Hos. 11:1). The former is a type of the eschatological adoption effected by Christ, which Christians receive (cf. 4:5). A careful study of Galatians 3 – 4, however, reveals that the entire sweep of the apostle's argument is not the Egyptian period of slavery as such; rather, Paul's focus is upon the *following* period of bondage and captivity that was inaugurated with the Torah. Byrne (1994: 290–291) rightly concludes, 'If Gal. 4:1–2 contains any anaphoric references to a period of slavery, it must be to that under the law, described so graphically in 3:23–25 and later (v. 3) presented as a subjection under the *stoicheia* analogous to the erstwhile pagan bondage of the Gentile Galatians (cf. 4:9). *The entire typology pattern, so central to the thesis here, breaks down at this point*' (my emphasis). See also Walters (2003: 42–76), who criticizes Scott's type (vv. 1–2) and antitype (vv. 3–7) approach as well: 'the present-tense of the verbs in verses 1–2 argue decidedly against this claim'. Ninan (1994: 196) makes the following observation contra Scott: 'The New Exodus scheme flounders in the specific case of Gal. 4:4–6 because there the redemption is not *eis nomon* but away from being under the Law. The presentation of the Torah in terms similar to the elemental spirits in Gal. 4:1–4 would in the scheme of Scott's correspondence require that the Torah is the Pharaoh. If ever there is any positive use of the Torah it is in Rom. 8:3 and not in Gal. 4:4. But here again the Christological mission while liberating the Torah, redefines the sonship of the redeemed in such a radically non-nomistic way that the nuances of the New Exodus are not primary. For these reasons the positive observations of Scott cannot be substantiated.' For a general critique of using exodus typology as the key to interpreting Paul see Seifrid 1994: 73–95.

[34] Martyn (1997: 386) identifies the more general notion of the sovereignty of the father in the illustration and application (see also George 1994: 294).

'pedagogue' (*paidagōgos*, v. 24). Now in chapter 4 Paul informs the Galatians that, under law, they are heirs, but because they are under age (lit. 'infants', *nēpioi*, v. 1), they are still regarded as minors. Indeed, Paul adds that their situation is 'no different from a slave' (v. 1, *ouden diapherei doulou*),[35] when they are under the temporary supervision of 'guardians' (*epitropous*) and 'trustees' (*oikonomous*) who were responsible for regulating their affairs. But the significant event that brings this period of supervision to an end is not the maturation of the 'heir-in-waiting' but the 'sovereign act on the part of the father' (Martyn 1997: 388–389)[36] (v. 2b, lit. 'until the time appointed by the father', *prothesmia [hēmera] tou patros*). This change in the minor's world is brought about by the action of the father, who himself decides to terminate his situation, a point Paul picks up in verses 3–7, where he goes on to explain and develop the legal analogy (vv. 1–2) by applying it to God in order to demonstrate his sovereign action in adopting us into his family.

The application: The divine Father (4:3–7a)

In verses 3–7 the apostle begins to apply the illustration: 'So also, when we were children,[37] we were in slavery *under the basic principles of the world*' (v. 3, *hypo ta stoicheia tou kosmou*).[38] By using the first-person plural 'we' here in verse 3, Paul includes himself with the Galatian Christians, which means that 'the Law ... [is] ... one of the enslaving elements of the cosmos' (Martyn 1997: 385). It is significant how Paul lumps together Jews and Gentiles – earlier in

[35] However, the heir *is* different from a slave, for the fact remains that he and his guardians know full well that one day he will be 'lord of the entire estate' (*kyrios pantōn ōn*, v. 1b). Thus Paul tailors his illustration to make it fit with the application coming later where he goes on to say that all human beings, Jews and Gentiles, are slaves (Walters 2003: 62).

[36] It is important to note this, as in the analogy (vv. 3–7) Paul does not go on to contrast maturity with immaturity but to a state of slavery, which, as Martyn rightly points out, is a 'condition one does not outgrow'.

[37] It is worth noting the way Paul runs back and forth between the first-, second- and third-person plural in these verses: 'We', v. 3; 'they', v. 5; 'we', v. 5; 'you', v. 6; 'we', v. 6; 'you', v. 7.

[38] There are three main ways in which the phrase *ta stoicheia tou kosmou* has been interpreted. First, it has been suggested that *ta stoicheia* (from the root word *stoichos*, a military term meaning 'rank' or 'row') refer to things that belong together; i.e. a set of philosophical or religious principles: the ABCs of the faith. Another interpretation of *ta stoicheia tou kosmou* has been to identify them with the four elemental substances that many ancients believed were the material components of the physical world: earth, water, air and fire. The third view is a development of the second, where the powers are not restricted to the physical realm but include an array of spiritual forces headed by Satan himself, whom Paul elsewhere calls 'the god of this age' (2 Cor. 4:4).

chapter 3 of this letter the apostle discusses the slavery of the Jews (3:22–25), but now he is ready to apply this to the pre-Christian experience of the Galatian believers, who were just as enslaved in their pagan idolatry as the Jews had been in their servitude to the Law. Douglas Moo (1991: 533; my emphasis) sums this up admirably:

> in ... Galatians ... Paul makes clear that the slave/son/heir language can be applied more generally to the status of *all* people within his salvation-historical scheme. Before the cross, the people of Israel, 'under the law,' lived as 'minors,' little better than slaves; in a similar way, Gentiles were enslaved under the 'elementary principles (*stoicheia*) of the world' (Gal. 4:9).

Paul is thus making the point that *all* have been in bondage of some sort from which they need salvation. A radical change however is underway that proves to be the turning point of the ages and that Paul puts in the following terms: 'But when the fullness of time had come God sent his Son in order that we might receive the adoption as sons' (*hote de ēlthen to plērōma tou chronou, exapesteilen ho theos ton huion hina tēn huiothesian apolabōmen*, vv. 4–5; my trans.).[39] This is followed by verse 6, which has rightly been described as 'the *locus classicus* for understanding the Fatherhood of God in Paul' (Thompson 2000: 126). 'Because you are sons, God sent the Spirit of his Son into our hearts, the Spirit who calls out, "*Abba*, Father" (*patēr*). The connection between the illustration (vv. 1–2) and the analogy (vv. 4–5) is now clear in that just as the human father was solely responsible for determining when his son should come of age, so also God the Father has a timetable in mind.[40] Stated negatively, and in the present context, this means that the clock of salvation history cannot be turned back to the Law. More positively, the whole sweep of salvation history has been sovereignly engineered by God the Father and has climaxed eschatologically in the action of his sending the Son into the world,

---

[39] On the basis of Roman law it has been suggested that Paul had in mind the Roman law *tutela impuberis* (guardianship of a minor) or, more specifically, *tutela testamentaria* (guardianship established by testament) according to which the son of a deceased father was under the supervision of a tutor nominated by his father until he was 14, and then under a curator until he was 25. See Gaius, *Inst.* 1.22–23; Hester 1968: 18–19, 59.

[40] George (1994: 300) is quite right when he states, 'in the analogy of the heir-in-waiting just developed by Paul, the time designated by the father for his son to enter into the inheritance corresponds to the time in human history fixed and appointed by God to the sending of his Son'.

culminating in our *huiothesia*.[41] Ben Witherington rightly concludes on the significance this has for Jews and non-Jews, 'The conclusion one must draw is that Paul views the status both of Jews under the Law and of Gentiles outside the Law as the same in ... that they both need ... adoption as sons, neither had this as a birthright' (1997: 283).

In all this we can see that Paul is making an important theological statement to show how God is the 'primary actor in the drama of salvation' (George 1994: 294).[42] The note of God's 'absolute claim' (Williams 1999: 65) is to the fore, where the Father exercises his sole prerogative in saving us through adoption into his family. This emphasis serves to underscore the fact that the background upon which Paul appears to be drawing is the Roman 'socio-legal customs ... of the authority of God as Father [in order] to stress the *authority of God as adopter*' (Ryken 1998: 14; my emphasis). Theologically, then, Paul presents God in the role of a supreme Father – the new *paterfamilias* – who exercises sovereign control, authority and power over his household, the church. Martyn (1997: 391) sums up what has taken place, 'We are taken by God into his own family. Thus, the ... change enacted by God in his sovereign act of timely redemption involves also the sovereign act of adoption by which he creates the new family of his church.'[43]

There is one final point we ought to note in the Galatian passage, which sheds some light on the background to Paul's adoption metaphor. In verse 5 Paul employs the compound verb *apolabōmen*, 'receives back' (which the NIV misses and translates with the simple 'receive', *lambanō*) in juxtaposition with *huiothesia*. Paul could have used the simple form above, but he uses the compound form instead, which is interesting and is consonant with the Roman legal procedure of adoption: when a father released his son from *potestas* by formally selling him (*emancipatio*), and this was done three times so that the

---

[41] Martyn (1997: 391) puts it well: 'The cosmic change enacted by God in his sovereign act of timely redemption involves the sovereign act of adoption by which he creates the new family of his church.' Scott (1992: 174) also comments, 'redemption is not an end in itself; the goal is rather redemption to a relationship with the Father established by "adoption" (*huiothesia*)'.

[42] Martyn (1997: 388) states that 'the sentence comprising vv. 3–5 is nothing less than the theological center of the entire letter'; George (1994: 294) also states that Paul is 'making a crucial theological point with these words'.

[43] Fitzmyer (1992: 500) states, 'For Paul *huiothesia* denotes a special status: because of faith ... Christians have been taken into the family of God, have come under the *patria potestas*, "paternal authority," of God himself, and have a legitimate status in that family, not simply that of slaves (who belonged, indeed, to the ancient *familia*), but of sons.'

son was finally free of his father's *potestas*. After two sales, however, the son could be manumitted (like a slave) back to his father, who could *receive him back* by a fresh act of *adoptio*. 'The son "emancipated," and then manumitted back, literally "receives back" ... by adoption the status of a son'. 'All this', Dunn has recently concluded, 'helps explain how Paul's thought could move easily from the thought of redemption (from slavery) to that of adoption to sonship' and underscores the fact that 'Paul had in mind the legal act of adoption by which a Roman citizen entered another family and came under the *patria potestas* of its head' (1993: 217).

The Father, the Spirit and the revelation of our adoption as sons

The role of God as Father adopting us into his family is, as already noted, a positive way of setting forth what the apostle Paul means by salvation. It is also important in another way in that 'it corrects the widespread notion of the universal fatherhood of God and provides against devastating implications' (Murray 1976: 233). That the apostle uses the expression *huiothesia* to describe what it means to be a Christian is important: our adoption as sons, according to Paul, is not our native or natural condition. God's family comprises solely adopted sons and daughters – there are no natural-born sons or daughters in his divine household. Stated another way, creatively God may be the Father of all humankind, since all are his 'offspring' (*genos*; cf. Acts 17:28b), but salvifically God is the Father only of those who are in Christ and are his sons and daughters by adoption and grace. There is only one who rightly qualifies as a natural son and that is Jesus,[44] a distinction rightly recognized by Augustine, the fourth-century theologian, when he states, 'Adoptionem propterea dicit'; 'ut distincte intelligamus unicum Dei filium' (We are adopted sons by grace; he is son by nature).[45]

But while every Christian would give mental assent to a belief in the fatherhood of God, not all of God's children have entered into the confident trust and willing obedience that that belief implies. Moreover, according to Paul, the knowledge that we are God's adopted sons and daughters and that he is our 'Father' is not merely a statement of faith, nor a conclusion we can arrive at with our own

---

[44] See chapter 5 and the discussion of Rom. 1:3–4.
[45] The citation is from Lightfoot (1975: 168–169). The translation is mine.

understanding. Rather, our comprehension of the fatherhood of God is revealed pneumatologically via the Holy Spirit. We shall look more closely at the role of the Spirit in adoption in chapter 6, but I signal the point at this stage that in Galatians 4 and Romans 8 Paul links the Spirit with the Aramaic *abba* and what it means to know God as *patēr*.

According to Galatians 4:4–6, the filial cry of *Abba* is less the spoken cry of the believer and more the Spirit's cry witnessing in the heart of the Christian (Smail 1980: 43). Paul writes, 'God sent his Son . . . that we might receive the full rights [adoption] of sons. Because you are sons, God sent the Spirit of his Son into our hearts, *the Spirit who calls out, "Abba, Father"*' (my emphasis). As Donald Guthrie states emphatically, '*No-one* would learn to approach God as Father in the familiar way indicated by the word "Abba" *except* through the Spirit' (1981: 545; my emphasis). Similarly, although with a slightly different emphasis, Paul states in Romans 8:15, 'For you did not receive a spirit that makes you a slave again to fear, but you received the Spirit of adoption [NIV]. *And by him* we cry, "*Abba*, Father"' (my emphasis). The Father God who sends the Spirit into the heart of the Christian is the same Father God who brings this paternal awareness to newly adopted sons that they have indeed come 'home'.

We now consider the expression '*Abba*, Father' in more detail, 'since a considerable amount of literature has grown up around this word' (Fee 1994: 411).

'*Abba*, Father': The familial cry of the son and the adopted sons of God

As already noted, Paul connects the expression '*Abba*, Father' (lit. *abba ho patēr*, or *abba*, the father) with the adoption metaphor in two passages (Gal. 4:6; Rom. 8:15). *Abba* is Aramaic, not Hebrew, which is not unusual, given the fact that Paul himself spoke Aramaic (cf. Acts 22:2). What is remarkable, however, is that an Aramaic expression is retained in two of Paul's letters written in *koinē* Greek that are addressed to predominantly Gentile congregations. The apostle's letters represent the earliest attestation of *abba* in the vocative form.

Abba, however, in the New Testament is not restricted to Paul's letters – it is found also on the lips of Jesus in the Garden of Gethsemane on the eve of his crucifixion, as recorded in Mark 14:36: 'Going a little farther, he fell to the ground and prayed that if possible the hour might pass from him. "*Abba*, Father," he said, "everything is possible for you. Take this cup from me. Yet not what I will, but what you will."'

But before we look at Jesus' use of *abba*, I shall respond to the feminist challenge that has called for the removal of this term from Christian vocabulary. First, we ought to take cognizance of the fact that Jesus' own practice of addressing God was to call him 'Father'. Moreover, Jesus also commanded his own disciples to use this language when addressing God in prayer: 'This, then, is how you should pray: "Our Father..."' (Matt. 6:9). These uses, often over-looked, represent 'a central argument against the feminist challenge' (Thompson 2000: 9),[46] and, as Meye Thompson (2000: 9) remarks, the 'normativity of Jesus' address to God as Father for shaping contemporary practices leads ineluctably to a second argument for maintaining the traditional language, namely, that such address to God *is the language of the Bible*' (my emphasis).

Although the biblical authors, in both Old and New Testaments, use female metaphors in respect of God (see later in chapter 8), there is no direct command to address God as 'Mother' in Scripture. '[E]verything that is distinctively Christian as opposed to merely Jewish, is summed up in the knowledge of the fatherhood of God, "Father" is the Christian name of God' (Packer 1988: 182–183).

Jesus' use of the term *abba* raises other questions; namely, whether Paul's use of the same expression demonstrates a knowledge of and a dependence upon the 'Jesus tradition'.[47] Why was *abba* retained and remembered by Paul, and what does the term actually mean? If it was not known and remembered by Paul's congregations, why does he not give any explanation of the meaning of this expression in his letters to the churches in Galatia and Rome, the latter of which he had never visited? And, in what way, if any, is the believer's adoption as son dependent upon Jesus' unique relationship of sonship to God?

Abba's Son and the adopted sons of God

One of the most influential discussions of *abba* in recent times has been that of the German scholar Joachim Jeremias. Jeremias argues that when Jesus prayed '*Abba*, Father' (Mark 14:36) in the Garden of

---

[46] For a sensitive survey of the feminist literature see Thompson 2000: 1–20.

[47] Generally speaking, scholars use this expression to explain whether or not Paul had any knowledge of and used the message and teaching of Jesus in his letters. There is good evidence that he did and that Paul was a follower of Jesus and not the founder of Christianity (see Wenham 1995). For the most recent robust defence of Paul's use of the Jesus tradition see Kim 2002.

Gethsemane on the evening immediately prior to his crucifixion, he was using a unique and unusual expression.[48] In other words, Jesus' utterance of these words, according to Jeremias, enables us to hear the *ipisissima vox Jesu* (the very voice of Jesus). Jeremias also concludes that *abba* was never employed in contemporary Judaism as a direct address to God: it was a family term used by little children within the confines of the home.[49]

Jeremias's views, however, have been heavily criticized, not least by the Jewish scholar Géza Vèrmes, who affirms that *abba* was not unique to Jesus but was used typically by charismatic Galilean Jews of later times. Vèrmes asserts that 'one of the distinguishing features of ancient hasidic piety is its habit of alluding to God precisely as Father' (1973: 210). Vèrmes cites the example of the Hasid Hanin, the grandson of Honi the Circle-drawer and cousin of Abba Hilkiah, the charismatic rainmaker (*b. Ta'an.* 23 b). This rabbinic text relates how during a drought some schoolchildren who came to Hanin to ask him to intervene in the situation uttered the cry *Abba, abba; habn lan mitraim*, which means, 'Father, father; give us rain.' Hanin prayed to God thus: 'Lord of the universe, render a service to those who cannot distinguish between the *Abba* who gives rain and the *Abba* who does not.' Vèrmes concludes (211), 'the central point ... appears to be that for the charismatic, as for Jesus, God is *Abba*'. What are we to make of this?

A careful comparison of this statement with Jesus', however, reveals that neither the children nor Hanin address God as *Abba*. Rather, Hanin is the one addressed as *abba*, who in turn addresses God by using the more formal expression 'Master of the Universe' (Witherington 1990: 216), which can hardly be equated with the more intimate term *abba*. A related issue here is whether *abba* was used by small children or adults to address their parents. Jeremias's views have also been prominent here. He argues that *abba* is 'child's babble or *lallwort*' (Ninan 1994: 123) and that *abba* was a word used only by children. Later, however, he changed his mind and concurred that adult sons too used this term when addressing their fathers. But even though the expression was also employed by 'adult children in an Aramaic home [this] does not thereby make it a more adult word'

[48] Jeremias (1971a: 67) states, 'the complete novelty and uniqueness of *Abba* as an address to God in the prayers of Jesus shows that it expresses the heart of Jesus' relationship to God'.

[49] Jeremias (1967: 60) writes, 'to address a father as *abba* is a mark of the everyday language of the family'. Jeremias was later to have a change of mind on this. See discussion below.

(Fee 1994: 411). *Abba* is most likely a family term used *both* by children and adults and expresses intimacy and affection for parents.

'Jesus' usage of the Aramaic term *abba* is still without parallel' (Thompson 2000: 50; see also Cullman 1995: 41),[50] and because *abba* is a Jesus word, the only credible solution as to why Paul retains it in his letters is the fact that it was an expression of Jesus' own making that was subsequently remembered. Jesus is the conduit who enables his disciples to employ the same language he himself used in addressing God as Father. If Jesus had not taken the initial step of addressing his Father as *abba*, which of his disciples would have, unless they had been previously taught by him to do so? The bilingual form '*Abba*, Father' suggests that this expression was used originally in congregations where Aramaic was spoken as well as Greek (i.e. not in the Pauline, Gentile, churches).[51] It was known as a Jesus term, and since congregations used it themselves, it seems likely also that they saw it as sanctioned by Jesus for use by his followers. The preservation of the Aramaic term *abba* in Christian usage as seen in Paul's letters (Rom. 8:15; Gal. 4:6) is, as I. Howard Marshall (1976: 59; see also Obeng 1988: 364; Witherington 1990: 218) rightly concludes,

> intelligible only if it was treasured as a word spoken by Jesus. It is sheer presumption that its use arose in the Aramaic speaking church when all the tangible evidence speaks in favour of its use by Jesus. The early church knew it was able to address God in this way because Jesus had invited his disciples to pray thus.

There is, however, one vital distinction that must be made between Jesus' usage of *abba* and that of his followers; namely, that whereas Jesus, the Son, uses the expression on the eve of the greatest

---

[50] Fitzmyer (1985: 28) states, 'There is no evidence in the literature of pre-Christian or first-century Judaism that 'abbā' was used in any sense as a personal address for God by an individual.' Even James Barr (1988b: 28–47), another of Jeremias's most outspoken critics, accepts that 'it may ... be quite true that the use of "abba" was original with Jesus and historically genuine. I have no wish to dispute this.'

[51] Witherington and Ice (2002: 31) state, 'What this strongly suggests is that we have here not only a relic of the earliest Aramaic-speaking Jewish Christians' prayer language, though that is true, but the juxtaposition of the two terms suggest this had become common prayer language for non-Aramaic-speaking Christians, both Diaspora Jewish and Gentile ones, as well. Witherington and Ice (31ff.) conclude, 'In the context ... Paul is emphasizing that his Gentile converts ... had been prompted by the Spirit to cry "*abba*," just as Jewish Christians such as Paul had been earlier prompted to do.'

challenge to his earthly career (the cross), we as his disciples and God's adopted sons employ *abba* on the postresurrection side of Calvary (Witherington & Ice 2002: 24 n. 13). As we shall see in the next chapter, the death of the eternal and unique Son of God is the means by which believers are adopted by God into his family and Paul is well aware of the distinction between Jesus' sonship and the adoptive sonship of believers.

What does abba *mean?*

Related to this discussion are two other points: first, what does the expression '*Abba*, Father' actually mean? And second, does '*Abba*, Father' constitute a prayer emitted by adopted sons?

If Paul was influenced by the Jesus tradition in the Gospels, that context may have much to tell us about its meaning and usage for the apostle. Many popular treatments of *abba* commonly assume that it means 'daddy', but James Barr has put forward linguistic arguments to demonstrate that 'Abba Isn't Daddy',[52] since *abba* was also used by adult children. That said, even though Barr may have answered the question of the origins of this term, as Fee (1994: 411) points out: 'its use by adult children in an Aramaic home *does not thereby make it a more adult word*. Most likely the word was in fact an expression of intimacy, used by children first as infants and later as children' (my emphasis).[53] In addition, *abba* can hardly mean just 'daddy' (in our day-to-day sense) when Jesus used the expression in the context of the Garden of Gethsemane as he faced the biggest challenge to his earthly mission (Mark 14:36). Here the translation 'daddy' would be overly sentimental, as it would fail to reflect adequately the sense of reverence or respect and would not take into consideration the sense of occasion as the cross loomed before Jesus – a time when he needed to exercise trust in God as *abba* as he had never done before.[54]

[52] The title of Barr's essay (1988b: 28–47).

[53] Fee (1994: 411 n. 154) also goes on to point out that while Barr 'is correct that it did not originate with the babbling of children (after all, why these sounds and not others?), that these (*abba* and *imma*) are the first words that most children would stammer needs to be noted. They do so, because these are the first words children are "taught," as it were (as in, "Say *abba*"). And in no language that I know are the more formal words for parents the first words they are "taught" to speak. Thus "origins" as such is irrelevant, but not so with usage and significance.'

[54] Trumper (2005: 74) admirably sums it up when he states, 'the trauma of Gethsemane reminds us powerfully that the appropriating language of *Abba* bespeaks not dripping sentimentality – as if daddy were a big softy to be manipulated at will – but the *seriousness of filial love*, devotion and obedience' (emphasis mine).

We should pay attention to Leon Morris's measured observation (1988: 315–116) when he states:

> Before we assume that it was used much like our 'Papa' or 'Daddy', we should reflect that the head of a family was an august figure in first-century society (the Roman *paterfamilias* still had the right to put members of his household to death, even if the right was used rarely; cf. Gen. 38:24).

Apart from leaving *abba* untranslated (which may be the best solution), perhaps 'dearest father' (Witherington & Ice 2002: 25) is nearer the meaning, because it emphasizes the respect and intimacy while also avoiding the overly sentimental connotations.

Second, does '*Abba*, Father' constitute a prayer? We have seen how Jesus used the term *abba* in the context of personal prayer and communion with his Father. In the Synoptic Gospels Jesus' relation to his Father was not just exceptional, distinct or even special; rather, his relationship to God was unique.[55] Given that Jesus used the expression '*Abba*, Father' as he prayed to his Father in the Garden of Gethsemane, it is possible that Paul's usage of the same expression in his letters was a short ejaculatory or extemporaneous response-prayer emitted by the newly adopted son, as an awareness of newfound filial status in the family *Dei* strikes home. Equally, Paul's use of *abba* in Romans (8:15) might also be a prayer, a *crie de coeur*, from the adopted son as he calls out in dependency upon God for help and strength.

According to David Wenham, there are parallels between Romans 8 and the Gethsemane story, one of which is the reference Paul makes to sharing in Christ's sufferings (Rom. 8:17). Just as Jesus, God's Son,

---

[55] Here Thompson's (2000: 88–89) argument is weak. She tries to argue that the references to God as the Father of Christians is carried over from early Judaism rather than being grounded in Jesus' own usage and experience of God as Father. But the Old Testament and early Jewish references to God as Father are few and far between and there are other anomalies. For example, she cites evidence from the intertestamental literature in the form of the Qumran literature, which depicts God as being addressed as Father. For instance, in the prayer of Joseph we read, 'My Father and my God, do not abandon me in the hands of the gentiles, do me justice, so the poor and afflicted do not die' (4Q372 1). There is one crucial difference with this text and that of Mark 14:36: in the former the language is Hebrew and not Aramaic. Witherington and Ice (2002: 60) draw the distinction between the Old Testament / early Judaism and Jesus' use of the term 'Father': 'what references we have almost never link the Father language to a particular relationship with one particular individual. Yet the New Testament usage almost always grounds the use of Father language in the relationship between Jesus and God.'

suffered, so the adopted son is called upon to share in Jesus' sufferings; and Paul goes on to develop the trials and struggles of God's children in Romans 8:18–23.[56] Wenham's view finds support in the use of the accompanying verb *krazō*, which, in the majority of occasions in Scripture, is used for an individual crying or calling out to God or during times of national emergency (e.g. Gen. 18:20; Exod. 2:23; 3:7; 1 Sam. 5:12). In the New Testament the verb is frequently used in the context of Jesus' ministry and work when helping individuals call out for help and deliverance (e.g. Matt. 15:22; Mark 9:23–24). And, of course, Jesus at the moment immediately prior to his death uttered the derelict cry 'My God, My God, why have you forsaken me' (Matt. 27:46).[57] With this in view, *abba* may not only be a prayer that signals the adopted son's new status but may also be a cry of dependency upon God the Father for support and strength in the days ahead. Thus, while *abba* may be a cry of 'familial joy' (Witherington & Ice 2002: 30), the other side of the coin is our present suffering as part of creation, depicted by Paul as our groaning and longing for the future and final adoption as sons, the redemption of the body (8:23).

What is also particularly striking about this prayer of the adopted son, recorded by the apostle Paul, is that his cry is not egocentric but theocentric: careful note should be taken of the fact that he does not call out '*I* am God's adopted son' but rather '*God* is my Father.' Were the believer to ponder the depths of this relationship, as Sinclair Ferguson (1981: 86) exhorts, words would defy and leave us fully unable to articulate what has taken place: 'Think of the privilege of calling the Creator of the ends of the earth "Abba, Father". It defies comprehension and calculation.' And yet, for all whom God has adopted as sons and daughters into his family it is true!

Abba*'s heirs*

In his letters to the Galatians and Romans Paul not only uses the term 'adoption' to describe believers but goes one step further by describing them as 'heirs' (*klēronomoi*). Thus in Galatians 4:5–6, after having mentioned adoption (v. 5), Paul goes on to state in verse 7,

---

[56] Wenham (1995: 279) writes, 'It seems possible, in light of the evidence, to think that Paul's reflections in Romans ... 8 on the Christian's struggles in the time of suffering ... have been influenced by the Gethsemane story.' See chapter 8 where this aspect is more fully discussed.

[57] It is interesting, if not significant, that this is the only occasion when Jesus does not address God as 'Father': when he as the Son of God bears the sins of the world and a *holy* God turns his back.

'you are no longer a slave, but a son; and since you are a son, God has made you also an heir'. In Romans 8:15–17 he puts it this way: 'you have received the Spirit of adoption ... [and] if we are children, then we are heirs – co-heirs with Christ' (my trans.).[58] In both instances it is important to note that 'adoption functions as a metaphor that gives nuance to what he wishes to communicate' about inheritance (Walters 2003: 42); in other words, it is the importance of the former and the consequences of first being an adopted son that throws light on to the latter and not the other way around. Paul's language of inheritance always harks back to the prior knowledge of being adopted sons.

The word 'inheritance' is an important one for the apostle Paul and has a background in the Old Testament, where the promise to Israel of an inheritance is prominent and was especially linked to a physical place, the land.[59] Abraham, for example, was promised an inheritance, the land of Canaan (Gen. 12:7) and this promise became fundamental in Old Testament theology (cf. Gen. 50:24; Deut. 34:4). Later in the Old Testament the inheritance was under-stood not as a physical concept but as a reward for the godly on the day of judgment (Isa. 57:7). When we come to the New Testament, the term takes on a different meaning rarely found in the Old Testament (although see Ps. 16:5), where it is linked with the notion of sonship and adoption, as Foerster (1991: 781–782) points out:

> A firm link is established between sonship and inheritance such as we hardly ever find in the Old Testament and later Judaism ... Thus, although he never calls Christ *klēronomos* he refers to Christians as *sunklēronomoi de Christou* in Rom. 8:17 and attrib-utes the inheritance of Christians expressly to their *huiothesia*.

However, as with adoption, a more suitable background to the analogy of heir is Roman law (Walters 2003: 42–76). While some might try to argue that the analogy of inheritance falls apart because

---

[58] Hester (1968: 63) states that Paul never refers to Christ as an heir but prefers to speak of him as 'Son' (e.g. Rom. 1:3–4; 5:10), because 'Son' by implication means he is also an heir. He remarks, 'if Paul did not use the title Heir for Jesus Christ, it was partly due to the fact that all the privileges of heirship are implied in the title Son, and that on the basis of the definition of heirship ... in the ... legal systems of his day, Paul felt that the title was better suited for Christians'.

[59] The term *klēronomos* comes from two words: *klēros*, 'lot', and *nemomai*, 'to possess'.

no-one is heir of the living, Williams (1999: 65) makes clear that this was

> not in Roman law (to which we believe Paul was referring). Here the heir was understood to be the embodiment of the testator – the father lived on, so to speak, in the son – not from the time of the father's death but from the time of the son's ... adoption.

And Lyall (1984: 110) says, 'The existence of heirs ... was not conditional on the death of their ancestor, for they had existence and status already by virtue of their relationship with him. Birth not death constituted heirship.'[60]

Paul states that believers are not only adopted sons but are also co-heirs with Christ (Rom. 8:17). But immediately prior to this he also asserts that believers are 'heirs of God' (Rom. 8:17), a phrase that can be understood in one of two ways. It can be taken as a subjective genitive, giving the meaning that God possesses the believer, or as an objective genitive, where the believer inherits God. Moo states that the noun *theou* is not the object of *klēronomoi*, as if God himself were what is inherited; rather, believers inherit what God has promised them (1996: 505). But what Paul says here is quite 'stunning', according to Schreiner (1998: 427), in that God's adopted sons and daughters are heirs of God himself.[61] The phrase suggests that believers are not only heirs of what God has promised but that 'we will inherit God!' (Peterson 2001: 161). Cranfield (1975: 419) states in this regard:

> Christians are men [and women] who have great expectations, that their expectations are based upon their being sons of God, that these expectations are of sharing not just in various blessings God is able to bestow but in that which is peculiarly His own, the perfect and imperishable glory of his own life.

Summary

Paul's adoption metaphor is situated in theological contexts where there is a clear trinitarian pattern. In this chapter I have focused on

[60] Lyall cites two examples: (1) Gaius (*Inst.* 2.157), who states that children 'even in their father's lifetime are considered in a manner owners'; and (2) Paulus (*Dig.* 28.2.11) declares, 'On the death of the father the heirs are not seen to inherit the property as rather acquire the free control of their own property.'

[61] This entails taking the description 'heirs of God' as an objective genitive, where the believer 'inherits God' (Wallace 1996: 129).

the Father's role and have demonstrated how Paul employs the term 'Father' (*patēr*) in his *huiothesia* passages as well as at the beginning of certain letters in order to emphasize God the Father's supreme role in saving and adopting us as his sons and daughters. In both Ephesians and Galatians the sovereign dimension to adoption is the overriding feature. In the former our *huiothesia* is deliberate and premeditated, having taken place outside time, in the eternal counsels of God the Father, while in latter the thrust is more eschatological in that the Father intervenes at the climactic moment of salvation history. By setting adoption against the prevailing Roman sociolegal and cultural context of the first century, Paul underscores the two aspects of God's initiative and absolute role as the new *paterfamilias* of a new family.

In both the above contexts we have also observed how Paul's discussion of adoption follows a clear outline: after discussing the implications of our adoption, he then goes on to present an ecclesiological focus whereby *huiothesia* functions inclusively – adoption into God's family (Eph. 2:20; Gal. 6:10) joins Jews and Gentiles into one household. Paul's many paternal references in these letters are also integrally related to his adoption metaphor and serve to heighten the fact that honour is ascribed to us because of our association with God as 'Father' and our belonging to his family. Indeed, this relationship also brings an accompanying moral responsibility for God's children to live in ways that bring glory to their adoptive Father and to his family name.

The expression '*Abba*, Father' also enables adopted sons to address God in prayer through the Spirit; and in doing so they use the same language Jesus, God's Son, used in communion with the Father. *Abba* was a term that found its way into the Gentile-speaking churches of Paul because Jesus had taught his disciples to address God in this way. And because *Abba*'s sons are also *Abba*'s heirs, the inheritance believers can look forward to is God himself.

Chapter Five

God the Son and
the adopted sons of God

Introduction

Philip Melancthon (1497–1560), the renowned German reformer and teacher, coined the often repeated expression 'to know Christ is to know his benefits'. 'To know Christ', according to Melancthon, is a circumlocution for 'union with Christ', and sinners cannot have a share in the benefits of salvation unless they are vitally united with the Son of God. Now adoption, as demonstrated earlier in this monograph, is one of the many benefits of the saving grace of God; indeed, it has been asserted that 'a major focus of the adoption texts is that *the believer is adopted by virtue of union with Christ, the Son of God*' (Cook 1978: 141; my emphasis; see also Stevenson-Moessner 2003: 93). That there is a relationship between Jesus Christ the Son of God and the believer's *huiothesia* is evident from a sample of the Pauline texts that deal with adoption (Gal. 4:4–5; Rom. 8:3; 8:17; Eph. 1:5).

The close association and connection between *huiothesia* and the person and work of God's Son was also recognized by Irenaeus, the early second-century church Father and theologian, who remarks (*Haer.* 3.11), 'it is incumbent upon the Mediator between God and men ... to present man to God, while He revealed God to man. For, in what way could we be partakers of the *adoption as sons, unless we had received ... through the Son* that fellowship' (Irenaeus 1995: 426; my emphasis).[1]

---

[1] Irenaeus is the earliest witness in church history outside the New Testament canon to the doctrine of adoption. It is well known that the central theme in Irenaeus' theological framework was recapitulation. In this respect Garner (2002: 275) remarks that Irenaeus 'viewed adoption as the means of salvific participation in God's recapitulative scheme ... the grand plan of recapitulation *consummates in biblical adoption*, and ... adoption is *equated with bodily redemption* realized in Christ' (my emphasis).

Likewise, the Westminster Confession of Faith (ch. 12; my emphasis) relates Jesus Christ and the believer's adoption in the following manner:

> All those that are justified, God vouchsafeth, *in* and for *his only Son Jesus Christ, to make partakers of the grace of adoption*; by which they are taken into the number, and enjoy the liberties and privileges of the children of God; have access to the throne of grace with boldness; are enabled to cry, Abba, Father; are pitied, protected, provided for, and chastened by him as a father; yet never cast off, but sealed to the day of redemption, and inherit the promises, as heirs of eternal salvation.[2]

And the Larger Catechism lists adoption as one of a triad of benefits of the redemption Christ has purchased for believers.[3] The Christian partakes of the blessings of salvation, including justification, adoption and sanctification, only because he or she has been effectually called to faith in Christ and has been united with him in his death and resurrection. Given all this, we shall examine in the following pages the 'essential role of Christ' (Cook 1978: 141) or, more theologically, the 'christological emphasis' (141) in respect of *huiothesia*.

But what exactly is the role of the Son of God, the second person of the Trinity, in relation to the adoptive sonship of believers? We have already observed in chapter 4 the Father's vital function in initiating our adoption into his family, but while he is wholly engaged in bringing us into his household, he does not act alone. Rather, the roles of Father and Son (and the Spirit, as we shall see in chapter 6) are complementary as far as our adoption is concerned.[4] In response to the Son's role, we have already noted, for example, how both Jesus (Mark 14:36) and the Christian (Gal. 4:6; Rom. 8:15) address God by using the same filial term, *Abba* (Dunn 1975: 24).[5]

---

[2] Whaling (1923: 226) is also of the view that one of the 'grounds of adoption ... [is] ... the union with Christ through the incarnation by which He became the Son of Man'.

[3] See §10, 'The Benefits of Salvation in This Life', nos. 32–36.

[4] Peterson (2001: 65) states that the 'Father has adorned his people with all spiritual blessings in union with his Son'. Schnackenburg (1991: 54) also comments, 'Christ is "the Beloved" the Son of God through whom we are adopted as sons of God.'

[5] D'Angelo (1992: 630) is of the view that 'Father' 'cannot be shown to originate with Jesus, to be particularly important to his teaching, or even to have been used by him'. D'Angelo fails, however, to give cognizance to the overwhelming evidence in the Gospel traditions of the application of 'father' to God (Matthew, 45 occasions; Mark, 5 occasions; Luke, 17 occasions; and John, 118 occasions). For more conservative views on the fatherhood of God see Thompson 2000; Witherington & Ice 2002.

This in turn prompts the question of whether the believer's filial relationship to God is the same or similar to that of Jesus, or if there is a distinction between the sonship of Jesus and the sonship of Christians. According to the nineteenth-century theologian R. S. Candlish, there is no discrepancy between the two, evident in his following remark: 'the only difference between our ... sonship and Christ's was that *Christ enjoyed the privileges of sonship before we do, but not in a different manner*' (cited in Ferguson 1981: 85; my emphasis). Is this distinction in sonship solely a matter of chronology, or is it much deeper and more far reaching than Candlish and others would have us think and believe? These are some of the questions and issues I shall focus on in this chapter. But first we need to examine an important text, Romans 1:3–4, which in recent years has become a test case in relation to the nature of the sonship of Jesus.

Jesus: God's 'adopted' Son (Rom. 1:3–4)?

At the outset of his letter to the church at Rome the apostle writes, 'Paul, a servant of Christ Jesus, called to be an apostle and set apart for the gospel of God – the gospel he promised beforehand through his prophets in the Holy Scriptures' (vv. 1–2). This opening statement is important for Paul's presentation of the person of Jesus in this letter, which sets the backdrop for the following verses. Romans 1:3–4 goes on to discuss the *content* of this good news,[6] which he says primarily 'concerns the Son of God' (*peri tou huiou theou*, v. 3a; my trans.).[7] The repetition of the noun 'Son' (*huios*, vv. 3, 4) underscores the fact that what Paul is delineating in these verses is nothing less than his 'Son-Christology' (Kim 1981: 111), where Jesus Christ, the Son of God, is the sum and substance of his apostolic message.[8] This Christological description is itself no small point, because divine

[6] Many scholars think that Rom. 1:3–4 is a pre-Pauline tradition; but see Scott (1992: 223–236) for a robust defence of Pauline authenticity. There are three main ways in which commentators have understood the contrast in these verses: (1) the human and divine natures of Christ; (2) the outward (*kata sarka*) and inward *(pneuma hagiōsynēs)*; (3) the redemptive-historical disjunction between the old and new ages; see Schreiner (1998: 41–45) for an elaboration of these viewpoints.

[7] Haacker (2003: 24) rightly makes the point that 'The Christology of Romans ... introduces Christ as *the* topic of his message in vv. 3–4, he uses the term "son of God" both as a heading (in v. 3) and as a climax of what he says (in v. 4)' (emphasis in original) (see also Hurtado 2003: 191).

[8] Kim (1981: 95) states, 'Paul likes to define or summarize his gospel in terms of the Son of God.' It is interesting, if not significant, how Luke records the fact that immediately after his conversion Paul's preaching was centred on 'Jesus ... the Son of God' (cf. Acts 9:20).

sonship language in respect of Jesus occurs seventeen times in the letters of Paul. On three of these occasions Paul uses the description 'Son of God' (Gal. 2:20; 2 Cor. 1:19; Eph. 4:13). He also uses the expression 'his [God's Son]' on thirteen occasions (1:3, 9; 5:10; 8:29, 32; 1 Cor. 1:9; Gal. 1:16; 4:4, 6; 1 Thess. 1:10) and a variety of other expressions such as 'his own Son' (Rom. 8:3), 'the Son' (1 Cor. 15:28) and 'the Son of his love' (Col. 1:13).[9]

Romans 1:3–4 raises many exegetical issues and it is therefore helpful to set these parallel verses side by side:[10]

verse 3	*verse 4*
'who has come'	'who was appointed'
'from the seed of David'	'Son of God in power'
'according to the flesh'	'according to the Spirit of holiness'
	'from the resurrection of the dead'

Paul begins by stressing that God's Son has 'come' or was 'born' (*gegomenou*, v. 3a) of 'the seed of David' (v. 3b), which clearly underscores Jesus' messianic status and credentials. Moreover, the Son of God came 'according to the flesh' (*kata sarka*, v. 3c), an expression many commentators understand as standing in contrast to the parallel statement 'according to the Spirit of holiness' (*kata pneuma hagiōsynēs*, v. 4b). What is not so clear, however, is the exact nature of the contrast Paul has in mind. Some commentators (Hodge 1972: 18–21; Mounce: 1995: 61) and Bible translations (e.g. NIV) view these clauses as contrasting the Son of God's divine and human natures.[11] As regards the divine nature, Christ would be born of the line of David, from whom would come a descendant and a kingdom that would last forever. In relation to the human nature, Jesus is the divine Son of God – a status that would be 'declared' to the world when he was raised from the dead. But the word 'flesh' (*sarx*) here has different meanings in Paul's letters and is mostly used by him to emphasize the weakness of the flesh (NIV, 'sinful nature'; e.g. Rom. 8:4, 5, 8). Thus, the human–divine nature is unlikely to be what Paul intends here.

---

[9] I owe these references to Hurtado (1999: 221–222).

[10] The literature on these verses is vast and the reader should consult the commentaries. A brief, useful guide is Moo (1996: 44–51).

[11] This interpretation also requires that we understand the verb *horizō* to mean 'declared', which, as I have discussed in the main text, is an unlikely translation. Evidence for the meaning 'declare' is also lacking in the LXX (Schmidt 1992, 5: 452).

It is probably better to understand Paul here in Romans 1:3–4 as contrasting two stages of the life on earth of Jesus the Son of God. In other words, the distinction is not between two human natures but two states, the pre- and postresurrection states or function of Jesus Christ the Son of God (Moo 1996: 48).[12] This view depends on an understanding of two other key exegetical issues that take us to the heart of the matter concerning Jesus' sonship: the meaning of *horisthentes* and the position of the phrase *en dynamei*, both in verse 4. I shall deal with *en dynamei* first.

The dative clause *en dynamei* (in power) can mean one of two things. It can be understood (1) adverbially, in which case it modifies the participle *horisthentes*, which some have taken to mean 'declared', 'designated' or 'appointed'; that is, 'declared with power to be the Son of God' (v. 4). Alternatively, the phrase can be taken (2) adjectivally and as qualifying 'Son of God', giving the translation 'appointed Son of God with power'. The latter is the better reading because it removes any suggestion of adoptionist Christology (that Christ *became* the Son of God by virtue of his resurrection; see n. 14 below). Thus, in accord with this second view, what we have here is a two-stage Christology, where the contrast is between the two phases or states of Jesus' existence: whereas during the pre-resurrection era Jesus was the Son of God in weakness and humility, in the postresurrection period he was appointed as the Son of God in power. The raising of God's Son in power is a Christological moment that not only inaugurates a new phase in the sonship of Jesus but is of huge soteriological significance, for he enables believers to become God's adopted sons.

Turning to the second issue of the participle *horisthentos* (v. 4a), some have understood this to mean 'declared' (Ferguson 1986: 87) or 'designated' (Leenhardt 1961: 36). In the majority of instances where this verb is employed in the New Testament, however, it usually means 'appointed'. For example, the same verb is used in Acts 10:42 in connection with the apostle Peter when he proclaims the good news to Cornelius and his household: 'He [God] commanded us to preach to the people and to testify that he is the one whom God appointed as

---

[12] Fee (1994: 478–484) puts the emphasis on the old age ('sphere of the flesh') and the new era ('the sphere of the Holy Spirit'), but the double usage here of the noun *huios* in vv. 3–4 puts the focus on the *person* of Jesus Christ, the Son of God, rather than the two epochs. Such a view also requires us to understand the phrase *pneuma hagiōsynēs* as a reference to the Holy Spirit, and Paul nowhere in his letters uses this as a designation for the *pneuma*.

judge of the living and the dead' (cf. Luke 22:22; Acts 2:23; 11:29; 17:26, 31; Heb. 4:7). Thus 'appointed' is the better reading.[13]

What has been particularly noteworthy since the 1980s has been the advancement of the argument for understanding *horisthentos* as having 'declaratory significance' and 'an unmistakable judicial tone' (Gaffin 1978: 118). Richard Gaffin is of the view that this 'suggests that the resurrection is a judicially constitutive declaration of sonship' (118). Gaffin (117–119) goes on to conclude, '*horisthentes* underscores what is already intimated in recognizing that "Son of God" is a messianic designation: the resurrection of Jesus is his *adoption* (as the second Adam)' (my emphasis).[14] This interpretation has most recently been taken up and articulated by James Scott, for whom it is an important part of the thesis in his monograph *Adoption as Sons of God*. Scott is in general agreement with this view and not only argues (1992: 255) that the phrase *horisthentos huioi theou* refers to Jesus 'as the adopted Son of God', but that this expression is also 'a circumlocution for the Adoption formula in 2 Sam. 7:14a' (242). To be sure, there are messianic overtones in this text (Son of David), but the key question in the midst of this discussion is whether it is proper to use the language of 'adoption' to describe Jesus' sonship.[15]

First, and most importantly, we have observed how Paul twice employs the more general term 'Son' (*huios*, vv. 3, 4) in reference to Jesus, rather than his own unique expression *huiothesia*, the latter being conspicuous by its absence from this passage. Indeed, if as is argued, Paul views this as Jesus' 'adoption', then Paul's letter to the Romans would be the locus where we would expect the apostle to employ his unique designation *huiothesia* in respect of the Son of God, given that *huiothesia* occurs most often in Romans (Rom. 8:15, 23; 9:4). But nowhere does Paul do so in this letter, or in any other for that matter; instead, he always reserves *huiothesia* for Christians and

---

[13] BDAG (2000: 443) gives the following meaning of this verb: 'to make a determination about an entity, determine, appoint, fix, set'.

[14] The most recent exponent of this position is David Garner (2002: 195–199), whose thesis title 'Adoption in Christ' is an apt one for this chapter. It should also be stressed that the scholars mentioned who arrive at this position do not understand Jesus' sonship in an adoptionist sense (Ferguson 1986: 87; Scott 1992: 223–244).

The heresy of adoptionism, which can be traced back to the early centuries of the church, is the view that Jesus was a blameless man who became the adoptive Son of God. 'In the early centuries of the church some maintained that the divine Spirit descended upon Jesus – a man of perfect virtue, sometimes granted to have been born of a virgin – at His baptism, and that He was deified after His resurrection' (Rowdon, 1978: 13–14).

[15] See chapter 3 for further discussion of Scott's thesis.

never for Christ. Thus to try to couch Romans 1:3–4 in terms of an adoption, as Scott tries to do, is to stretch the text beyond its limit.

Second, Scott tries to argue that the term *horisthentos* can be equated with the Pauline expression *huiothesia*, but he overlooks that *huiothesia* is a soteriological term for Paul (as I have consistently argued), whereas *horisthentos* most certainly is not. Rather, *horistheis* 'is a *Christological* term, denoting the exaltation of the Saviour of the world, who was God's own Son prior to his becoming a man and it specifies his Cosmic Lordship as the saviour of mankind' (Ninan 1994: 171; my emphasis).[16]

Third, Paul has already used the participle *genomenon* (coming, v. 3b), which not only implies pre-existence (cf. Rom. 8:3) (Moo 1996: 46; Byrne 1996: 44), but is also indicative that Jesus is already in possession of a unique status of sonship that cannot be bettered or improved upon. Ninan (1994: 346) says rightly, 'there was never a time when he was not the Son' – Jesus is intrinsically by nature the eternal Son of God. Indeed, there is a certain reluctance on the part of Paul to juxtapose *huiothesia* with the sonship of Jesus, which functions to safeguard 'the unique nature, status and function of the incarnate Son of God' (Ninan 1994: 203). Harold Hoehner (2002: 197) is right when he posits, 'Adoption is never used of Christ because he has always been the Son of God by nature, and unlike humans, he does not need to be adopted from his natural state into a new relationship with God as father.'

This matchless quality of Jesus' sonship is further substantiated by the 'consistent syntactical feature in all these references to Jesus' divine sonship ... the use of the definite article' (Hurtado 1999: 222) (cf. Rom. 1:3–4, 9; 8:3; Gal. 1:16; 2:20; 4:4, 6; 1 Cor. 1:9; 15:28; 2 Cor. 1:19; 1 Thess. 1:10; Eph. 4:13; Col. 1:13). Jesus is not a son but *the* (unique) Son of God. What is also interesting is that the bulk of these references are heavily concentrated in two of Paul's capital epistles where adoption is also found (Galatians and Romans), thus deliberately linking the divine sonship of Jesus and the salvation of Christians expressed in terms of *huiothesia*. Moreover, it is precisely the uniqueness of Jesus as the pre-existent Son of God that qualifies him to be the divine conduit through whom others are enfranchised as God's adopted sons and daughters (Hurtado 1993: 905). Jesus as the eternal Son of God is uniquely equipped to exercise a salvific role as the only one through whom people can become God's children by

---

[16] Ninan (1994: 171) concludes, 'Scott's ingenious idea of the identity of the terms *horistheis* or *huiothesia* needs to be rejected as representative of the mind of Paul.'

adoption (Gal. 4:4–5). His deity, a characteristic not shared with any other except the Father and the Holy Spirit, immediately sets him and his sonship apart from the believer's sonship by adoption, a point Smail (1980: 144; my emphasis)[17] rightly recognizes in the following remark:

> It is he who in the uniqueness of his resurrection is designated the Son of God in power (Romans 1:4) while we are sons through an act of *huiothesia* (adoption, son-making) which Paul always relates to the ... finished work of Christ ... Thus the distinction between Jesus and us needs to be carefully observed. The *language of incarnation belongs to him, and the language of adoption to us ... and if we try to reverse them confusion will result.*

In sum, 'Christ is not only the means of our adoption, he is the definition of all that sonship means' (Smail 1980: 144), and our *huiothesia* is inextricably linked with and *dependent* upon Jesus' unique relationship to God as Son. As we have seen, the more general notion of sonship, not adoptive sonship, is what dominates Paul's understanding of Jesus' filial relationship to his Father, and it is this aspect that drives through the *corpus Paulinum*. In brief, *sonship* is Pauline-speak to describe Christ; *adoption* is Pauline-speak to describe Christians.

We now turn to Paul's references to Jesus as God's Son, which occur most often and are concentrated in Romans and Galatians – where they occur eleven times (Hurtado 2003: 191). We begin with Romans.

God's Son and our adoption as sons in Romans

The revelation of God's Son for our adoption (Rom. 8:3)

Romans 8 has rightly been regarded as an important chapter for its teaching on the Spirit, but at the outset and throughout this chapter Paul also strikes an important Christological note that is crucial for what he goes on to discuss in regard to *huiothesia*.[18] The apostle begins

---

[17] See also Marshall (1967: 101–102), who states that we need 'also bear in mind that "Son of God" was at least in process of becoming a messianic title, [and] it became all the more unlikely that the early church saw in the resurrection of Jesus his Adoption by God to sonship'.

[18] Trumper (1997:106) rightly points out in this respect, 'While we confess that the Christology of Romans 8 is implicit rather than explicit ... nevertheless we cannot understand the chapter's pneumatology without the Christological background.'

by stating that 'what the law was powerless to do' (v. 3a; cf. vv. 29, 32) God did by sending his own Son. 'Through Romans 8 the language of divine sonship runs like a silver thread' (Hurtado 1999: 229) and Paul, as Hurtado (1993: 905) has observed, 'explicitly connects ... the sending of the Son of God in Rom. 8:3 with ... both present and future consequences of divine adoption' (8:15, 23).[19] A somewhat similar but fuller statement is made in the related adoption passage (Gal. 4:4, see below), where we ought to note in passing the similarity in syntactical patterns between the two texts. In Romans 8:3–4 Paul states, 'God did by sending his own Son in the likeness of sinful man ... *in order that* the righteous requirements[20] of the law might be fully met in us' (my emphasis), while in Galatians 4:4–5 he remarks, 'God sent his Son ... *in order* to redeem ... in order that we might receive the adoption as sons' (my trans.). In both instances 'God' is the subject of the sentence, followed by a verb of sending as predicate, and the object is 'Son'. In both, a final purpose clause, introduced by the particle *hina*, provides the explanation that elaborates on the soteriological significance or purpose of the sending.

Returning more specifically to Romans 8:3, the language Paul employs is personal and emphatic: 'God did by sending *his Son* in the likeness of sinful man' (v. 3; my emphasis). The participle 'sending' (*pempsas*) is unusual – the closest parallel is Galatians 4:4: 'God sent (*exapesteilen*) his Son', which has much in common with Romans 8:3–17 (Moo 1996: 478 n. 40) 'and implies pre-existence' (Witherington with Hyatt 2004: 420–421).[21] Fundamentally, this sending denotes the climactic moment when the Son of God stepped out of eternity into history by taking upon himself the full human condition.

Careful note should be taken of the fact that Paul does not say the Son came only in flesh; rather, he qualifies this with the word 'likeness' (*homoiōma*) in order to combat false views about the incarnation. God's Son took on flesh and blood, thus becoming a real, physical human being, thereby refuting the second-century heresy Docetism, which taught that Jesus only seemed or appeared

---

[19] It is too simplistic to say, as Fee (1994: 562) does, that Paul's emphasis in Gal. 4:4–7 is Christological/soteriological, whereas in Rom. 8:12–17 it is pneumatological: 'in the present passage the focus is altogether on the Spirit, so much so that the "adoption as sons" which Christ effected in Gal. 4:5 is now referred to as the Spirit's thing'. Granted the Spirit is predominant in Rom. 8, but the Spirit is not responsible for effecting adoption (as Fee understands it) and the Christological emphasis is in evidence earlier in Rom. 8:3, immediately prior to the adoption passage itself.

[20] The original Greek word translated as 'requirements' by the NIV is in the singular and not plural form.

[21] Ninan (1994: 208) comments, 'the son who is sent was the son before his mission'.

to be human (Gk *dokeō*, 'to seem' or 'to appear'). God's Son took on real flesh and blood and so did not 'seem' to be a human being. Simultaneously, Paul does not state that the Son came in 'sinful flesh' but in the *'likeness* of sinful flesh', because in his humanity Jesus was without sin (cf. John 7:18; 8:46; 2 Cor. 5:21; Heb. 4:15; 1 Pet. 2:22). In short, the Son of God's humanity was both real and sinless at the same time and here we immediately begin to see that 'Jesus has a primacy as Son' (Wenham 1995: 117) that sets him and his sonship apart from all others of the human race.

Paul goes on to give the reason for the Son of God's coming into the world, which was not only incarnational but also sacrificial (i.e. 'to be a sin offering', Rom. 8:3c) (Byrne 1979: 95). This latter phrase can be understood as a general statement 'for sin' or 'to deal with sin' without specifying the means by which this was achieved. It is also a technical term, as there are clear sacrificial allusions: the expression *peri harmartias* in forty-four of its fifty-four occurrences in the LXX (e.g. Lev. 5:6–7, 11; Num. 6:16; 2 Chr. 29:23–24; Neh. 10:33; Ezek. 42:13) means 'sin offering'. Wright states in this regard, 'There can be no longer any room for doubt that when Paul wrote *kai peri harmartias* he meant the words to carry their regular biblical overtones, i.e., "and as a sin offering"' (1991: 220–225). The full, sinless humanity of the Son of God eminently sets Jesus forth as one who uniquely 'possesses the necessary requirement to act as our substitute' (Moo 1996: 481) on the cross for our sins. It is highly significant for Paul, then, that it was in his humanity and in the earthly sphere that Jesus the Son of God lived, moved, and died on our behalf, and it is within that same sphere that our *huiothesia* was secured and in which God's adopted sons and daughters are now called to live and move (Rom. 8:14ff).[22]

Adopted as sons and joint heirs with Christ through his death (Rom. 8:17)

Our second 'Christological reference' (Smail 1980: 150) is 'Romans 8:17 [where Paul also] links adoption to union with Christ' (Peterson

---

[22] Ninan (1994: 349) argues that Paul's usage of the language of sonship and adoption is not simply his systematic application of any existing Jewish eschatological hope (*pace* Scott) nor the reworking of the Jewish idea of adoption (*pace* Byrne). 'These concepts', states, Ninan, 'lack a built-in mechanism to justify a non-nomistic definition of God's people.' Rather, 'Paul's radical departure from Jewish patterns ... calls for a different legitimatization ... that ... comes by the correspondence of Christian experience of sonship to the story of Jesus as the Son of God and also the experience of the Spirit as the Spirit of sonship.'

2001: 67). Immediately prior to this verse, Paul uses three different terms to describe God's spiritual 'offspring': 'sons' (*huioi*, v. 14), 'adopted sons' (*huiothesia*, v. 15) and 'children' (*tekna*, v. 16), which he then goes on to connect with the notion of being heirs in verse 17: 'joint heirs with Christ' (*synklēronomoi de Christou*). By using the latter expression Paul works on the common assumption in the ancient Roman world that if one is a son or an adopted son, then he is most assuredly an heir as well (cf. Gal. 4:6). Indeed, one of the primary purposes of adoption was to provide a suitable heir, as Francis Lyall (1984: 110) points out, 'Whether children were natural children or adopted children was irrelevant; children of either source were heirs.'[23]

Contextually, Paul is talking about how God's adopted sons and daughters are already heirs (v. 17a), but they can also look forward to the time when they will receive their full inheritance.[24] Paul, however, does not take this for granted and qualifies this with a conditional clause: '*if* we share in his sufferings in order that we may share in his glory' (*eiper sympaschomen hina kai syndoxasthōmen*, v. 17c; my emphasis).[25] Verse 17 needs to be understood within the wider context of verses 18–27, where behind Paul's thinking seems to be the struggle Jesus had as he faced the looming prospect of the cross (Kim 2002: 269). With this in view, 'the Sonship of Jesus the Messiah … becomes paradigmatic for the adopted sons' (Ninan 1994: 289). Moreover, 'the reality of the Christians' participation in Christ's suffering' (cf. Phil. 3:10ff.; Col. 1:24) (Kim 2002: 269) means that God's adopted sons and daughters are *identifiable*, as Peterson (2001: 67) remarks:

---

[23] See also the comment by Berger et al. (2003: 12–13), who remark, 'The effect of *adoptio* … was to place the adopted person for all legal purposes in the same position as if he … had been a natural child in the power of the adopter. *The adoptee* took the adopter's name and rank and *acquired rights of succession*' (my emphasis).

[24] In many legal systems an heir does not exist until after a person has died; until then there exists only an heir apparent. However, this does not apply in the case of Roman law, as Wansink (2000: 991) states: 'Under Roman law … the heir was seen as a continuation of the *paterfamilias*'s legal personality, not as a separate legal entity, and, as a result, he had legal standing as heir *during* the life of the *paterfamilias*. One was heir not through the father's death but through one's … adoption' (my emphasis) (see also Lyall 1984: 110; Williams 1999: 65). Gaius (*Inst.* 2.157) states that children 'even in their father's lifetime are considered … owners'.

[25] Schreiner (1998: 428) states in this regard that the 'word *eiper* should not be understood as a fulfilled condition or as a fact. It denotes a real condition that must be met for believers to enjoy the inheritance'; Dunn 1988: 456; contra Cranfield 1975: 407.

They are in union with Christ in his death and resurrection, and that union manifests itself as believers suffer with him now. That union will also manifest itself in the future, as believers share in his glory. Here Paul regards union with the crucified and risen Son as undergirding the adoption of God's genuine sons and daughters.

This 'christological connection' begun in verse 17 'is then carried through to the end of the paragraph by Paul's use of the verbs *sympaschomen* [suffer with] and *syndoxasthōmen* [glorified with] where he associates adoption with the "redemption of our bodies" (v. 23)' (Cook 1978: 141). This time the link between the sonship of Jesus and the *huiothesia* of believers may be more subtle, but it is no less distinct or real for all that because adoption is dependent upon the resurrection of Jesus Christ. Without Christ being raised from the dead there can be no redemption of the body and no consummation of adoption.[26]

The Son, sonship and *huiothesia* of believers in Galatians

'Sons of God' – 'seed of Abraham' (Gal. 3:26–29)[27]

We noted in chapter 3 how the general theme of sonship cuts across the entire biblical corpus and is the larger biblical idea of which adoption is an integral part. Kinship language, and in particular the issue of sonship, is addressed in Galatians 3:26–29 and for this reason merits further discussion. But there are other important reasons for considering this text. First, Galatians 3:26–29 is one of two main conclusions to Paul's argument (Gal. 4:4–5 is the second; see below) begun earlier in Galatians 3:1ff., where the apostle insists that the Torah has run its course (Fee 1994: 395). Second, there are several important parallels in these two passages where a number of themes are recapitulated (see table below).[28] And third, and most importantly, the context of these verses suggests that Paul's opponents are making

---

[26] See chapter 8, pp. 189–190 for further discussion of this point.

[27] This heading reflects the main title of Byrne's (1979) monograph, which emphasizes the priority of allegiance for the Galatians (see also Hansen 1989: 138). For a fuller treatment of this argument see Burke 1994: 43–60. McKnight (1995: 195) also states, 'Essentially, the argument from sonship may be put like this: ... being a "son of God" means that a person is also a member of Abraham's seed, because one becomes associated with Christ, who is the Seed of Abraham (v. 29).'

[28] The table is taken from Dunn (1993: 210), although I have slightly amended the contents. For a discussion of the parallels in these two passages see Walters 2003: 61–65.

kinship or sonship to Abraham a prerequisite for the Galatians' inclusion into the community, a theme Paul merges with a newly redefined kinship or sonship to God through Jesus Christ, God's Son (Fung 1988: 166–167).

The following table (Dunn 1993: 210) helps illustrate the parallel between Galatians 3:23–29 and 4:1–7:

Galatians 3:23–29	Galatians 4:1–7
v. 23 before the coming of faith we were held in custody under the law confined until the coming of faith . . .	v. 1 as long as the heir is a child . . . v. 2 he is under guardians and stewards until the time set by the father.
v. 24 the law was our custodian until Christ . . .	v. 3 as children we were enslaved under the elemental forces . . .
v. 25 but when faith came we were no longer under a custodian v. 26 for you are all sons of God through faith in Christ	v. 4 but when the fullness of time came . . . v. 5 in order to redeem those under the law. In order that we might receive the adoption as sons.
v. 27 you were all baptized into Christ . . .	v. 5 God sent the Spirit of his Son . . .
v. 29 so then you are Abraham's seed, heirs in accordance with promise.	v. 7 so that you are no longer a slave but a son, and if a son, also an heir . . .

Table 5.1

Paul mentions three major historical figures in Galatians 3:6–19: *Abraham* the patriarch, *Moses* the lawgiver and *Christ* the Son of God, although Paul does not deal with them in that order (see below). The person of Abraham is vital to Paul's argument from verse 6 onwards – 'Consider Abraham' (v. 6) – whom he repeatedly mentions throughout chapter 3 (vv. 6, 7, 8, 9, 14, 16, 18, 29). But it is important to note that the patriarch is broached only as a way to lead on to the One who is the fulfilment of the Abrahamic promise, Jesus Christ, the Son of God (3:16, 26). Essentially, what Paul presents in this passage is a Christocentric and Christological reinterpretation of the Abrahamic covenant (Hansen 1989: 199).

We shall shortly consider 3:16ff., but before doing so we need to note the context and problems the church at Galatia was facing. The major difficulty confronting the mainly Gentile community at

Galatia was the compulsion upon its members by Judaizers to embrace aspects of the Jewish Law, including circumcision (2:12; 6:12) and keeping special days (4:10). In other words, and in accordance with Jewish *nationalistic* understanding, if the Galatians wished to become true sons of Abraham, they needed to embrace the Mosaic Law. Paul in Galatians 3, however, argues against this emphasis of Jewish observances by sketching for his readers a new form of kinship (Esler 2000: 173–180)[29] and view of salvation history, borne out by the fact that the covenant promises given to Abraham *preceded* the giving of the Mosaic Law. The promises are therefore of greater priority and cannot be set aside, and those who endeavour to attain the inheritance of the Law have not only failed to understand the real meaning of the promise but have singularly failed to grasp the outworkings of God's plans for the salvation of humankind.

At the outset Paul reminds the Galatians of the need to emulate Abraham's faith because it is through faith (not by 'observing the law', 3:2, 5) that they become the 'children of Abraham' (*houtoi huioi eisin Abraam*, v. 7).[30] The apostle's redefinition of kinship belonging is clearly evident here, because he is not speaking of Abraham's *physical* descendants but those who are his spiritual progeny, men and women, including Gentiles, who share his faith.[31] Paul then moves from a scriptural argument to a human analogy in verses 15–19, where he is still talking about Abraham; only this time he raises the issue of the promises made to the patriarch. In response to the nationalistic emphasis of the agitators' emphasis on circumcision, Paul seeks to erase this misunderstanding by *dissociating* the promise from the Law, where Galatians 3:16 is pivotal to the whole of his argument. The apostle argues that just as a human covenant cannot be set aside, so it is with the promises. But more importantly, these very promises 'were spoken to Abraham and to his seed' (3:16, *Abraam eppethēsan ... kai*

---

[29] See also Burke (2001: 128–133) for a discussion of the preponderance of kinship language used in the letter and how Paul employs adoption as a means of resocializing the Galatian believers into the distinctively Christian way of life; Hellerman (2001: 120) also recognizes that Paul's argument in Galatians is heavily reliant upon kinship terms.

[30] Longenecker (1990: 114) is right to assert that this latter expression is 'polemically based. The Judaizers' message undoubtedly focused on being rightly related to Abraham and God's covenant with Israel ... the Judaizers' approach, and so the Jewish question as to who really were "sons of Abraham" was probably often on their lips.'

[31] Esler (1997: 131) makes the following observation: 'Since the Jews and Jewish Christ-followers in Galatia advocating circumcision were probably (and reasonably) proposing kinship with Abraham as one of the glittering prizes for taking the step, Paul redefines Abrahamic lineage as obtained by faith.'

tō spermati autou). The Scripture does not say "and to seeds", meaning many people, but "and to your seed" (3:16, *kai tō spermati sou* – your), meaning one person, who is Christ' (3:16, *hos estin Christos*).[32]

Now the Jews and Jewish Christ followers in Galatia who were proposing kinship with Abraham were utterly convinced that the 'seed' in Galatians 3:16 referred to those who were the physical descendants of Abraham. Paul, however, takes the quite 'audacious' (Esler 1997: 131) step of redefining Abrahamic lineage by the introduction of Christ, Abraham's seed (3:16) through whom kinship to God (3:26) is realized. And crucially to become a son of God in God's household, the most honourable of all households, is only through faith in Jesus Christ, the Son of God. As noted above, Paul dissociates the promise from the Law, evident by the fact that there is no talk of the Law until after Christ is mentioned. Paul sandwiches between the promises and the Torah the person of Christ, and by deliberately using the singular 'seed' (*sperma*)[33] the apostle leapfrogs

---

[32] A huge body of literature has grown up around this text and in particular Paul's usage of the singular word 'seed', which would undoubtedly have caused a jarring note for his Old Testament readers. However, the promise referred initially to Isaac, and then to his descendants. The fact that Paul is aware of the ambiguity is evident because he goes on to employ the term 'seed' in a collective sense in Gal. 3:29.

[33] The latter half of v. 16 ('The Scripture does not say "and to seeds", meaning many people, but "and to your seed", meaning one person, who is Christ') involves an exegetical argument that turns upon the singular use of the word *sperma*. Some have branded Paul's argument as nonsensical. 'Seed' in the Abrahamic promise is a generic singular that was always understood within Judaism to refer to the posterity of Abraham, excluding those who descended through Ishmael and Esau (cf. *b. Šab.* 146a; *b. Pes.* 56a). The Jewish people prided themselves on being the 'true sons of Abraham' and being the recipients of the promises given to Abraham. The Targums take this corporate understanding of God's promise to the patriarch as so much a matter of fact that they use the plural form 'and to your sons'. But for Paul physical descent is no guarantee of a spiritual relationship (e.g. Rom. 9:6–7). Rather, Paul argues instead that Christ is the 'seed' in view in the Abrahamic covenant and goes on to say that those 'in Christ' (v. 29) are not only the seed of Abraham but are also heirs according to the promise.

Daube (1956: 440–444) has argued that some rabbis in an attempt to solve the divergence between Gen. 15:13 ('four hundred years') and Exod. 12:40 ('four hundred and thirty years') in regard to Israel's bondage in Egypt, understand the thirty-year difference as the time between God giving the covenant to Abraham and the birth of Isaac. Hence 'seed' in Gen. 15:13 ('Know for certain that your descendants will be strangers in a country not their own, and they will be enslaved and ill-treated four hundred years') is a singular, and specifically refers to Isaac. However, Paul does not appear to understand 'seed' as a specific singular but as a generic singular, evident by the way he treats 'seed' in v. 29 as a collective noun (cf. Rom. 4:13–18). Thus, as Longenecker (1990: 132) states, 'Paul is invoking a corporate solidarity wherein the Messiah, as the true descendant of Abraham and the true representative of the nation, is seen as the true "seed" of Abraham – as are, of course, also the Messiah's own, as v. 29 insists.' In short, Paul is reinterpreting the Abrahamic covenant, where the priority is to belong to Christ, and *all* who are in him, Jew and Gentile alike, also qualify as the seed of Abraham.

over the Mosaic law as a channel for receiving the inheritance of the Abrahamic covenant. Instead, Christ, the Son of God, is the only means whereby these promised blessings can be entered into and enjoyed, as Schreiner (1998: 39) aptly comments:

> if Jesus is God's true Son, then membership in the people of God depends on being rightly related to Jesus. As Paul says ... he is the singular seed of Abraham (Gal. 3:16), and thus the blessing of Abraham (Gal. 3:14) is available only to those who belong to the Messiah Jesus.

Paul clinches the argument in Galatians 3:26–29 with a Christological statement, thereby redefining his understanding of kinship belonging. He prioritizes the need for the Gentiles to belong to Christ. This is evident by his use of the dative expression 'in Christ', which he links with the notion of sonship: 'You are all *sons of God through faith in Christ Jesus*' (*pantes gar huioi theou este dia tēs pisteōs en Christō Iēsou*, 3:26; my emphasis), the Son of God (Gal. 1:16; 2:20; 4:5). The word 'all' (*pantes*) here is in the emphatic position in the sentence and is inclusive in its scope – Gentiles are also 'sons' and are included in God's household (cf. 3:8). Paul concludes, '*There is neither Jew nor Greek*, slave nor free, male nor female, *for you are all one in Christ Jesus*' (3:28; my emphasis). Undoubtedly, this was a 'shocking declaration for any Jew to hear' (Hansen 1994: 111) because under the old economy only Israel and the Israelites were the 'sons of God' (e.g. Exod. 4:22; Deut. 14:1–2; Isa. 1:2–4). But now in accordance with the purposes of God, the scope of blessing is more far reaching because the Son of God opens up the way for Gentiles to be included and receive this filial status as well.

Paul brings his argument to a conclusion with a conditional and profoundly Christological statement in 3:29, where once again the position of the noun 'Christ' in the sentence takes precedence and where the overriding emphasis is upon the unique role of the Son of God: '*If* you belong to Christ, *then* (*ara*) you are Abraham's seed, and heirs according to the promise' (3:29; my emphasis).[34] Unfortunately, the Galatians had reversed the order because their first loyalty was to Abraham, when it ought to have been to Christ. Paul's Christocentric and Christological argument is complete: the Galatian Christians

---

[34] Kim (1981: 316) sums up what has taken place: 'It is Christ who is properly called the Son of God ... So we ... are by faith ... united with him and incorporated in him, we participate in his divine sonship.'

needed to give their allegiance to Christ, since it is through faith in him that they become sons of God. This in turn *also* 'qualifies' them as the seed of Abraham (i.e. 'Sons of God' – 'Seed of Abraham'). By clinging to circumcision and the Law instead the Galatians were in fact putting back the clock of salvation history.

The sending of God's Son: Redemption from slavery unto adoption (Gal. 4:4–5)

The Christological emphasis seen in the last section, which had begun earlier in Galatians 3:1ff. continues and comes to a climax and 'final conclusion' (Fee 1994: 400) in Galatians 4:4–5, where Paul moves from the general notion of 'sons' (*huioi*, vv. 26–29) to a delineation of his thesis of adoption (*huiothesian*, v. 5) as sons.[35] These verses represent 'the centre of the entire epistle' (Martyn 1997: 406),[36] where Paul compresses much theology into two verses. *Huiothesia* is especially tied to the person and work of Christ, God's Son, as illustrated by the chiastic structure suggested by J. B. Lightfoot (1975: 168):

A   God sent his Son
   B   born under law
   B′ in order to redeem those under law
A′ in order that we might receive the adoption as sons
    (*huiothesian*)

The chiastic structure above is immediately preceded by the temporal clause 'when the time had fully come' (*ēlthen to plērōma tou chronou*, v. 4), which indicates the climactic moment when God sent his Son into the world. This phrase does not mean that time had ripened of its own accord or automatically, or even that it was the time of man's greatest need, which is undoubtedly true. Rather, the hour was the moment of divine disclosure, the dawn of redemption and adoption, when God decisively took action and intervened with the revelation of his Son. Some commentators view this sending formula as a reference to the commissioning of Jesus in the same way God sent the prophets of the Old Testament on a mission (Dunn 1993: 215). However, far more is involved, as Witherington (1997: 288; my emphasis; see also Longenecker 1990: 171) rightly notes:

---

[35] Fee (1994: 400 n. 121) states, 'This passage is often termed "christological"'; it is that, too, of course, since in Paul one cannot have soteriology without Christology.

[36] Fee (1994: 400) also states, 'It is scarcely accidental, therefore, that the theological basis of the argument of the whole letter comes in one of the more soteriological passages in the corpus.'

Paul is *not talking about a prophetic sending* that comes after birth in the case of Amos or an Isaiah, and being set apart is not identical with being sent. The latter presupposes the former, and of course one cannot exist before one can be sent. God can even intend to set someone apart in advance. But God cannot send someone in advance of their existing.

Pre-existence is also evident by the apostle's use of the definite article in the clause 'God sent his Son' (*exapesteilen ho theos ton huion autou*, v. 4), an indication that Paul 'views Jesus' sonship as unique' (Hurtado 1993: 903). As in other related references to the pre-existent Son (e.g. 1 Cor. 8:6; Phil. 2:5–8; Col. 1:15–17), there is also here 'an affirmation of the deity of Jesus' (Hansen 1994: 118). The description 'Son of God' here shows just what a 'high Christology' is involved.[37] Moreover, this description identifies Jesus' 'unique relationship to God his "Father"' (Hengel & Schwemer 1997: 102; my emphasis) and has

a central role in Galatians as compared to other letters of Paul. For Paul, *the Son* is pre-existent and is sent by the Father as a human being into the world in order through his death to 'ransom' human beings who have fallen victim to judgement and death as a result of the inexorable demand of the law.

Thus even prior to the incarnation, the pre-existent Son was set apart by God to set slaves free and make them his children by adoption.

Closely allied to Jesus' deity is his full humanity as Son of God, evidenced by the fact that he is 'born of a woman' (*genomenon ek gynaikos*, v. 4). Here the emphasis lies with the fact that Jesus was born in the human manner (cf. Job 14:1; Matt.11:11; Luke 7.28; Josephus, *A. J.* 7.21), just as Paul earlier in the letter says he was himself (1:15).[38] By his conception the Son of God became

---

[37] Paul's primary concern is not with the pre-existence, but the cumulative weight of evidence 'presupposes preexistence'. As Fee (1994: 402 n. 126) points out, 'Given the parallel in v. 6, it is hard to imagine that the Galatians would have heard this only in terms of commissioning, on the basis of the circuitous parallels which Dunn alleges. Here it can only mean "God sent *forth* his Son," the presupposition of which is prior existence with God from whom he was sent forth.'

[38] Some take the expression 'born of a woman' as implying the virgin birth, but the emphasis here lies more with Jesus' humanity than Paul's knowledge or awareness of the virginal conception of Jesus (Longenecker 1990: 171; Martyn 1997: 390; Witherington 1997: 288).

what he had not been before (a human being), but he did not cease to be what he had always been (the Son of God).[39] The significance of the incarnation, Christ becoming a man, is preparatory and with a view to the sons of men becoming the adopted sons of God. Irenaeus, the early church theologian, captures (Irenaeus 1995: 448–449; my emphasis) the linkage in these twin ideas when he remarks:

> For it was for this end that the Word of God was made man, and He who was the Son of God became the Son of man, that man ... receiving the adoption, might become the son of God. For by no other means could we attain to incorruptibility and immortality, unless we had been united to incorruptibility and immortality. But how could we be joined to incorruptibility and immortality, unless, first, incorruptibility and immortality had become that which we also are, so that the corruptible might be swallowed up by incorruptibility, and the mortal by immortality, *that we might receive the adoption as sons.*

John Calvin (*Instit.* 2.12.2; my emphasis) echoes similar sentiments when he states that adoption was the purpose for the incarnation of the Son, the second person of the Trinity:

> What the Mediator was to accomplish was no common thing. His task was to restore us to God's grace as to make of the children of men, children of God ... Who could have done this had not the selfsame Son of God became the Son of man, and had not he so taken what was ours as to impart what was his to us, and to make what was his by nature ours by grace? There relying on this pledge, we trust that we are sons of God, *for God's natural Son fashioned for himself a body* from our body, flesh from our flesh, bones from our bones, *that he might be one with us ... adopted ... as his brothers.*

But the incarnation, the act of God in Christ taking upon himself flesh and blood, was not in and of itself sufficient to secure our

---

[39] Martyn (1997: 390 n. 8) states, 'We have here one of the roots of the later affirmations that Christ was fully divine and fully human. For in Paul's view Christ was the Son of God whom God has sent into the world, but that sending involved his being born fully under the malignant power of the cosmic elements, just as in every other human being.'

huiothesia.[40] Stated another way, Jesus' identifying with us in our humanity does not *ipso facto make* us adopted sons. Paul goes on to spell out in clear soteriological terms how this was brought about: 'God sent his Son in order to *redeem* us . . . *in order that we might receive the adoption as sons*' (Gal. 4:4–5; my trans. and emphasis). Jesus the incarnate Son of God went to the cross by virtue of which all who are spiritually united with him in his redemptive death (and resurrection) are adopted into the family of God. Moreover, Jesus was uniquely 'qualified' to achieve God's salvific purposes, as John Stott (1968: 106) notes: 'If He had not been a righteous man, He could not have redeemed men. If He had not been a righteous man, He could not have redeemed unrighteous men. And if He had not been God's Son, He could not have redeemed men for God or made them sons of God.'

A reversal of fortunes takes place by virtue of the redemption accomplished by Jesus Christ, the Son of God, in the sense that we become what we never were (adopted sons, 4:5) and cease to be what we had always been – slaves to sin (4:7). Although Paul here in verse 5 does not tell us how the Son redeemed us, we *are* told in Galatians 3:13, where the apostle employs the same verb: 'Christ *redeemed* us from the curse of the law by becoming a curse for us' (*Christos hēmas exēgorasen ek tēs katras tou nomou genomenos hyper hēmōn katara*) (my emphasis). The apostle's mentioning of redemption or 'buying back' draws in the related metaphors of slavery and adoption, which require some explanation lest we conclude prematurely that Paul has confused them.[41]

Probably in Paul's mind here is the Roman practice of adoption (see Porter 2003: 148–166). Here Paul's thought includes the legal process of a father's releasing his son from *potestas* by formally selling him (*emacipatio*) in accordance with Roman law; if this was done three times, the son was finally free of his father's *potestas*. After two sales, however, the son could be manumitted (like a slave) back to his father who could receive him back by a fresh act of *adoptio*. All this explains how Paul can move from speaking about slavery, then redemption, to adoption (Dunn 1993: 217).

[40] Peterson (2001: 59) captures the thrust of this when he distinguishes between the incarnation and the work of Christ: 'The Son's *incarnation* was essential preparation for our union with him and our adoption flows from it. Because Jesus is the unique Son of God, he is perfectly qualified to do the *work* needed for us to be spiritually joined to him by adoption through the Father' (my emphasis).

[41] Ridderbos (1977: 197) states, 'The new relationship between God and men . . . effected by Christ's substitutionary work as Mediator (atonement, ransom), finally finds expression in the important concept adoption of sons (*huiothesia*).'

But can we be even more specific than this? The shift in Paul's metaphors here makes better sense when we consider that the person to be manumitted was not a citizen but a *slave* because the 'redemption of a slave was a prerequisite ... [and] actually a step toward adoption' (Theron 1956: 10; Stibbe 1999: 162). I. A. H. Combes asserts that 'adoption of a slave within one's household was in the Graeco-Roman world of the first century ... not uncommon ... and many did, obtain freedom from (and even adoption by) their masters' (1998: 69; see also Rollins 1987: 108). With this background in mind we are in a better position to grasp what Paul is saying in these verses. Here Paul links a triad of interconnected metaphors – slavery, redemption and adoption. He moves from one to the next in describing his readers as *slaves* (Gal. 4:3; cf. Rom. 8:15), their need of *freedom* (redemption, 4:5) and then receiving *adoption* (4:5; cf. Rom. 8:15). In all this the mediating role and function of Jesus Christ is fundamental, as Smail (1980: 146) concludes, it is 'only as a result of an event of son-making and adoption (*huiothesia*) whose objective basis is in the work of the Son [that] ... we are now able to address God as *Abba* and to enter into the inheritance that belongs to those who are his children'.[42]

In sum, the goal of God's unique Son coming into the world was to secure the believer's adoption.

Adoption through union with Christ the Son of God (Ephesians)

Most commentators agree that the author's main purpose in Ephesians 1:5ff. is to present an extended eulogy of praise to God, a eulogy that according to Peter O'Brien (1999: 91) sets forth God's saving purposes 'from eternity to eternity' (see also Lincoln 1990: 43; Fee 1994: 665). There is, as noted earlier, a clear trinitarian emphasis in verses 3–14, which is evident by the way in which Paul begins the letter: he stresses that God the Father is the source and origin of salvation.[43] However, '*the sphere of activity* within which the divine

---

[42] Fee (1994: 407) also remarks, 'Paul sets forth the work of Christ as an objective, historical, once-for-all reality. In that objective, historical work the Son procured "sonship" for all who believe in him, which Paul makes personal for him and for them by the final purpose clause "so that we might *receive* adoption as sons."'

[43] Many commentators have taken note of the fact that Paul is making use of a Christianized version of the traditional Jewish 'blessing' of God. Moreover, in keeping with my emphasis in this chapter, and as Lincoln (1990: 43) makes clear, 'The *Christological* focus marks off this *berekah* from its Jewish counterparts' (my emphasis).

blessings are given and received is God the Son, the Lord Jesus Christ' (O'Brien 1999: 91; my emphasis). The roles of the Father and the Son (and the Spirit) are complementary and stress that the 'Father has adorned his people with all spiritual blessings *in union with his Son*' (Peterson 2001: 65; my emphasis). We observed earlier how in Ephesians the Father is fully involved in our *huiothesia*, but our adoption as God's children is brought about only through his Son, Jesus Christ. The picture portrayed of God by Paul is not of a Father reluctantly trying to hold back his Son; to the contrary, the latter is sent into the world at the former's behest in order to accomplish and bring about adoption.

As the opening eulogy proceeds, Paul explicitly informs his readers that 'God … has blessed us in the heavenly realm with *every spiritual blessing in Christ* (*en pasē eulogia pneumatikē en Christō*, v. 3; my emphasis). The sum total of the Christian's spiritual blessings and inheritance is expressly connected and related to union with Christ, the Son of God. The aorist participle ('blessed') in verse 3 can be taken to refer to 'the completed action of God' (Best 1998: 114), but it can also describe the panoply of blessings bestowed upon the Christian and of which he now partakes (O'Brien 1999: 95; Mawhinney 1987: 46). According to the latter, Paul is saying that these varied and manifold blessings are only accessed 'in and through Christ'.

The expression 'in Christ' and its equivalents (e.g. 'through Christ') is distinctively Pauline and used thirty-nine times in Ephesians (Hoehner 2002:173).[44] Paul uses a proliferation of prepositional phrases in the opening verses of his letter to the Ephesians, as the following makes clear:

'in Christ' (v. 3)	'in him' (v. 9)
'in him' (v. 4)	'in him' (v. 11)
'through Christ' (v. 5)	'in Christ' (v. 12)
'in the One he loves' (v. 6)	'in him' (v. 13)

Seifrid (1993: 433) succinctly sums up the essence of this Pauline prepositional phrase as 'God's saving purposes … decisively effected *through Christ*' (my emphasis).[45] We need some appreciation of

---

[44] Even though Paul does on occasion say that 'Christ lives in me' (Gal. 2:20), the notion that the believer is 'in Christ' is much more common in the Pauline literature.

[45] According to Seifrid, 'in Christ' (*en Christō*) occurs on 151 occasions in the writings of Paul.

Paul's use of the phrase 'in Christ' that has a semantic range and meaning in accordance with the context. Four categories have recently been identified by Barcley (1999: 106): (1) Paul can use the expression in a 'local' sense when referring to individuals or groups of believers 'in Christ'; (2) more frequently, however, it refers to the salvific benefits accruing to Christians (e.g. justification, redemption) 'in Christ'; (3) Paul often expresses the actions that believers do (instrumentally) 'in Christ'; (4) Paul declares that 'in Christ' God works to bring reconciliation to a needy and helpless world (e.g. 2 Cor. 5:19).

Ephesians 1:5, 'in love he [God] predestined us to be adopted as his sons *through Jesus Christ*' (my emphasis), falls into the fourth category 'and although this category ... may not be as frequent as Paul's other uses, it forms the basis' (Barcley 1999: 108) for the other three categories. Christ, the Son, is God's agent through whom adoption is secured. Just as in the ancient Roman world the father (the *paterfamilias*) initiated the adoption, so for Paul, God the Father is always the architect and prime mover in adopting the believer into the new divine household; uniquely for the apostle, however, Christ, the Son of God is the agent through whom he accomplishes his saving purposes.

The multiplicity of blessings (e.g. election, redemption) Paul lists here are enjoyed only through union with Christ.[46] Having mentioned the diverse nature of the spiritual benefits that are ours in Christ (v. 3) Paul also includes the fact that we have been '*adopted as sons through Jesus Christ*' (*huiothesian dia Iēsou Christou*, Eph. 1:5). Ephesians stresses that the privilege of adoption into the Father's family 'is through the agency of Christ (*dia Iēsou Christou*, v. 5)' (Lincoln 1990: 25), an assertion found also in other passages (e.g. Gal. 4:4–5) 'that link believers' reception of adoption as sons with the life and work of Christ as God's Son' (1990: 25). The prepositional phrase 'through Jesus Christ' identifies the one *through whom* the adoption is executed: 'it is through or by means of the work of Christ ... that ... it [is] possible for the sinner to be adopted into the family of God' (Hoehner 2002: 197).[47] John Murray (1961: 170) puts the matter well when commenting on Ephesians 1:

---

[46] Snodgrass (1996: 18) remarks, 'All the privileges of life are found in *union with Christ* ... Ephesians presents a gospel of union with Christ more powerfully than any other New Testament letter' (my emphasis).

[47] Fee (1994: 667) makes a similar point: 'this "adoption" was effected for us historically through the death of Christ'.

we cannot think of adoption apart from union with Christ ...
union with Christ and adoption are complementary aspects of this
amazing grace. Union with Christ reaches its zenith in adoption
and adoption has its orbit in union with Christ.

For the apostle Paul, those whom God has adopted into his household
constitute those who have been united through the shed blood of his
own Son – Jesus alone is the one through whom Christians are
enfranchised as adopted children, which immediately underscores a
qualitative distinction between his sonship and the adoptive sonship of
the Christian (Best 1998: 125). The point Paul is making is unmis-
takably Christological;[48] namely, that adoption into God's household
is uniquely and exclusively through Jesus Christ, God's Son. Stated
differently, adoption into the *familia Dei* does not, better cannot, take
place without or apart from Christ, the Son of God (Cook 1978:
142).[49] In all of this it is worth noting that this is another instance
where we find the overlap between adoption in the ancient social
context and in Paul's thought breaking down, since the notion of
union with the Son of God 'has no antecedent in the sociolegal
practices of Rome or the OT world' (Ryken et al. 1998: 15).

Summary

In this chapter I have examined the role of Christ the Son of God in
respect of sonship and our adoption as sons. I began by noting how
the more general term 'Son' (*huios*) is Paul's preferred expression to
describe the sonship of Jesus and that the expression *huiothesia* is
always reserved for believers/Christians and never used of Christ.
This distinction between the unique sonship of Jesus and the
believer's adoption as son for the apostle Paul is important and needs
to be upheld and carefully maintained.[50] To use the latter in regard to
Christ's role or status as Son is to blur the distinction between his
unique sonship and our *huiothesia* as believers.

[48] O'Brien (1999: 92) writes in relation to Christ, 'There is an important christological dimension to the paragraph as well. Christ, who is the mediator and sphere of
divine blessing, has the Father's glory as his goal.'

[49] Esler (1997: 131) also states that it is only 'through Jesus, the Son of God, [that we
can] become God's adopted sons'.

[50] It should be noted that while the apostle Paul configures the distinction between
Jesus' sonship and the sonship of believers by using the expression *huiothesia* in respect
of the latter, other New Testament writers have their own way of making similar
distinctions. E.g. in John the term *huios*, 'Son', is reserved exclusively for Jesus, whereas
believers are called *tekna*, 'children'. See the comment in Carson 1991: 126.

Paul discusses adoption in his letter to the church at Rome within the context of God sending his own Son into the world in human flesh. It is important to note here that Paul prefaces his talk about adoption (Rom. 8:15) with talk of the incarnation and work of God's Son as a 'sin offering' (8:3). In Romans 8 Paul also states that adopted Christians are heirs with Christ (v. 17) provided that they suffer with him (v. 17). Indeed, suffering not only identifies the adopted children of God but also points forward to the consummation of their adoption, the redemption of their bodies (v. 23).

In addition to using the term *huiothesia*, Paul in Galatians 3 – 4 uses the more general and frequently occurring term 'son' (*huios*) to describe believers. Here agitators were trying to foist circumcision on to the Galatians, claiming that the true sons of Abraham were those who could trace their physical descent back to the patriarch. Paul, however, presents a Christocentric and Christological reinterpretation of the Abrahamic covenant and uses the patriarch to redefine the meaning of kinship. He stresses that the Galatians' first allegiance should be anchored not in Abraham but in the One who is the Seed of Abraham, and that through faith in this Son they become the sons of God.

In Galatians 4:5 Paul presents a similar argument to that in Romans 8:3, only this time he links together three metaphors: slavery, redemption and adoption. Paul explicitly strikes a Christological note by making the death of Christ, the Son, the objective basis for our redemption from slavery in order that we may be adopted into the divine household.

Finally, adoption in Ephesians 1:5 is situated within the context of a plethora of spiritual blessings that are ours only in and through God's Son, Jesus Christ. Once again the Christological emphasis is clear in the sense that although the Father initiates adoption into his household, he does so through the agency of his Son.

We can conclude, then, that the two ideas in the mind of the apostle Paul of the sonship of Jesus and the *huiothesia* of believers are at all times related: God always adopts his sons and daughters through Jesus Christ his Son.

Chapter Six

Adoption and the Spirit

Introduction

We turn our attention in this chapter to the role of the Holy Spirit and the Christian's adoption as son. Earlier we observed how Paul is the only author in the New Testament to use the expression 'adoption' and that he does so on five occasions in three different letters. But as Mawhinney (1987: 45 n. 24) has recently observed 'in ... four New Testament instances in which *huiothesia* is used with regard to Christian sonship the *Holy Spirit* is also mentioned: Romans 8:14–15; 8:23; Gal. 4:4–6; Eph. 1:3–14' (my emphasis) (see also Cook 1978: 141). Moreover, in one of these instances Paul joins the twin notions of the Spirit and adoption in the genitival phrase *pneuma huiothesias*, 'Spirit of adoption' (Rom. 8:15).[1] The expression *pneuma huiothesias* is a *hapax legomenon* (one saying) in the New Testament and has been variously interpreted by commentators; indeed, this phrase and the general context of Romans 8:12–17 raises a number of questions concerning the precise function of the Holy Spirit in regard to adoption: is the Spirit responsible for *making* Christians God's sons by adoption,[2] or does the Spirit merely enable the believer to *express* or confirm an already existing filial relationship to God?[3] And what is the significance, if any, of Paul joining the two ideas of the Spirit and adoption at what is not only the midpoint of the chapter but of the letter as well? These are some of the questions I shall address in this chapter.

---

[1] Calvin refers to the expression 'Spirit of Adoption' as the 'first title of the Spirit' (*Instit.* 3.1.3), as noted by Ferguson 1996: 182. According to Ferguson, Calvin's description corresponds 'to ... the highest of the privileges of redemption, namely, sonship' (see further on this in Griffith 2001: 135–154).

[2] E.g. Wanamaker (1980: 379), who is of the view that the expression *pneuma huiothesias* means 'the Spirit ... works adoption'; Cranfield (1975: 397) also interprets this expression to mean 'the Spirit who brings about adoption'.

[3] E.g. Moo (1996: 502), who mentions the latter as a possible interpretation: 'the Spirit who confirms adoption', but then rejects this on the grounds of being 'overly subtle'.

The 'familial' role of the Spirit in our adoption as sons

Before we consider these issues, it is worth noting how theologians tend to focus more on the roles of the Father and the Son in relation to the Christian's adoption into God's family. This is due to the fact that it is easier to conceive of the Father and the Son in personal terms and of their familial roles as members of the Godhead and the respective roles they have to play. The same, however, cannot be said of the Spirit – we do not have a clear understanding of the importance of the Spirit's personal and 'familial' function in regard to *huiothesia*, and as a consequence we have underplayed the vital role and activity of the *pneuma* in this area of Paul's theology.[4] A careful study of his letters reveals that Paul never describes the activity of the Spirit by using inanimate or impersonal terms (e.g. wind, water, fire etc.) (Witherington & Ice 2002: 130). Rather, 'Paul's stress [is] on the *personal* nature of the Holy Spirit' (130),[5] evidenced by the way that the ' "Holy Spirit" is coupled with verbs that indicate a personal agency' (130; Fee 1994: 829–831).

This aspect is repeatedly seen in Romans 8. For example, Paul in Romans 8:5 juxtaposes two ways people can choose to live: literally to 'live according to the flesh' (*kata sarka*) or literally to 'live according to the Spirit' (*kata pneuma*). To follow the dictates of the former is to have one's mind set on what that nature desires, but to obey the leading of the Holy Spirit is to have one's mind 'set on *what the Spirit desires*' (v. 5; my emphasis).[6] In Romans 8:9 Paul goes on to state that the Spirit of God *dwells* within the believer (*pneuma theou oikei en hymin*). Personal references or characteristics of the Holy Spirit like these are particularly striking in the adoption passage where the Spirit is said to 'cry out', '*Abba*, Father' from within the adopted son (*to pneuma tou huiou autou eis tas kardias hēmōn krazon, Abba ho patēr*, Gal. 4:6). The Spirit is also responsible for *leading*

---

[4] This oversight is also seen in doctrinal or theological studies on the subject of the Holy Spirit – there is rarely a chapter devoted to a discussion of the difficult expression *pneuma huiothesias* or of the role of the Spirit in adoption. There are two exceptions of which I am aware. Palmer (1958) has a chapter entitled 'The Holy Spirit and Divine Sonship', which comprises a short subsection entitled 'Adoptive Sonship'. Buchanan (1966: 251–268) in a devotional work has a chapter entitled 'The Work of the Spirit as the Spirit of Adoption'.

[5] See other related, insightful remarks in Witherington & Ice (2002: 108 n. 7).

[6] Dunn (1999: 83 n. 1) points out that the Greek word is *phronēma*, which means 'way of thinking' and occurs only in Paul's letters in this chapter (i.e. 8:6–7 and 8:27). Note, however, the use of the cognate verb in Phil. 1:7; 2:2, 5; 3:15, 19; 4:5.

God's sons (*hosoi gar pneumati theou agontai*, Rom. 8:14), and to stress the Spirit's personal role further, Paul goes on to describe the *pneuma* as 'the Spirit of *his Son*' (*to pneuma tou huiou autou*, Gal. 4:6) and 'the Spirit of *sonship*' (*pneuma huiothesias*, Rom. 8:15). In the verse immediately following, Paul also states that the Spirit *bears witness* with/to our human spirit that we are indeed God's children (*auto to pneuma symmartyrei tō pneumati hēmōn hoti esmen tekna theou*, Rom. 8:16). This latter phrase is especially noteworthy because here Paul employs the *personal* pronoun, which in the original Greek is situated emphatically in the sentence: 'the Spirit *himself*[7] (*auto to pneuma*) bears witness with/to our spirit'.

Another clear indication of Paul's familial and personal presentation of the Spirit is the manner in which the actions attributed to the Father and the Son are also ascribed to the Spirit. For example, in Romans 8:26–27, a passage clearly linked to the earlier adoption passage (Rom. 8:15–23) (Dunn 1975: 241), Paul informs the Roman Christians that the Spirit intervenes for them at critical moments ('We do not know what to pray for, but the Spirit . . . intercedes for the saints in accordance with God's will', vv. 26–27), an action he credits to Christ a few verses later ('Christ Jesus, who . . . is at the right hand of God and is also interceding for us', 8:34). The role of the *pneuma* here is particularly noteworthy, as Paul is 'the first to speak clearly of the Spirit as an intercessor' (Obeng 1986: 621–632), where the activity described in verse 27 is not the Christian's but the Spirit's. God, Paul tells his readers, is the one who searches the heart and knows what is the mind of the Spirit or what the Spirit urges and desires.

When we consider the cumulative weight of all of these personal/familial references and pneumatic activity, Witherington (2004: 226; my emphasis) rightly concludes that

the Spirit is spoken of in profoundly *personal* terms. Paul does not see the Spirit as merely some sort of force or power or even just the

---

[7] Calvin (1899: 300 n. 1) points out here, 'The words *auto to pneuma* seem to mean the divine Spirit . . . The reference is to "the Spirit of God" in verse 14. "This selfsame Spirit," or "*He* the Spirit," for *autos*, or *auto*, may be rendered, especially when the article intervenes between it and the noun. See Luke 24:15; John 16:27' (my emphasis). Fee (1994: 569) also rightly concludes regarding Rom. 8:16, 'By both the intensive pronoun, "the Spirit *himself*" and the verb "bears witness with," Paul asserts the Spirit's personal existence. One does not speak of "the influence itself" as "bearing witness with" another person . . . this text opens up for us the personal dimension of the Spirit that will not allow anything less' (emphasis in original).

presence of God. The Spirit prays, which is a profoundly personal act, and we are told here the Spirit intercedes for the saints.

And Dunn says, 'This clarification of the *character* of the Spirit, beyond the older more animistic or dynamistic talk of the Spirit as an inspiring or empowering presence, *is one of Paul's most important contributions to Christian thought and spirituality*' (1996: 84; my emphasis). The Holy Spirit is not only God's empowering presence, to coin a phrase,[8] but God's *personal* (and inseparable member of the divine family) presence at work in and through his adopted offspring. Moreover, this aspect of the Spirit's work and this witness in the church and the life of the believer have not been sufficiently recognized as dimensions of Paul's pneumatology. Given that the Pauline corpus is the earliest witness at the beginning of the early church in relation to what was thought about the Holy Spirit, these personal characteristics and familial references in respect of adoption are highly significant.

We now need to return to the opening questions above concerning the role of the Spirit in adoption, where it is striking to note how Paul's references to the *pneuma* (and *huiothesia*) in Galatians and Romans are prefaced by a discussion of the subject of the Law.[9] Indeed, Paul's thinking is dominated by the subject of the Law in these two letters and this interest intensifies in Galatians 3 and Romans 7,[10] two chapters immediately prior to Galatians 4 and Romans 8 where we find many pneumatological statements in juxtaposition to Paul's sonship metaphor. This is significant as we shall now see.

---

[8] The informed reader will recognize this as the main title of Gordon Fee's excellent *magnum opus* on the Holy Spirit.

[9] Paul's attitude to the Law is complex, but it is neither inconsistent nor contradictory. Paul employs the noun *nomos* in Romans and Galatians with different nuances. E.g. in regard to the former, *nomos* is employed generically (4:15b; 7:1a), refers to a 'principle' (3:27a; 7:21, 23a) and also denotes a part of OT Scripture (e.g. Rom. 3:19a). However, Paul uses this noun most frequently in reference to the Mosaic Law (Rom. 2:12–14a, 15, 17–18; 4:13–15; 5:13, 20; 6:14–15; 7:2–9, 12, 14, 16, 22, 23b). For more on the apostle's use of *nomos* and related expressions see Seifrid 2000: 96–98.

[10] There is no reason to doubt that the law was a major reason for Paul writing Galatians. In the case of Romans, Thielman (1993: 529–542) rightly argues that the suspicions about Paul's Jewish credentials in general and his view of the Law in particular (cf. Acts 21:20–21) were also prevalent in Rome (Rom. 3:8; 6:1, 15). 'Hence,' states Thielman (1993: 540) 'Paul's purpose in Romans was probably at least in part to correct misunderstanding about his view of the Law.' See also Francis Watson (1991: 206), who proposes two separate congregations in Rome marked by 'mutual hostility and suspicion over *the question of the law*' (my emphasis).

The old era of the Torah (Gal. 3/Rom. 7) and the new epoch of the *pneuma* (Gal. 4/Rom. 8)[11]

Paul's letters to the churches at Galatia and Rome contain his most extensive treatment of the Law. These two letters have the highest incidence of Pauline usage of the term *nomos* – out of a total of 119 occurrences in Paul's letters this term is employed 72 times in Romans and 32 times in Galatians.[12] More specifically, *nomos* is mentioned 21 times in Romans 7,[13] but the word *pneuma* occurs only once, whereas in Romans 8:1–27 the *pneuma* is referred to on 21 occasions,[14] *nomos* only 5 times. Similarly, in Galatians 3:1–24 the Law is mentioned 13 times and the Spirit only 3 times, whereas in Galatians 4 – 6 the Spirit and its cognates are referred to on 14 occasions, the Law on only 5 occasions. From these statistics we can see that there is a profusion of references to the Law in the two chapters (Gal. 3; Rom. 7) immediately preceding the chapters (Gal. 4; Rom. 8) where Paul primarily discusses the Spirit, which he then goes on to relate to adoption.

If we probe a little further, we find that in Galatians 3 and Romans 7 Paul makes a number of pejorative remarks concerning the Law that sit alongside other more positive statements where he also affirms the Law as wholesome and good.[15] For instance, Paul refers to the Law in Romans 7 as making him conscious of sin: 'I would not have known what sin was except through the law' (Rom. 7:7; 4:15). Furthermore, Paul says 'the sinful passions aroused by the Law were at work in our bodies' (Rom. 7:5). Earlier in Romans Paul states that the Law actually increases and intensifies the degree of sinfulness in the world, 'so that the trespass might increase' (Rom. 5:20), a point echoed in Galatians 3:19: the Law 'was added because of transgressions'. In both the above chapters Paul states that to be under Law is to be under slavery (Rom. 7:25) and 'held prisoners by the law' (Gal. 3:23; cf. Rom. 7:6). Hence, the Law is unable to impart life (Gal. 3:21); on the contrary, it is the very instrument by which individuals are

---

[11] See Turner (1996: 116), where he uses a similar title.

[12] These statistics are from Morris 1988: 143. Morris also calculates that the noun *nomos* occurs 191 times in total in the NT.

[13] Rom. 7 has provoked much discussion as to the identification of the person (i.e. Christian, non-Christian) or people (i.e. Israel), but the issue of anthropology is subordinate to that of the Mosaic Law (Stendahl 1976: 21).

[14] Moo (1996: 468) states concerning the significance of these references in Rom. 8, 'This means that the Spirit is mentioned in this chapter almost once every two verses, while its closest competitor, 1 Cor. 12, mentions the Spirit a little over once every three verses.'

[15] I am indebted to Fee (1994: 814–816) for some of the points adduced here.

condemned to death: 'the very commandment that was intended to bring life actually brought death' (Rom. 7:10; cf. 7:5). In fact, to try to live in accordance with the Law, which was only temporary and given 430 years after the promises, was tantamount to turning back the clock to the old era (Gal. 3:23ff.).

This is a point Paul also makes in Galatians 3:1–5 (the only passage outside Galatians 4 – 6 in the letter where we find references to the 'Spirit'), the reason being that Paul is astonished at his Galatian converts' behaviour in deserting the true gospel for another gospel that 'is really no gospel at all' (1:6–7). Actually, the situation was more serious and personal than this because not only were the Galatians guilty of turning away from a message, but they were in serious breach of 'walking out' on the living *God* (cf. 1:6, 'I am amazed that you are so quickly turning away *from him who called you*', *apo tou kalesantos hymas*) (my trans. and emphasis).[16] Here Paul, in the midst of speaking about the Law, bombards the Galatians with a series of stinging rhetorical questions to underscore his amazement at their having begun the Christian life with the Spirit only to abandon it by turning back to the Law (Gal. 3:1–5; my emphasis):

> You foolish Galatians! Who has bewitched you? . . . I would like to learn just one thing from you: Did you receive the *Spirit* by observing the *law*, or by believing what you heard? . . . After beginning with the *Spirit*, are you now trying to attain your goal by human effort? . . . Does God give you his *Spirit* and work miracles among you because you observe the *law* . . . ?

In Romans 7:6 Paul sounds a clear note of discontinuity between the old era of the Law and the new epoch of the Spirit: 'by dying to what once bound us, we have been *released from the Law* (*katērgēthēmen apo tou nomou*) so that we serve in the new way of the Spirit (*en kainotē pneumatos*), and not in the old way of the written code' (*palaiotēti grammatos*) (my emphasis). And, to underscore the break from the

---

[16] Because of the repetition of the noun *euangelion*, 'gospel' (vv. 6 and 7), commentators have made much of the Galatians' desertion of the *gospel*. However, it needs to be recognized that the substantive participle 'the one who called you' clearly indicates that it is *God* whom the Galatians have forsaken. Paul, elsewhere in the letter uses the same participle to refer to God (1:15; 5:8), and, as Martyn (1997: 109) states, 'in Paul's preaching the Greek participle, *ho kalōn*, "he who calls," virtually functions as a name for God (1 Thess. 2:12; 5:24; Rom. 9:12). Paul never uses the verb "to call" with himself or any other person as the subject.'

past, Paul stresses to the Galatians how the old era of the Law has now been eclipsed by the new era of the Spirit: 'if you are led by the *Spirit*, you are *no longer* under law' (Gal. 5:18; my trans. and emphasis).[17] 'By this he [Paul] means that in the new era of the Spirit in which the Christians live, they serve God in and by the Spirit, rather than by Torah observance, which characterized the old era' (Fatehi 2000: 234).

On the other hand, Paul has a number of positive remarks to make concerning the Law. Paul repeatedly insists that the Torah was a God-given gift, 'a peculiar favour entrusted to Israel' (Westerholm 1997: 89). For instance in Romans 7 the apostle states that the Law is 'holy' (7:12), 'righteous' (7:12), 'spiritual' (7:14) and 'good' (7:16). A little later in the same chapter Paul even declares, 'in my inner being *I delight* (*synēdomai*) in God's law' (7:22). The apostle also strikes a positive note in Galatians 3:24,[18] where he states that the Law was a 'means of grace' that God uses to bring a person to Christ: 'the law was *put in charge* (lit. *paidagōgos*) to lead us to Christ'.[19] And earlier in Romans Paul also insists that despite the revelation of Christ, the Law is still necessary, useful and authoritative for all God's people – faith does not 'nullify the law'; on the contrary, 'it establishes and upholds it' (Rom. 3:31; my trans.). While some aspects and functions of the Law have reached their omega point (e.g. circumcision), one thing is for sure: the keeping of God's commandments has clearly not (cf. Rom. 13:8; 1 Cor. 7:19). In short, an important note of continuity is sounded as far as Paul's understanding of the Law is concerned.

The Spirit: An eschatological gift

The above pattern and diversity in relation to Paul's understanding of the Law have been understood and 'solved' by scholars in different ways. This is not the place to go into an in-depth discussion of the

[17] Fee (1994: 383) states, 'even though Paul's expressed contrasts for his present purposes are between "faith" and "works of Law," the ultimate contrast in this argument is between life under Law (= slavery) and life in the Spirit (= adoption as children).'

[18] Thielman (1993: 539) compares Galatians (e.g. 5:14; 6:2) with the Corinthian correspondence and states that both 'showed a similar pattern of regarding the Mosaic legislation as obsolete but then referring to the Law in positive ways'.

[19] The *paidagōgos* (v. 24), 'guardian', was an important member of the ancient household and was primarily responsible for the general supervision of a child as well as taking him to and from school. A guardian, usually employed at the request of the father, was not given any didactic responsibilities, as the instruction of a child was a normal social expectation of the parents in antiquity (Longenecker 1990: 148; Burke 2003b: 107–108).

tortuous subject of Paul and the Law but to note that while some scholars (e.g. Räisänen 1983) regard the apostle's thinking on this subject as inconsistent and self-contradictory,[20] others have sought to resolve Paul's struggle along national (Dunn 1983: 95–122; 1985: 523–542)[21] and sociological (Watson 1986) lines.[22]

These discussions of the Law, however, take little cognizance of the vital role the Spirit has to play in Paul's thinking in general and in these chapters in particular. If the portrait of the Law painted here is correct, then at its heart is the connection that the old covenant inaugurated at Sinai has been superseded by the new covenant predicted in the Old Testament by the prophets Jeremiah and Ezekiel (see later on this). This general pattern (the replacing of the old covenant with the new) as we have seen, is depicted in Galatians and Romans in terms of the *old epoch of the Law* (Gal. 3/Rom. 7) and the *new epoch of the Spirit* (Gal. 4/Rom. 8). The change of covenants was necessary because no individual could fully keep the stipulations of the old covenant, a fact Israel had repeatedly demonstrated at national and individual levels.

Gordon Fee (1994: 816) rightly recognizes that the old epoch has been overshadowed by the dawning of the new era and concludes that 'the *key* to Paul's view of the Law lies with the gift of the eschatological Spirit' (my emphasis).[23] This is seen clearly at the

[20] Räisänen (1983: 199) states, 'Contradictions and tensions have to be accepted as a constant feature of Paul's theology of the law.' For a strong rebuttal of this position see Weima 1990: 219–235. See also van Spanje 1999.

[21] Dunn understands the phrase 'works of Law' not in terms of Paul attacking 'good works' in a general or meritorious sense. Rather, it is argued, Paul was thinking of the 'badges' of Jewish belonging that marked Israel's sense of distinctiveness. In particular, Dunn thinks Paul is referring to circumcision, food laws and the keeping of special days, which were the 'identity markers' of Jewish imperialism and inevitably led Israel to boast of her favoured status. Certainly, Paul was against all and any kind of Jewish exclusivism, but the phrase 'works of law' cannot be understood as narrowly as Dunn contends, because Paul excludes righteousness by Law in a *general* sense (cf. Gal. 2:21; 3:11–12; 5:4). Moreover, as we have seen, much of Galatians centres on the temporary nature of the Mosaic covenant (Gal. 3:15 – 4:7), and it stretches the argument too much to say that only a part of the Law is in view when Paul speaks of 'works of Law'. See Moo 1983: 73–100; 1987: 287–307. For a very useful discussion of the subject of Paul and the Law within the context and argument of each Pauline letter see Kruse 1996.

[22] Watson advances the thesis that Paul at first engaged in a mission to the Jews, only later turning to the Gentiles and jettisoning the demands of the Law (e.g. circumcision) in order to overcome a practical problem. Watson's argument, however, reduces a theological problem to a sociological one.

[23] Hafemann (1993: 674) concurs: '*the centrality of Paul's eschatological conviction* that Christ has initiated the beginning of the new creation with the establishment of the new covenant, in fulfillment of Jeremiah 31:31–34 and Ezekiel 36:26–27, *needs to be taken seriously as a key to Paul's understanding of the Law*' (my emphasis).

beginning of Romans 7, where the apostle lays down the main markers by which he intends to proceed: 'the old way of the written code' has been replaced by 'the new way of the Spirit' (7:6). All this anticipates what Paul is about to discuss in greater detail about '*another law* (viz. that of the *pneuma*)' (Coetzer 1981: 182; my emphasis), which he then goes on to relate to his adoption metaphor in Romans 8. This shift as we saw earlier was evident in Galatians 3:1–5 when Paul confronted his readers with a number of questions, about which Gordon Fee states, 'for Paul the Spirit marks the effective end of Torah, ... because the coming of the Spirit fulfills the eschatological promise that signals the beginning of the new covenant, thus bringing the old to an end' (1994: 815).

That Paul was aware of the fact that the old covenant, written on tablets of stone, would be replaced by a new covenant written by the Spirit on people's hearts is clear elsewhere in his writings: 'You show that you are a letter from Christ, the result of our ministry, written not with ink but with the Spirit of the living God, not on tablets of stone but on tablets of human hearts' (2 Cor. 3:3). The practical outworkings of this change, as Norman Hamilton (1957: 30) comments, are that

> the Spirit replaces the function of such a code and by His determining influence produces regulated action without any code. In harmony with this replacing of the Law, the Spirit takes over the former function of the Law as the norm and guide for all life.

To be sure, this does not mean that believers in the Old Testament under the old covenant lacked the Spirit of God; the Spirit was indeed active at strategic moments in Israel's history. Whereas the Spirit was intermittently at work in the lives of Old Testament believers, assisting them in times of worship (Exod. 31:3), in accomplishing God's will (Judg. 3:10; 6:34) and on special occasions of inspiration bringing about deliverance for his people (1 Sam. 10:6, 10), this has been redefined by the inauguration of the new covenant, where the Spirit is permanently vested in God's people and is the distinguishing mark of the end-time believer (Rom. 8:9; 1 Cor. 3:16; 6:19) (C. J. H. Wright 2001: 298 n. 72). Whereas the Holy Spirit was the primary deposit on mediating figures (prophet, priest and king) or specially endowed figures (e.g. Bezalel and Aholiab) in the old covenant, the Holy Spirit is bestowed on *all* of the covenant people of God under the new. Paul goes even further to state that the Spirit now enables

God's people to do what the Law could never accomplish: 'in order that the righteous requirements of the law might be fully met in us' (Rom. 8:4). As F. F. Bruce (1985: 153) puts it, 'God's commands have now become God's enablings.'

But before he goes on to speak at length about the Spirit and adoption, Paul grounds it all in the work of God's Son (Rom. 8:3). It is crucial to note that 'it is not the reception of the Spirit which is objectively the cause of being set free from the law, but Christ's advent' (Ridderbos 1977: 200 n. 63, citing S. Greidanus) and atoning death on the cross. Thus, says Romans 8:3 (cf. Gal. 4:4), God sent his Son 'to be a sin offering' (*peri hamartias*) 'and so he "condemned sin"' (v. 4, *katekrinen tēn hamartian*), so that the 'righteous requirements of the law might be fully met in us' (v. 4). This latter phrase has been interpreted in two main ways. First, some rightly understand the clause in purely juristic terms (Gundry 1985: 1–38): only *Christ by his death* (v. 3) has fully met the righteous requirements of the Law and because of this, believers are free from any condemnation and counted as righteous in him. Other commentators understand the clause as referring to the *person* in Christ. In other words, God's intention was not just to deliver people from condemnation, but to make possible 'the righteous requirements of the law'.

There seems no good reason, however, for divorcing (Morris 1988: 304; Schreiner 2001: 327) the above two opinions: Christ by his once-and-for-all-sacrifice has alone fulfilled the righteous requirements of the Law, but it is only as Christians are 'in Him' that they can ever live as God intended – in the power of the Spirit of God.[24] The gift of the Spirit for those who are justified by faith in Christ brings about an obedience from the heart that the Law demanded, as prophesied in Ezekiel 36:27: 'I will put my Spirit in you and move [lit. 'I will make it happen'] you to follow my decrees and obey my laws' (cf. Isa. 11:1–10; 32:14–18; Jer. 31:31–34; Ezek. 11:17–20).[25] Similar Jewish hopes are also evidenced in the eschatological promise in later rabbinic literature where the dawning of the age to some was associated with the bestowal of the Spirit: 'And I will create for them a holy spirit, and I shall purify them so that they will not turn away from me that day and forever. And their souls will cleave to me and to all my

---

[24] Fee's (1994: 530) comment is apt: '*Primarily* through the work of Christ, but in the *last instance* through the work of the Holy Spirit God has brought the time of the Law to an end' (my emphasis).

[25] Wright (2001: 298 n. 72) points out that because the Spirit was active in OT times, 'it is not necessary to regard Ezekiel's prophecy as *exclusively* eschatological' (my emphasis).

commandments. And they will do my commandments' (*Jub.* 1:23–24). And similar views were shared by the Qumran sectarians: 'It is through a holy spirit uniting him to his truth that he shall be purified from all his iniquities. It is through a spirit of uprightness and humility that his sin shall be wiped out' (1QS 3:6–8; 1QS 4:5, 11, 18). The main difference for the apostle Paul is that the Spirit represents the inbreaking – the first fruits of the Spirit (Rom. 8:23) – of the last days into the present as the portion of life and the power of the future ages to come.

Sonship: An eschatological gift

The Spirit, as we have seen, is a key element to understanding Paul's view of the Law,[26] but the Spirit is also crucial to what Paul has to say in relation to his thesis of sonship by adoption. Romans 8 is '*the* great Spirit chapter' and is undoubtedly 'the high point of Paul's theology of the Spirit' (Dunn 1998: 423; my emphasis). This entire chapter is saturated with the language of the Spirit, where the range and activity of the *pneuma* is clearly manifest: the Spirit is referred to as 'Spirit' (*pneuma*, v. 4); 'Spirit of life' (*pneuma zōēs*, v. 2); 'Spirit of God' (*pneuma theou*, v. 9); 'Spirit of Christ' (*pneuma Christou*, v. 9) and 'the Spirit of him who raised Jesus from the dead' (*pneuma tou egeirantos tov Iēsoun ek nekrōn*, v. 11). So integral is the Spirit to sonship by adoption that Paul joins the two in the expressions 'those who are led by the Spirit of God are sons of God' (v. 14) and 'the Spirit of adoption' (*pneuma huiothesias*, v. 15). In Romans 8 Paul's pneumatological language takes over – references to the Spirit exceed that of all other chapters in the New Testament.

But even though the Spirit is mentioned more times in Romans 8 than any other chapter in the Pauline corpus, it is important to grasp that 'the *pneuma* is not the principal issue that is discussed: rather it is subservient to spelling out the eschatological sonship of Christians' (Ninan 1994: 316). The sonship of the Christian is inextricably bound to Jesus the Son of God (Rom. 8:3). It is also interesting, as Bornkamm (1970: 156) observes, how 'Romans 8 ... contains not a single verb in the imperative'. Perhaps, then, it is significant that

[26] Fee (1997: 168) states, 'The Spirit plays the absolutely critical role in Paul's Christian experience, and therefore a crucial role in his understanding of the gospel. So significant is the Spirit to Paul's understanding of the Christian life that in the final analysis, there is no aspect of thought – at least, no feature of his theology – in which the Spirit does not play a leading role.'

whereas in Romans 7 the apostle is mostly dealing with the Mosaic Law (the *Command*ments), now in chapter 8 where the Spirit is in view the believer has a new freedom and energy to live as God intended.[27] This is due to the fact that life in the Spirit is controlled and lived out not by an external regulatory code (Rom. 7:7) but through the indwelling power of the *pneuma* (Rom. 8:4, 9).

Why does Paul join the Spirit and sonship (vv. 14 and 15) in this way? The reason lies in the fact that just as the Spirit was an eschatological blessing, so also is sonship.[28] For example, the Old Testament prophets looked forward to a time when 'the Israelites will be like the sand on the seashore, which cannot be measured or counted. In the place where it was said of them, "You are not my people", they will be called "sons of the living God"' (Hos. 1:10).

This Jewish hope was also expressed in the later rabbinic literature: 'I will be a father to them and they will be called "sons of the living God"' (*Jub.* 1:25). Indeed, such a hope was especially anticipated during the intertestamental period, where, significantly, the two notions of the Spirit and sonship are joined in the following promise: 'He will pour down upon us the *spirit* of grace. And you shall be his true *sons* and you shall walk in his commandments first and last' (*T. Jud.* 24:3–4; my emphasis).

There is no doubt Paul would have understood such expectations given his Jewish background, and this is evidenced by the way in which he combines references to the Spirit and sonship in Romans 8:14, Galatians 4:6a and 8:15 (see further below). The importance of this for Paul is that the Spirit and not faithfulness to the Law is the primary reference point in defining sonship (Dunn 1988: 451). Again, the main difference for Paul is that such an eschatological hope has already dawned, evidenced by the present tenses in verses 14 (*eisin*, 'they are') and 16 (*esmen*, 'we are').

Having noted how Paul links the two ideas of *the Spirit* and *sonship*, we need now to look further at these, especially in the light of the vigorous scholarly debate concerning their relationship. The issue centres primarily on the proper order or the timing/chronology of our receiving the Spirit and our sonship to God (Longenecker

---

[27] Dunn (1998: 203) states in this regard, 'Paul the apostle identifies the Christian as one who has received the Spirit and lives in accordance with it. Membership in God's family is no longer defined as being a *bar mitswah* ("son of the commandment"), but as one who has been adopted by God and shares the Spirit of God's Son.'

[28] Ninan (1994: 306) rightly states, 'Sonship of God and the experience of the Spirit of God are *the distinctive marks of the eschatological humanity*' (my emphasis).

1990: 173). We begin by considering Romans 8:14 and Galatians 4:6a, which will provide the groundwork for discussing the key, related expression: *pneuma huiothesias*, 'Spirit of adoption' (Rom. 8:15).

The Spirit and sonship (Rom. 8:14), sonship and the Spirit (Gal. 4:6a)

Romans 8:14 is located within the wider context of verses 12–17, which comprise a close nexus of connecting particles that function as links in a chain binding the unit. Verses 12–15 (my trans.) are of immediate concern to us, where the links are obvious:

> *Therefore* (*oun*) brothers and sisters we are in debt not to the flesh ... (v. 12), *for* (*gar*) if you live according to the sinful nature you will die but if you put to death the misdeeds of the body you will live (v. 13), *for* (*gar*) those who are led by the Spirit are the sons of God, (v. 14), for (*gar*) you have not received a spirit that makes you a slave again to fear but you have received the Spirit of adoption.[29]

In addition to the many connecting particles, note should be taken of 'the shift of imagery to "sons"' in verse 14 that is 'both sudden and unexpected' (Fee 1994: 564) and requires some amplification, which Paul goes on to provide in order to show that the sons he has in view are 'adopted sons' (Rom. 8:15; my trans.).

Romans 8:14 and Galatians 4:6a have often been interpreted as contradictory aspects of Paul's pneumatology, and it will therefore be helpful to set these two texts side by side in order to get a clearer picture of the issues involved:

Romans 8:14	*Galatians 4:6a*
Those who are led by the Spirit are the sons of God.	And *because you are* sons God sent the Spirit of his Son into our hearts ... (my emphasis)

On the one hand, in Romans 8:14 Paul states that sonship is the result of the gift of the Spirit, which appears to be at variance with what he says in Galatians 4:6; namely, that sonship precedes the gift of the

---

[29] For a discussion of how v. 16 is linked to the preceding verses see pp. 148–150.

137

Spirit, where the latter is sent as a sequel to the former. How, if at all, can we reconcile these two positions?

Verse 14 is the more straightforward of the two texts where, as noted above, Paul appears to be stating that sonship is a consequence of having first received the Spirit. Understood in this light, a wedge is driven between the timing of the believer's sonship and his or her reception of the Spirit. But before we can arrive at a definitive conclusion on this text we need to look at the corresponding and more difficult text Galatians 4:6a, and especially how we are to understand the Greek particle *hoti*. The word *hoti* can be taken in one of two ways: we can either understand it in a causal ('because') or a declarative ('that') sense. According to the former, sonship is the reason God sent the Spirit of his Son into our hearts; put another way, our becoming God's sons *precedes* the reception of the gift of the Spirit. But the 'causal' view, as Max Turner rightly points out, is 'classical Pentecostal' teaching, and he goes on to state, 'this is no second blessing' (1996: 120 n. 17) or doctrine of subsequence, because Paul never argues in this manner in Galatians or Romans or in any other of his letters for that matter.[30]

Other commentators understand *hoti* in a declarative sense ('that'), where the particle denotes the Spirit's cry as 'proof' of the Galatian Christians' sonship: 'And that you are sons – God sent the Spirit of his Son into our hearts'. But as David Lull (1980: 108) rightly points out, 'the declarative *hoti* clause does not answer our original question *as far as the priority of adoption and our receiving of the Spirit is concerned*' (my emphasis).[31] We cannot arrive at a satisfactory conclusion to this matter by considering Galatians 4:6a in isolation; rather, we need to consider what Paul states here in relation to the Spirit within the wider context of the letter. The first point we ought to note is that Paul in Galatians 4:6a is 'working from a Christological confession and so speaks of sonship as the basis for God's gift of the Spirit' (Longenecker 1990: 173). However, in the earlier central theological section of the letter this order is reversed, where Paul, Longenecker points out, 'in 3:2–5 ... *begins* his *probatio* by reminding his converts of their experiences as recipients of the *Spirit*

---

[30] Turner (1996: 120 n. 17) writes, 'This gift [the Spirit] ... is nothing less than the matrix of our sonship to God. This conclusion is further assured by the close parallel of Rom. 8:15, where the Spirit is referred to as *the Spirit of adoption* by whom we cry "Abba! Father"' (emphasis in original). Interestingly, Turner also notes that Gordon Fee, a Pentecostal New Testament scholar, does not subscribe to a two-stage, second-blessing view, either (Fee 1994: 406–412; Dunn 1970: 113–115).

[31] Lull (1980: 108) states that this view 'is consistent with the declarative *hoti*-clause'.

in order to lead them on to the climax of his argument as to their status "sons of God" (3:26)' (1990: 173; my emphasis), a conclusion that concurs with Paul's corresponding statement in Romans 8:14 (Longenecker 1990: 173; see also Witherington 1997: 290).[32] Another matter we should also bear in mind in the discussion here is that Paul's letters are not systematic treatises (although most scholars and commentators agree that Romans comes the closest to it), but a response to situations facing the communities to whom he wrote. This occasional nature[33] of Paul's letters is important, as Longenecker (1990: 173; my emphasis) says, because

> for Paul ... sonship and receiving the Spirit are intimately related that one can speak of them in either order ... with only the *circumstances of a particular audience*, the issue being confronted, or the discussion that precedes *determining the order to be used at a given time or place*.

Most importantly, 'Paul is not here setting out stages in the Christian life, whether logical or chronological'; 'rather his emphasis is on the reciprocal relation or correlational nature of sonship and the reception of the Spirit' (Longenecker 1990: 173; see also Witherington 1997: 290).[34] Sonship and the reception of the Spirit of God are not regarded as separate in the mind of Paul, but are instead inextricably linked: '*the Spirit comes with sonship* ... it is in no way dependent on law-keeping' (Cosgrove 1988: 52; my emphasis).[35] Put another way, sonship and the Spirit are not 'two stages in the Christian life, but ... two mutually dependent and intertwined features in the ... experience of salvation' (Longenecker 1990:174). The crucial point for Paul is that in Romans 8:14 and Galatians 4:6 sonship accompanies the Spirit, and there is a 'shared assumption' between the two texts in that

[32] Dunn (1993: 219) states of Gal. 4:6a, 'it is most unlikely that Paul wished to suggest that the Spirit was a gift subsequent upon their being made sons. Such an inference would have been quite counter to his basic argument: that the Galatians' receipt of the Spirit was the beginning of their experience as Christians (iii.2–3) and amply demonstrated their full acceptance by God, that is, as ... sons of God (iii.7, 26). It would also run counter to the parallel thought expressed in Rom. viii ... where it is clear that possession of the Spirit is coterminous with the sonship (Rom. viii. 14).'

[33] I am of course using the term 'occasional' in the more technical sense, to refer to the historical reasons that gave rise to Paul's writing of this letter.

[34] Witherington (1997: 290) also states, 'The two things [sonship and the Spirit] go together, the status and the condition and experience of sonship.'

[35] Scott (1992: 260) states in regard to Rom. 8:14ff., 'the Spirit is inseparable from sonship'.

all who are God's sons have the Spirit and all those who have the Spirit can rightly be called the sons of God.[36] But what of the related expression *pneuma huiothesias* (Rom. 8:15) – can we arrive at any consensus regarding this phrase and our interpretation of Romans 8:14 and Galatians 4:6a?

The Spirit of adoption

Paul employs the phrase *pneuma huiothesias* (Rom. 8:15) alongside the expression *pneuma douleias*, and commentators have understood this contrasting couplet in different ways. Paul writes, 'For you did not receive a spirit that makes you a slave again to fear, but you received the Spirit of adoption' (8:15). He makes a similar remark in his letter to the Corinthian Christians, where the positive and negative distinctions are also in evidence: 'We have not received the Spirit of the world but the Spirit who is from God' (1 Cor. 2:12). Some take these phrases in 8:15 as a rhetorical device or as expressions of opposition between God and evil (1Q3S 3:18; *T. Reub.* 5:3; *T. Levi* 2:3; 9:9; *T. Jud.* 13:3) (Cranfield 1975: 396). Others understand the antithesis to be between two human 'spirits': the 'spirit of slavery', which Paul says Christians have *not* received (*ou ... elabomen*), and the 'spirit of adoption', which we have received (*elabomen*). This is unlikely given the fact that in verses 14 and 23 (cf. Gal. 4:6) the Spirit is connected with adoption and must refer to the Holy Spirit. Another possible interpretation is to take both as capital 'S' in the sense that the Holy Spirit is operative in the old era of the Law and the new era of the *pneuma*. Certainly, this fits the context of Romans 8, and so the phrase *pneuma huiothesias* must refer to the Holy Spirit. Indeed, it is likely Paul is contrasting the old dispensation, the Law (Rom. 7), as one of fear and bondage, *pneuma douleias*, with the new era, characterized by the Holy Spirit and adoption (Rom. 8) (Cranfield 1975: 397).

Understood in this light, the contrast is not between two actual spirits but two possible conditions the Spirit might bring about. That is to say, Paul is making it clear to his readers that the Spirit they have

---

[36] Morris (1960: 43) states, 'It must never be forgotten that the ministry of the Spirit is bound up inseparably with that of the Son'; Cosgrove (1988: 74) agrees when he writes, 'In Rom. 8:15 Paul points to the fact of the Spirit as evidence that his readers count as "sons". In Gal. 4:6 he moves in the other direction, from the fact of the Galatians' sonship to their reception of the Spirit on that basis. *The unity of Rom. 8:15 and Gal. 4:6 lies not in their respective arguments but in their shared assumption that God gives the Spirit to his sons*' (my emphasis).

received is not associated with / does not lead to slavery (as if God's Spirit could do such a thing!) but is associated with / leads to the 'adoption as sons'. There are two other points to note: first, Paul uses the Greek word *palin* (cf. Gal. 4:8) to refer to the state from which the Roman believers have been delivered, which in turn emphasizes that they are no longer slaves but adopted sons; second, Dunn alerts us to the use of the expression 'adoption' rather than 'son', which heightens the contrast with the term 'slavery' in that it underscores the double gulf between the two: the believer's status has been changed not only from slave to freedman, but also from freedman to adopted son (Dunn 1988: 452).

Paul had earlier in his letter to the church at Rome emphasized the universal guilt of humankind and how all without question are under the dominion and slavery (or the *potestas*) of sin: 'Jews and Gentiles alike are all under sin' (3:9). And a little later in the same chapter and at the climactic conclusion to the first part of his letter he writes, 'all have sinned and fall short of the glory of God' (3:23). Because adoption in the ancient world brought about so stark a change in someone's status, it is a telling metaphor for Paul, which he harnesses for his own theological purposes to describe the believer's position in the family of God. God has graciously and absolutely intervened and freed us from the *potestas* of sin and evil, and now we are in subjection to the *potestas* of God through adoption as his children. Paul makes a similar point by using different language in his letter to the Colossians that captures the essence of what adoption is all about: '[God] has rescued us from the dominion of darkness and brought us into the kingdom of the Son he loves, in whom we have ... the forgiveness of sins' (Col. 1:13).[37] No longer are we in bondage to or driven by sin, the flesh or Satan, but as God's son and daughters by adoption we serve and are empowered by the energizing Spirit who lives within.

The genitival expression *pneuma huiothesias* (Rom. 8:15) highlights for us a much debated issue: whether what Paul states here concerning the relationship of sonship by adoption to the Spirit contradicts what he states in Romans 8:14 and Galatians 4:6a. In this regard, a number of scholars think that the expression 'Spirit of adoption' is an objective genitive that 'functions as a predicate, indicating the *effect* of the Spirit's presence' (Fee 1994: 566; my emphasis). Thus the Spirit who does not lead to slavery is more positively regarded as God's

---

[37] Early church Fathers such as Origen, Gregory of Nyssa, Augustine and Gregory the Great understood Christ's death as a ransom to Satan (Stibbe 1999: 172).

agent or 'the Spirit who brings about adoption'.[38] This reading, however, can be contested on two counts. First, it is hard to find a grammatical category that allows for the genitive to be taken in this way (Scott 1992: 261 n. 143), and second, *huiothesias* could not be taken objectively because, if it were, the verbal noun would not as here stand in the genitive.[39] Moreover, as observed in chapter 4 of this monograph, the *Father* – not the Spirit – is the chief instigator as far as our adoption into God's family is concerned, as John Murray (1960: 295) notes:

> It is the Father who, by way of eminence, is the agent of adoption. The evidence particularly in the Pauline epistles, indicates that it is to the father believers sustain the relation of sons by adoption and it is therefore the Father who adopts.[40]

Others understand this expression to mean 'the Spirit which anticipates adoption' (Barrett 1991: 153) and view adoption in purely eschatological terms (v. 23). The anticipatory dimension, as it relates to the consummation of adoption, is certainly part of Paul's thesis of adoption, but this by itself does not sufficiently acknowledge the 'now' or 'present' aspects adduced earlier in verses 14 and 16.[41] Still others take the phrase to mean 'the Spirit who expresses adoption' (Murray 1960: 295), in the sense that the Spirit does not actually make us God's adopted sons but assists us in testifying to this new filial disposition. This is true, but the witness of the Spirit is more relevant to Paul's argument in verse 16, which follows (see below).[42]

A better solution is to understand the expression *pneuma huiothesias* as a genitive of quality, where the connection between adoption and the Spirit is such that the 'Spirit "goes with" ... *huiothesia*'.[43]

---

[38] E.g. Cranfield 1975: 397; Fee 1994: 566 n. 277.

[39] Byrne 1979: 100; contra Fee 1994: 566 n. 277.

[40] And as Swete (1931: 204) comments, 'The Spirit of the Son is sent into the hearts of the adopted sons ... it does not make them sons, for they are such by their union with the Incarnate Son, but it makes them conscious of their sonship.'

[41] Swetnam (1967: 102–108) does not accept *huiothesian* (v. 23) as part of the original text, and tries unsuccessfully to reconcile the two positions between the 'now' and the 'not yet' by taking the verb *ekdechesthai* to mean 'infer' and not 'wait'. He arrives at the following translation: 'Not only creation but we ourselves who have the first fruits of the Spirit, we also lament to ourselves, arriving at sonship by inference.' Swetnam, however, does not take into consideration the apostle Paul's usage of the same word in the same context (i.e. vv. 19, 25), where it must mean 'await'.

[42] Moo (1996: 502) argues that the Spirit is *both* the agent and assurer of adoption.

[43] Byrne 1979: 100; Scott 1992: 261 n. 143; Michel 1975: 260. For other examples of this usage of the genitive see BDAG (2000), '*Pneuma*', 835 (§5e).

Understood in this way, the Spirit and adoption are not only closely connected but are in fact inseparable; stated in another way, they are reciprocally related.[44] Indeed, if as Paul states earlier, the presence of the Spirit is inseparable from Christian *beginnings* (cf. Rom. 8:9; cf. Gal. 3:3, *houtōs anoētoi este enarxamenoi pneumati*), then Paul by using the phrase *pneuma huiothesias* is also saying there can be no such possibility of adopted sons of God without that same Spirit. Adoption and the Spirit are mutually dependent and interrelated aspects of the Christian's experience of salvation rather than separate developments in the believer's life (Longenecker 1990: 174).[45] As James Dunn succinctly and clearly puts it, 'no Spirit, no Christian' (Dunn 1998: 494).

This interpretation is assured by what Paul goes on to say in Galatians 4:6, where he uses another distinctive phrase: the 'Spirit of his Son' (*to pneuma tou huiou autou*), not found anywhere else in the Pauline corpus, to demonstrate how sonship and the Spirit are inseparable parts of the earthly life and ministry of Jesus. What Paul wishes to drive home to the Galatian Christians by the use of the phrase 'Spirit of his Son' is that just as it is impossible to think of the Spirit divorced from the sonship of Jesus, so it is equally inconceivable to think of that same Spirit apart from the Christian's adoption as son (cf. Rom. 8:14; Gal. 4:6a; Rom. 8:15, *pneuma huiothesias*).

Adoption, the Spirit and the moral imperative

As noted earlier, Romans 8:12–17 is a closely knit unit, evident by the way in which the apostle employs a number of connecting particles: verse 12, 'therefore' (*oun*), and verses 13, 14 and 15, 'for' (*gar*). Thus verse 12 is connected to the verses following rather than

[44] Ridderbos (1977: 199) states, 'There is in the Pauline pronouncements a peculiar relationship of reciprocity between adoption as sons and the gift of the Spirit.'

[45] Turner (1996: 120) writes that the gift of the 'Spirit is nothing less than the matrix of our sonship to God'. Lloyd-Jones (1974: 272) devotes four chapters to v. 15 alone and understands the expression 'you have received the Spirit of adoption' as an experience subsequent to conversion. He describes this as a 'very special form or type of assurance ... a second type of assurance ... that is given to Christians ... but is not necessary for salvation'. But the assurance of which Lloyd-Jones speaks is too subjective and the natural reading of the phrase 'we have received the Spirit of adoption' as John Stott (1994: 236) rightly points out 'is surely the experience of *all* believers'. Stott (1994: 236) concludes, 'There is no indication in these ... verses that a special, distinctive or overwhelming experience is in mind, which needs to be sought by all although it is given only to some. On the contrary, the whole paragraph appears to be descriptive of what is, or should be, common to *all* believers' (my emphasis).

being an exhortatory aside. Having stated that 'the Spirit of him who raised Jesus from the dead is living in you' (v. 11), Paul now states that there is a moral obligation upon the Roman Christians (v. 12). The apostle states this negatively in that believers are not in debt to the flesh (v. 12), which causes the reader to expect the phrase 'but they are in debt to the Spirit'. But Paul does not go on to state this. What he does say in verse 13b (see below) forms the framework and the moral context for his discussion of sonship by adoption in verses 14–15:[46] 'if by the Spirit you put to death (*thanatoute*) the misdeeds of the body, you will live, because (*gar*) those who are led by the Spirit of God are sons of God. For (*gar*) you did not receive a spirit that makes you a slave again to fear, but you received the Spirit of adoption' (vv. 13b–15).

In verses 12–13 Paul also moves 'from indicative to the imperative mood' (Esler 2003: 247), where the verb 'put to death' (*thanatoute*, v. 13b) is a strong one that means 'to kill someone, hand someone over to be killed, especially of the death sentence and its execution' (BDAG 2000: 443). Moreover, this verb is in the present continuous tense, hence our putting to death the sinful nature is a lifelong activity and not a once-and-for-all act. Further still, *thanatoute* is in the 'active' (as opposed to passive) voice and denotes that this is an action for which God's adopted sons must take the initiative and for which they are responsible. This is why Ridderbos is right to insist that 'this adoption as sons *must* make believers live in the true relation of sonship' (1977: 201; my emphasis). What is involved here is nothing less than 'Paul's Spirit ethic' (Dunn 1998: 643) in relation to our adoption as God's sons,[47] and the apostle's teaching is immensely practical. Paul's intention is that adopted sons must demonstrate a certain ruthlessness towards all/any sin in their lives: they are to kill it off, starve it of its oxygen supply and not allow it any room to breathe. *These* (the pronoun *houtoi* is in the emphatic position) are the sons who are led by the Spirit (v. 14).

But can we be more precise in determining the 'leading' to which Paul refers in verse 14 immediately above? Ernst Käsemann (1980) argues that the passive verb (*agesthai*) means 'driven by' the Spirit

[46] Fee (1994: 560) states, 'What begins in v. 14 as a further explanatory word to v. 13 becomes in vv. 15–17 further explanation of v. 14 and thus a further description of life in the Spirit in its own right.'

[47] Although the eighth chapter of Romans is not usually viewed as a locus for Pauline morals, Bornkamm (1970: 156) points out that 'Rom. 8 deals expressly with the counter movements to the thoughts and endeavours of the "flesh" … and clearly outlines Paul's "ethics".'

and is the language of 'ecstatics' or 'enthusiasts' (1 Cor. 12:2); hence to translate it as 'led by' would be to weaken its meaning. Several reasons count against Käsemann's view: first, there is little in the context to suggest that the problem of the 'ecstatics' in Corinth affected the church at Rome; second, the lexical evidence is lacking, because nowhere is this verb translated 'drive';[48] and third Paul is here more concerned with a *relationship* between the believer and God via adoption than he is with any experience as such (Dunn 1999: 85). Being led by the Spirit is not restricted to a few 'enthusiasts' but is a distinguishing mark of *all* God's adopted sons. The one necessarily includes the other – all God's sons are led by the Spirit and all who are led by the Spirit are the sons of God (Schreiner 1998: 422). The leading to which Paul refers here can be partly understood against those Old Testament texts which teach that 'God "leads" the people of God in the ways of God' (Fee 1994: 563),[49] as seen in Psalm 23:3, 'He guides me in paths of righteousness for his name's sake.' Thus as God's sons we are led by God into paths of righteousness for his name's sake where his character – for that is what is bound up in the Old Testament understanding of God's name – and reputation are upheld and honoured by the members of his family.

However, the specific 'leading' to which Paul refers must also be understood against the immediately preceding context of verse 13b ('put to death the misdeeds of the body') and how this relates to his thesis of sonship by adoption (vv. 14–15) (Ferguson 1981: 88). Some commentators think that by using the expression 'led by the Spirit' Paul has the general subject of guidance in mind and how such 'guidance' under the Spirit's direction can assist believers to take a course of action they deem to be in accordance with God's will (i.e. 'I was led/guided by the Spirit' in this or that direction).[50] To be sure, there is truth in this (cf. John 16:13) but that is not what Paul means in this context. Rather than dealing with the unknown or even general guidance per se he is here more concerned with the *known* and revealed 'will of God', which has a clear moral focus (Schreiner 1998: 422). In these verses it 'is the demand the Spirit makes on those it introduces to the new world; it is the *nova obedientia*' (Dillon 1998: 698) of the Spirit that is in view. In the present context the phrase 'led

---

[48] BDAG (2000) does not include 'drive' as a possible meaning for the verb *agō*. Rather, it has this passage under 'be led/allow oneself to be led', which is very different from 'be driven'.

[49] I owe the point that follows to Fee.

[50] So, rightly, Fee 1994: 563.

by the Spirit' is pregnant with moral content, where Spirit-led sons of God are responsible for killing off/mortifying all sin in their lives. Sinclair Ferguson (1981: 88; his emphasis) helpfully identifies the thrust and context of what Paul is driving at here when he remarks:

> the leading of which Paul speaks has a very clear and definite content here. It is connected intimately with the help the Spirit is said to give in verse 13, to 'put to death the misdeeds of the body'. The *guidance the Spirit provides is that of clear-cut opposition to sin*. To claim to experience the ministry of the Spirit of adoption and yet to dally with sin is to be utterly deceived. The Spirit of adoption is the same Person as the Spirit of Holiness of whom Paul had spoken earlier (Rom. 1:4). *His presence brings a new attitude to sin*.[51]

Our adoptive relationship to God as Father, then, should provide '*the motive for ... authentically holy living*' (Packer 1988: 247–248; my emphasis) that must not only be expressed in our sense of filial dependence but also be demonstrated in the family likeness (Stott 1979: 40).[52] While as God's adopted sons we might still bear some of the marks of what we once were, it is with the help of the Holy Spirit that we must daily and continually starve the sinful nature. Indeed, there is a clear difference between acknowledging that one is an adopted son of God and behaving as one, as L. H. Marshall (1960: 259) identifies:

> The ethical implications of Adoption are obvious. A 'son of God' must behave in a manner worthy of his august descent, and only those who behave so are truly 'sons' ... only as men behave like God can they really prove themselves to be the sons of God.[53]

---

[51] Hester (1968: 94) also states, 'The "indicative" of living in the Spirit is tempered by the "imperative" of walking in the Spirit. There is a moral restraint in the imperative of sonship and this moral restraint is an obligation of sonship.'

[52] I am therefore unable to concur with Francis Lyall's (1984: 68) statement 'in Romans 8:15, Ephesians 1:5, and Galatians 4:5 the metaphor points to the selection of believers as sons: their justification in their entry into sonship, and from the point of view of His guidance and authority (in legal terms, under his *potestas*), *irrespective of how they actually live*' (my emphasis). If, as Lyall rightly agues, the Roman background is in view, how sons and adopted sons conducted themselves mattered a great deal to the reputation of the father and the family name, and this is also true in the spiritual realm.

[53] Cranfield (1975: 395) aptly sums up the moral thrust of the 'leading' to which Paul refers here: 'The daily, hourly putting to death of the schemings and enterprises of the sinful flesh by means of the Spirit is a matter of being led, directed, impelled, controlled by the Spirit.'

To sum up this section, Paul's presentation of sonship by adoption is inextricably linked to the Spirit in that both are eschatological gifts and there is a clear moral responsibility to conduct oneself as a member of God's family. We have here what could be more appropriately called the ethics of the eschaton – the duty of all God's adopted sons to live circumspectly in the last days (see Burke 1992: 25–29; 2001: 318–320).[54] It is a salutary thought, as Paul states a little later in this chapter, that the goal[55] of our *huiothesia* is our transformation 'into the image (*eikonos*) of God's Son' (Rom. 8:29; my trans.).[56] Indeed, Ninan (1994: 329) states, '*huiothesia* is conformity to the image of Jesus as the Son of God'. It is possible that in verse 29 Paul is talking about progressive conformity: 'it is by the work of the Holy Spirit that we are being transformed into the full adoption of children of God' (Stevenson-Moessner 2003: 94; cf. Cranfield 1975: 432). Thus, as *we* with the help of God's Spirit 'put to death the misdeeds of the body' (Rom. 8:13b), *God* is also at work changing us; in this way God's sovereignty and human responsibility join hands in the final adoption. The emphasis in Romans 8:29 is on the latter, since the verb 'be conformed' refers to an inner change, and the divine surgery Paul has in view is of the more deep, invasive kind rather than that of the superficial, cosmetic variety (Rogers & Rogers 1998: 331).[57]

But in understanding what it means to 'be conformed' it is also important to be mindful of the context here, and Paul's earlier remark concerning the suffering of God's Son, which might provide a contextual clue in relation to how we understand the verb *symmorphous* in verse 29. When Paul uses the preposition *syn* in verse 17

[54] In this respect deSilva (2004: 143) makes the insightful remark 'nothing seems to drive New Testament *ethics* quite so much as kinship topics, from showing oneself as a true child of God by embodying the characteristics of God and of Christ (the motif of "like parent, like child") ... in the household of faith' (my emphasis).

[55] The 'goal' or event in view here is that of the resurrection (Scott 1992: 247 n. 93).

[56] Kim (1981: 329) argues a strong case for Paul having received the totality of his 'soteriology ... by his experience at the Damascus Christophany. The characteristics of his doctrine of justification by faith *sola gratia* and *sola fide* ... developed out of his Damascus experience [and] it was by seeing the risen and exalted Christ as the Son and image of God who has restored the divine image and glory lost by Adam that Paul developed his soteriological conception of the believers' being adopted as sons of God.'

[57] The same verb *proorizō*, used in Eph. 1:5, is again brought into service by Paul in Rom. 8:29 to make the point that just as God had 'predestined' us unto adoption before time began, so he also had 'predestined' those same sons to be changed into the image of the Son par excellence.

(Leenhardt 1961: 233), he has in mind the growing conformity of God's adopted sons to God's Son *in suffering and obedience* (Peterson 1995: 120). The considerable closeness between 'glory' and 'form' also suggests this and 'facilitates the transition from the idea of "conform" to that of "glorify together with" '(v. 23) (233). Verse 30 picks up the notion of glorification again where the focus is eschatological, but this eschatological thrust ought not to rule out a present dimension, because 'the believer has been destined (*proōrisen*, v. 29) from conversion onward to conform to Christ's pattern of suffering followed by glory' (Moo 1996: 534; see also Peterson 1995: 120; Witherington with Hyatt 2004: 219). The apostle's use of the word *prōtotokos* in verse 29 also signifies that Jesus 'as divine Son . . . is the prototype as well as the agent through whom others are enfranchised as sons of God' (Hurtado 1993: 905) by adoption. The linkage here of God's Son and adopted sons means that the way to be conformed to the Son's likeness and glory is via suffering and treading a similar path to the one Christ trod.[58] The family marks of adopted sons are not only obedience, as observed earlier, but also suffering in the present life with the prospect of glory to come. Just as suffering and sonship were inextricably linked during the historical career of Jesus (cf. Rom. 8:17), so suffering and sonship by adoption are also interwoven (cf. Rom. 8:23) in the lives of Christians (cf. 1 Pet. 4:12), even though the former is of an entirely different order and nature to the latter.[59]

Adoption and the dual witness of the Spirit with our spirit

There is no connecting particle or conjunction between Romans 8:15 and 16, but this does not mean that verse 16 is unrelated to what the apostle has stated previously. Rather, the connection is thematic and, as David Williams (1999: 65; see also Fee 1994: 567) rightly points out, what Paul says regarding the witness of the Spirit clearly indicates that he 'still has the metaphor of adoption in

[58] Smail (1980: 151) puts it well when he comments, 'Shared Sonship means shared suffering.' I use the term 'similar' rather than 'same', as Christ's suffering was unique.

[59] Our suffering is linked to Christ's suffering in the sense that just as his life was not easy, so the Christian life is not easy either. But there is an aspect of Christ's suffering that is unique: he did not suffer for his own sin but suffered vicariously for the sins of others.

mind'.[60] Indeed, it is in this verse that the 'adoption is given its existential reality by the presence and witness of the Spirit' (Dunn 1998: 424).

The major interpretative issue in verse 16 has to do with our understanding of the compound verb *symmartyrei*. Commentators disagree concerning the meaning of this verb, which has resulted in two main readings: either 'the Spirit bears witness *to* our spirit that we are God's children',[61] or 'the Spirit bears witness *with* our spirit that we are God's children'.[62] Cranfield's (1975: 403) view is representative of the former when he states, 'What standing has our spirit in *this* matter? Of itself it surely has no right at all to testify to our being sons of God' (emphasis in original). Most scholars however, are persuaded that the associative view is better, where our spirit joins with God's Spirit in bearing witness to our adoption as sons (Witherington with Hyatt 2004: 219).[63] There are at least two reasons for this: first, the above verb has the meaning 'to' in only two New Testament passages (Rom. 2:15; 9:1); second, this word was still used to mean 'bear witness with' in papyri dating back to the second century. As Moo (1996: 540 n. 40) states, this 'additional nuance makes excellent sense in a context where two "spirits" are prominent'.[64] Moreover, the idea of dual witnesses is well attested in Scripture. For example, in Deuteronomy 19:15 we read that 'A matter must be established by the testimony of two or three witnesses,' and Paul demonstrates an awareness of the principle of multiple witnesses, as 2 Corinthians 13:1

[60] Moo (1996: 504) also states, 'Paul refers to the human spirit here because he wants to stress that the witness of "the Spirit himself" about our adoption as sons affects the deepest and innermost part of our beings'; contra Scott (1992: 177 n. 199), who too easily dismisses the significance that the witnesses of the public act of Roman adoption may have on this text: '[that] the witness of the Spirit in Rom. 8:16 reflects the witnesses in the Roman act of adoption hardly deserves serious consideration'. See Sherwin-White (1978: 149), who states that the certification of any matter in Roman law (which would have included adoption) required several witnesses (cf. Hester, Williams, Dunn, Atkins).

[61] Few, if any, modern translations adopt this reading. Commentators who take this view include Godet, Leenhardt, Cranfield and Morris.

[62] Most translations adopt this reading; e.g. AV, NIV, NASB, RSV, JB etc. Grammatically, the issue is whether the definite article (*tō pneumati*) is a dative of association (with our spirit) or a dative of indirect object (to our spirit). Commentators who adopt the former reading include Hendriksen, Dunn, Fee and Moo.

[63] Another phenomenon that adds weight to the associative view is the fact that this is the first of nine *syn*-compound verbs (verbs preceded by the Greek preposition *syn* [together with]) within the space of fourteen verses.

[64] Moo (1996: 503) is right when he says, 'This is ... the only occurrence of *pneuma* in Rom. 8 that does not refer to the Holy Spirit.' Stacey (1956: 132) states, 'In Rom. 8:16 Paul invokes the Spirit of God and the Christian's spirit, as separate witnesses to the sonship of the believer, and the distinction between the two is patent.'

149

makes clear. Thus a better translation is that 'the Spirit of *huiothesia bears witness with* our Spirit to us that we are indeed God's adopted sons and daughters'. Put another way, the Spirit of God strikes a chord with the human spirit of the adopted son, indicating to him that he has indeed 'come home'.

In this respect the Holy Spirit plays a critical role in assuring adopted sons of their new filial disposition. But this is no mystical experience, as though the Spirit subjectively whispers to us 'You are God's son.' This 'would amount to a new revelation from God *over and above* the revelation given to us in Scripture' (Ferguson 1989: 73; my emphasis). Rather, the Holy Spirit makes us aware of our adoption into God's new family. Thus the work of the Holy Spirit is reiterative rather than innovative, because the Spirit always acts on the basis of what Christ has already done and Paul had earlier struck an important Christological and soteriological note in Romans 8:3 (cf. Gal. 4:5). God's Spirit is sent into our hearts to let us *know* we are his adopted sons, for when doubts start to creep in, as they invariably do, knowledge of our standing before God is important. It is at such moments that the witness of the Spirit with our human spirit is both crucial and affirmative.

This dual witness – the Holy Spirit with our spirit – is one more piece of evidence that Paul in verse 16 is still thinking about regarding the Roman practice of adoption. In the ancient Roman world adoption was a public act where the '*manicipatio* was carried out in the presence of witnesses, to ensure that the legality of the adoption could be established beyond doubt by reference to one or more of the witnesses' (Williams 1999: 65; Sherwin-White 1978: 149; Hester 1968: 60–62; Dunn 1993: 219). Those same witnesses would be used if a person's adoption was disputed (e.g. over a matter of inheritance; cf. Rom. 8:17), where the adoptee's testimony coupled with that of the witnesses would prove so crucial. Our adoption as God's children 'is permanent' (Thompson 2000: 121) and irreversible and it is interesting as well as significant how later in this chapter Paul envisages accusations and charges being brought against God's elect (Rom. 8:32), accusations coupled with the reminder that nothing nor no-one can ever separate us from the love of God (Rom. 8:39), our adopting Father (Eph. 1:5).

Summary

The role of the Holy Spirit in relation to our adoption as sons has long been overlooked, despite the fact that the *pneuma* is mentioned in four of the five relevant passages. Moreover, important personal and familial characteristics usually associated with God the Father and God the Son are ascribed to the Spirit, a member of the 'Divine Family'.

In the two adoption passages in question (Gal. 4 and Rom. 8) Paul's many references to the Spirit are deliberately set against the backdrop of earlier references to the Law (Gal. 3; Rom. 7). This is no accident, because the Law, in accordance with Jewish hopes in the Old Testament and intertestamental periods would be fulfilled and eclipsed by the eschatological Spirit and sonship. Paul would have been clued into these Jewish expectations, evidenced by the way in which he links the Spirit and sonship in Romans 8:14 and Galatians 4:6a. For Paul the Spirit and sonship are not only eschatological gifts but are viewed as indissoluble, rather than being separate or subsequent stages in the Christian life – all God's sons are led by the Spirit, and all those who are led by the Spirit are God's sons. This interpretation is further supported by Paul's use of the related expression *pneuma huiothesias* in Romans 8:15, by which he means that the Spirit cannot be severed from *huiothesia* but goes with or accompanies our adoption as sons. Just as it is inconceivable to think of the Spirit separated from God's Son (Gal. 4:6), so it is equally unimaginable to consider the Spirit apart from the believer's adoption as son.

Given that adoption and the Spirit are blessings of the eschaton, the command to 'put to death the misdeeds of the body' (Rom. 8:13b) also brings an additional moral responsibility for all God's adopted sons to conduct themselves circumspectly as those who live in the last days (vv. 14–15). God's sons and daughters, in the energy of the *pneuma*, are exhorted to kill off all sin in their lives continually, knowing also that God is at work changing and conforming them to the ultimate goal of adoption: the *eikōn* of God's own Son (Rom. 8:29). This same Spirit, moreover, has a vital role to play in assuring us or making us aware of our *huiothesia*, and this dual witness – God's Spirit with our human spirit – would have resonated with Paul's readers, since a plurality of witnesses was required for the public verification of adoption in accordance with ancient Roman legal practice.

Chapter Seven

Adoption and honour

Introduction

We saw earlier that adoption is probably a metaphor drawn from the ancient Roman social context of Paul's day. We also saw in chapter 3 how adoption in the ancient world was an important means by which the adoptee was given a status and honour not previously enjoyed.[1] In this chapter we shall look more closely at the relationship between adoption and honour. For example, what kind of honour was bestowed upon adopted sons in the ancient world and what can this tell us, if anything, about the honour God confers upon those he adopts into his family? And given that concord was a core social value within the natural family, is there any evidence in Paul's letters where he employs his adoption metaphor as a means of resolving the problems and difficulties between the family of believers?

I begin by tracing the ancients' understanding of honour and noting points of contact with adoption.

Adoption and honour in antiquity

The twin aspects of honour and shame were the 'foundational social values' (deSilva 2000: 23) upon which first-century culture and society were built.[2] Honour was not only the most cherished but also the most jealously guarded of all ancient social values in the eastern Mediterranean culture. The reason for this was that 'one's reputation defined the core of personal identity' (Spencer 2003: 19).[3] Honour could be *achieved* when, for instance, a person performed some

---

[1] Strom (2000: 65) states, 'Wealth, education, marriage, *adoption*, administrative or rhetorical talent, piety, virtue and citizenship *could* each *offer a platform for status*' (my emphasis).

[2] For a brief and accessible synopsis of how important honour was to the ancients see Witherington 1998: 44–48. Moxnes (1993: 167–172) makes the point that outside the family one belonged to the wider group of kin, tribe (clan) or people.

[3] Spencer's treatment of important ancient values in the life of Jesus such as 'family', 'friendship', 'body', 'money', 'work' and 'honour' is most insightful.

virtuous deed, thereby establishing a reputation or name for himself (deSilva 2000: 28).[4] On the other hand, honour could be *ascribed* and 'is always presumed to exist within one's own *family* of blood, that is among all those one has as blood relatives' (Malina 1993: 38). Most especially, one's parents, the father in particular, were the figures from whom honour as a social value was seen to derive. Unlike today's twenty-first-century Western society, 'who you are' individually was of much less importance in the group-oriented world in antiquity, where the 'one to whom you belong' took precedence.[5] We find this notion at work in the Old Testament, where 'accretions of honour by one family member add to the honour rating of the whole family' (Esler 2000: 152),[6] as for instance in the case of Eliakim, who is made the chief controller of Hezekiah's household: 'He will be a seat of honour for his father's family ... On him will hang the whole glory of the family, even to the meanest members – all the paltriest of vessels whether bowl or pot' (Isa. 22:23–24, REB).

This second understanding of honour, *ascribed* honour, is also well exemplified in the intertestamental era when Ben Sira remarks, 'A person's honour comes from his father' (Sir. 3:11). Here Ben Sira goes on to trace the deceased person's honour by recalling the honour of his ancestors and parents. Conversely, he writes a little later, 'Children will blame an ungodly father, for they suffer disgrace because of him' (Sir. 41:7).

Now adoption falls under the rubric of the latter category of *ascribed* honour. In the ancient world it was well known that matters of life and death were in the hands of the *paterfamilias*, and so for a father to decide consciously to adopt another brought immense prestige to the adoptee, a point well illustrated in the case of Octavian, later to become the emperor Augustus. Julius Caesar adopted Octavian as his son, with the result that Octavian's 'honour rating rose considerably by that grant' (deSilva 2000: 28). Octavian's adoption is ascribed (as opposed to achieved) honour, not only because it occurred later in life, but also because of the new association and attachment to his adoptive father, the emperor. To be sure, natural sonship ascribed status, but in the case of adoption such honour was greatly accentuated – it brought esteem not previously enjoyed, because of the adoptee's relationship with his new father and new family to which he had now come to belong.

---

[4] I am indebted to deSilva's stimulating insights for some of what follows.
[5] Malina and Neyrey (1996: 153–174) call this a dyadic personality.
[6] I also owe the following Scripture reference to Esler.

When an individual was adopted in accordance with Roman law, benefits accrued to the adoptee, as Suzanne Dixon (1992: 112) explains: 'children ... inherit ... concrete goods such as houses, land, businesses, slaves ... [and] ... *adoption* was an obvious means of gaining virtually all the benefits listed above' (my emphasis). Dixon asserts (111) that all Roman sons, including those by virtue of their adoption, inherited 'the family name and *honour* and obligations that go with them'. The corollary of this also meant that all children, including those who had been adopted, 'could bring *glory or discredit* on it [the family] by their behaviour' (110; my emphasis). This may have been one reason why adoption was delayed until adulthood, by which time the father had a good idea of the sort of son and heir he was getting (Rawson 1986: 12).

With this brief background in view we now turn to the texts. We begin with Galatians before we turn to a consideration of Paul's letter to the Romans.

Adoption and honour in Galatians

Paul's letter to the church at Galatia is the only capital epistle that lacks a formal thanksgiving section at the beginning. Unlike his other letters, where he addresses his readers as 'sanctified in Christ Jesus' (1 Cor. 1:2) and those 'loved by God' (Rom. 1:7), Paul finds no time for such salutations in his letter to the Galatians. Evidently, there were serious problems facing Paul in a church he himself had established (cf. Gal. 4:19).[7] The apostle immediately gets to the heart of the problem by registering his astonishment at how his converts were 'so quickly deserting the one who called you by the grace of Christ and are turning to a different gospel – which is really no gospel at all' (1:6). Crucially, Paul couches the desertion in personal (more correctly, paternal; see below) rather than impersonal terms: 'the *one* who called you' (1:6; my emphasis). We shall return to this point later.

The difficulty facing Paul in respect of the church at Galatia was the infiltration of agitators who were boasting of their acquired

---

[7] See Gaventa (1990: 189–201) on this text. In Gal. 4:19 Paul uses a tortuous metaphor when he states, 'My dear children, for whom I am again in the pains of childbirth until Christ is formed in you...' In the first instance, Paul describes how *he* is in pains *again* (twice for the one child!) of childbirth, which is interesting for at least two reasons: first, it is most unusual for an ancient male to employ female imagery to describe himself thus; and second, having described the Galatians as the child within his 'womb', it is not the Galatians of whom Paul says he gives birth, but Christ!

honour. This was partly based upon their success in getting the Galatians circumcised: 'For those who are circumcised do not even keep the law themselves but they desire to have you circumcised, *that they may boast in your flesh*' (Gal. 6:13, *hina en tēhymetera sarki kauchēsōntai*; my trans.) (Russell 1997: 97).[8] Clearly, there was nothing wrong in boasting per se, as Paul himself states elsewhere, 'Let him who boasts boast *in the Lord*' (1 Cor. 1:31; my emphasis). Indeed, Paul states earlier in Galatians, 'let each one examine his own work, and then he will have reason for boasting in regard to himself alone, not in regard to another' (Gal. 6:4; my trans.). Paul, like the agitators, in his preconversion days had every reason to boast of his Jewish credentials and his acquired honour, as he states, 'I was advancing in Judaism beyond many Jews of my own age and was extremely zealous for the traditions of my fathers' (Gal. 1:14). Ever since his life-changing encounter with the risen Christ, however, Paul wishes to do only one thing, as he writes, 'May I never boast except in the cross of our Lord Jesus Christ, through which the world has been crucified to me, and I to the world' (Gal. 6:14). Paul's acquired honour in the past 'pales in comparison to the *ascribed* honor bestowed upon him (and thereby the Galatians) by Jesus Christ and the Father' (Russell 1997: 97; my emphasis).[9]

This is the point the apostle picks up and develops in relation to adoption. Paul in Galatians 1:6 identifies God at the beginning of the letter as the 'the one who called you by the grace of Christ' (*tou kalesantos hymas en chariti Christou*), a description to which he returns at the end of the letter: 'You were running a good race. Who cut in on you and kept you from obeying the truth? That kind of persuasion does not come from *the one who calls you*' (*tou kalountos hymas*, 5:7–8). Immediately prior to 1:6, however, Paul specifically identifies this 'One' on three occasions as none other than the 'Father' (Gal. 1:1, 3, 4). The Galatians were not merely deviating from a doctrine, but were also failing in their loyalty to their Father. Indeed, this 'Father' whom the Galatians had deserted was the very one who had willed their deliverance from 'the present evil age' (Gal. 1:4) and the One to whom 'glory' (Gal. 1:5; i.e. *honour*) was due (Russell 1997: 96). For the Galatians to allow themselves to be circumcised was tantamount to entering into the community of their oppressors and 'therefore ... [to come] under a different father' (99).

[8] I owe this point and some of the discussion that follows to Russell.

[9] I am following Russell here.

We observed in chapter 4 how the designation 'father' functions in Paul's letter to the Galatians as a means of underscoring God's sovereign role as *paterfamilias* (head of the household) in adopting individuals into his family. Another reason why Paul prefaces this letter with a proliferation of paternal language is in order to trace believers' origin and sense of belonging to God their Father. This paternal language, then, comes full circle in conjunction with Paul's adoption metaphor in Galatians 4:6.

This same sense of belonging is, interestingly, stressed by the Synoptic evangelists Matthew and Luke, who in their genealogies preface their discussion of the events of the earthly career and ministry of Jesus by focusing on his origins and belonging. The genealogies of the first and third Gospels are sometimes passed over as unimportant but they provide insights and clues into their authors' purposes for writing. In both Gospels the writers emphasize that a proper understanding of the Jesus story and the Jesus of history is not comprehensible unless they first mark out where he came from. One of their main functions is to show derivation and by so doing ascribe honour to the person by emphasizing the one to whom he belongs.[10] In other words, the genealogies underscore the fact that the person in question comes from 'the most noble stock' (deSilva 2000: 52). Thus Matthew 1:1 is a form of title to this Gospel that opens 'A record of the genealogy of Jesus Christ ... the son of Abraham' (*Biblos geneseōs Iēsou Christou ... huiou Abraam*)', where the evangelist goes on to show how the Jewish ancestry of Jesus – which is important to this author and his readers – can be traced back to the patriarch Abraham, the honourable father of the Jewish race. Luke, on the other hand, follows Jesus' lineage back to Adam the father figure of the human race (3:38) (deSilva 2000: 159).[11] As such, Jesus is indeed the Son of God and the Son of Joseph, but for Luke the universal thrust (evident throughout the whole Gospel) depicts Jesus at the very outset of this Gospel as the 'Son of Everyman' (Spencer 2003: 37).

Certainly, I am not suggesting that Paul's paternal references at the beginning of his letters are in the same category as the Gospel

---

[10] It could also be argued that Matthew's reason for including a number of persons who brought dishonour to the line of Jesus (e.g. Rahab the prostitute, Ruth the Moabitess and Bathsheba the adulteress – who was already compromised by being married to a Canaanite) magnifies the amazing grace of God by the bringing forth of his son, Emmanuel, from a line so full of promise yet so full of disgrace.

[11] Luke wants his readers to grasp the fact that just as Adam was a historical figure, so too was Jesus.

genealogies.[12] Nevertheless, the manner in which the apostle traces the origin of the Galatians' Christian life back to their heavenly 'Father' is not devoid of content or meaning.[13] We observed earlier in Galatians how paternal language highlights God's absolute authority in the believer's adoption. Another fascinating reason why Paul repeatedly broaches the subject of the paternity of God (e.g. 1:1, 3, 4) at the start of the letter and then climaxes in the adoption passage (Gal. 4:6) is to confirm 'to the believers in Galatia that by adoption into God's family ... God ascribes [the] *honor* of God's own household to the believer' (deSilva 2000: 73; my emphasis).[14] Being included in God's family brings an unsurpassed honour to the adopted child of God. Certainly, Jesus as the Son of God is uniquely honoured, but Christians too as God's adopted children are given a share in that honour. As adopted sons the Christians' *honour* is ascribed from their divine parentage, from having 'no less a father than God himself' (deSilva 2000: 206).[15] And 'God, of course, depends on no source of honor, for God is himself the source of honor' (Neyrey 2004: 155). Contextually, then, Paul is stressing to the Galatian Christians that they not only owe their very existence to

---

[12] Perhaps the nearest Paul comes to composing a 'genealogy' comparable to those found in Matthew and Luke is in Rom. 1:1–4, where he writes, 'Paul, a servant of Christ Jesus, called to be an apostle and set apart for the gospel of God – the gospel he promised beforehand through his prophets in the Holy Scriptures regarding his Son, who as to his human nature was a descendant of David, and who through the Spirit of holiness was declared with power to be the Son of God...' Duling (2003: 236) states in this regard, 'Paul probably recognized that one basic indicator of status and ethnicity is a genealogy. He *might* have had a genealogy in mind when he cited the formula that Jesus was descended from David "according to the flesh" (Rom. 1:3)' (my emphasis). See chapter 5 for a treatment of these verses in respect of Jesus' alleged 'adoption'.

[13] Esler (2000: 175) states that the terminology of 'kinship (the fatherhood of God) or fictive kinship language ... contribute(s) to the ... dimensions of group-belonging' and demonstrates Paul 'is tapping into the high regard for one's family typical of the Mediterranean'. Russell (1997: 96) makes the following observation: 'In one sense the whole theme of Galatians is this amazingly rapid and uncalled-for defection of the Galatians as children from their Father God and the Lord Jesus Christ.'

[14] Moxnes (1988a: 216) also comments in regard to honour, 'Who are the people of God, the sons of God? (Rom. 8:14–17)'; to which he responds, 'believing that they were "sons of God", Christians considered themselves to be in an *honoured* position' (my emphasis). It should be pointed out that here Moxnes is thinking of the general notion of 'sonship', even though the text he cites (Rom. 8:14–17) also contains the expression we are primarily interested in: 'adopted as sons' (*huiothesia*). Moreover, *huiothesia* is used on two occasions in Rom. 8 (vv. 15, 23). See also Esler 2003: 249.

[15] DeSilva (2000: 206) goes on to state that those whom God adopts as his sons and daughters 'enjoy the great honor of being children of no less distinguished Parent than the God of the universe'. I have attempted to show elsewhere (Burke 2001: 119–134) how Paul employs paternal language in relation to adoption to underscore the deep resocialization that occurs as a result of being made God's sons by adoption.

God the Father in adopting them as his sons and daughters but they also owe him their continued allegiance and loyalty (Russell 1997: 98). The Galatians by their possible defection were bringing the gospel into disrepute and dishonouring the Head of their family (99).[16] They needed to demonstrate the same loyalty to their Father that Paul himself had so clearly shown since his conversion to Christianity (Gal. 1:11–12).[17] Fidelity and obedience were expected norms of the father–son relationship in the ancient world; hence Paul exhorts his readers to continue the Christian life as they had begun it (Gal. 3:1–5).

According to the apostle Paul, to become a follower of Jesus Christ is conceptualized as *huiothesia*. As a consequence, we have a share 'in the honour of the head of . . . God's family . . . as believers came to be associated with the highest and most honourable "head of the household" in the cosmos' (deSilva 2001: 11).[18]

For Paul, then, the believer's entrance into the household of God came about through Jesus, God's Son, who willingly suffered a dishonourable death (Gal. 4:5) of crucifixion so that we might be honourably accounted God's adopted children (Gal. 4:5).

One other important point to make here is that Paul also employs his *huiothesia* term as a means of resocializing the Galatians into the distinctively Christian way of life. Wayne Meeks (1983: 88) asserts:

> the image of the initiate being adopted as God's child and thus receiving a new family of human brothers and sisters is a vivid way of portraying what a modern sociologist might call the resocialization of conversion. The natural kinship structure into which the person had been born and which previously defined his place and connections with society is here supplanted by a new set of relationships.[19]

[16] Russell (1997: 98) states, 'In one sense the whole theme of Galatians is this amazingly rapid and uncalled-for defection of the Galatians as children from their Father God . . .'

[17] Interestingly, there are two ways of looking at paternal terminology in this letter. God is the Father of the Galatians, but Paul also regarded himself as their 'father' (Gal. 4:19) in the sense that as God's instrument he had established the church when he first brought the gospel to them.

[18] Malina and Rohrbaugh (1998: 82) also state, 'By using the Greco-Roman metaphor of adoption, Paul notes this . . . change in honour status for those who become God's kin.'

[19] Witherington (1998: 77) writes, 'A careful sociological analysis of what happened to *Paul* on the road to Damascus would have to conclude that he *underwent* a thorough *resocialization*' (my emphasis). See Burke (2001: 124–128) for a discussion of 'adoption' as a term Paul uses to resocialize the Galatians into the distinctively Christian way.

Christian adoption not only signifies a deep resocialization that has taken place but also points up the fact that if God's adopted sons and daughters are to be properly nurtured and established in the faith, then the environment in which they will develop and mature is when the *ekklēsia* (church) best resembles a 'family-like fellowship' (Sandnes 1994: 14). Indeed, it ought to be within the arena and context of the church family itself (not to mention society at large or those on the periphery of the church) that God's adopted offspring should bring honour and blessing, rather than shame and dishonour, as they demonstrate genuine, practical service and love towards others within the household of faith. Paul states towards the close of his letter, 'Do good to all people, especially to those who *belong to the family of believers*' (*tous oikeious tēs pisteōs*, Gal. 6:10). Whenever Christians buy into the dishonouring ways of the world and the prevailing culture and fail to honour the Father, they not only deny their adoption but also negate the work of God in Christ through the Sprit in bringing them into God's family.

Having considered how adoption and honour are related in Galatians, we turn to a consideration of Paul's letter to the Romans where the context and the apostle's approach to these matters takes on a different complexion.

Adoption and honour in Romans

Context

Paul's letter to the church at Rome is his longest and arguably most theologically important. Paul had diverse reasons for writing this letter:[20] primarily, he here provides the most detailed discussion of the gospel of the 'righteousness of God' (*dikaiosyne theou*), a righteousness enjoyed and entered into by faith alone (Rom. 1:16–17).[21] The first eleven chapters take up this theme of God's plan for the salvation of humankind: humankind is sinful (Rom. 1 – 3) but God justifies people through the Lord Jesus Christ (Rom. 4 – 8), which is for the Gentile as well as the Jew (Rom. 9 – 11), a point struck by Paul in the introductory 'theme' of the letter (Rom. 1:14–16). One reason

[20] The generally accepted view today is that the apostle Paul had several *reasons* in mind when he wrote this letter. See Wedderburn 1988. See also the recently revised and edited volume by Donfried 1991.

[21] There has been much debate concerning the place of justification by faith in Romans and whether or not it is the 'centre' or 'central' to Paul's thinking' (Moo 1996: 89–90; Seifrid 1992).

Paul writes at length concerning justification by faith is that he is not the founder of the church at Rome, nor has he ever visited the church (though he has intended many times to do so: Rom. 1:13; 15:24), and he wants his readers to be in no doubt concerning his understanding of the gospel of Jesus Christ. He writes to alleviate the concern of Christians in Rome who may be suspicious of his teaching on the Law (e.g., Rom. 3:8). Paul also writes this lengthy doctrinal exposition because of his impending missionary expedition to Spain – he wants to secure the support of the whole church.

In addition to these primary reasons for the composing of this letter are other secondary reasons, chief of which is that the apostle is addressing 'a troubled church ... a church with real tensions and struggles [with] divisions and resentments' (Lane 1998: 198).[22] Today scholars are increasingly of the view that there were dissensions within the community, especially between Jew and Gentile, thus enabling some rightly to conclude that '*one* of Paul's purposes [for writing] was to heal this *division* in the Christian community in Rome' (Carson & Moo 2005: 406; my emphasis).[23] Also it is noteworthy how Paul 'does not address this letter, as he does so many of his others, to the "church" (compare e.g., 1 Cor. 1:2; 1 Thess. 1:1). What this probably means is that there was more than one "local church" in the city of Rome' (Moo 2001: 36). Indeed, it seems there were different house churches in existence in Rome, where Christians met for worship and fellowship, an arrangement mirrored earlier when Jewish communities worshipped in segregated synagogues (Wedderburn 1988: 146).[24] In this regard, the final chapter of the letter to the Romans (16)[25] provides an important hermeneutical key to the problem of disunity in the church at Rome.[26] The difficulty centres round the fact that there were not one but two types of house churches in existence in the metropolis that were 'organized along lines of ethnicity' (Jeffers

[22] See also the discussion in Carson and Moo 2005: 407.

[23] Miller (2001: 338) also comments, 'a growing number of scholars locate the purpose of the letter in Paul's desire to *unite* divided Christians in Rome' (my emphasis) (see Schreiner 1998: 22). Talbert (2002: 12) also states, 'A consensus seems to be building ... that the main need in the Roman church addressed by Paul was that of resolving the disunity between Jews and Gentiles.' Lane (1998: 199) also comments, 'The issue at stake was whether there was to be one church or two' (see also Lincoln 2002: 177).

[24] Wedderburn cites inscriptions that testify to these various groupings.

[25] Most commentators now accept Rom. 16 as part of the original letter (Donfried 1991: 44–52).

[26] Weima (1994: 215–230) has shown by a study of epistolary analysis, including Romans, how the ending of a letter can provide insights into the problems and difficulties that confronted a particular Pauline community.

1999: 86).[27] Francis Watson comes to this conclusion when he states, 'Paul's argument does not presuppose a single congregation ... it presupposes *two congregations*, separated by mutual hostility and suspicion ... *which he wishes to bring together into one congregation*' (1991: 206; my emphasis).[28]

A close reading of Romans 16 shows that there was a separate Jewish house congregation meeting at the home of Priscilla and Aquila (16:4–5). On the other hand, Paul's greetings to Asyncriticus, Phlegon, Hermes, Patrobas and Hermas (16:14) and to Philologos, Julia, Nereus and his sister Olympas (16:15) identifies separate Gentile house churches (Wedderburn 1988: 45).[29] The double reference to 'the brothers with them' (16:14) and 'the saints with them' (16:15) further suggests that these 'probably refer to house churches' (Moo 2001: 36).[30] These ethnically separated house churches were a manifestation of a much deeper issue Paul deals with earlier in Romans (14 – 15), where the so-called 'weak' (Jewish believers) and the 'strong' (Gentile Christians) disagreed over the eating of certain foods. Moo (2000: 505) is of the opinion that there is probably a link between the separate house churches and the issues raised in Romans 14:1 – 15:13. He comments:

> It was probably the case ... that certain house churches were composed entirely of believers 'weak in faith' and others of believers 'strong in faith' (see comments on 14:1 – 15:13). Paul's plea for acceptance of one another, then, is seeking reconciliation among various 'churches' in Rome.[31]

[27] Some scholars posit as many as five house churches in Rome. For more on this see Lampe 1991: 216–230; Jewett 2003: 92. Lampe (2003: 36) comments in regard to the separate worship services in the different churches in Rome, 'Each circle of Christians may have conducted worship services by itself in a house or apartment, so that it can be referred to as a house church.' A similar problem prevailed in the house churches in Corinth (Burke 2003b: 95–113).

[28] Sampley (1995:121) states, 'In Romans we have ... *an ethnically grounded struggle over leadership and position in the Roman house-churches.* Romans is a sustained, cohesive, comprehensive address of the Roman factions in a quest for unity' (my emphasis).

[29] Jeffers (1999: 86) states that different 'ethnic groups in the cities ... lived in certain quarters of the town'. He continues, 'Jews tended to settle in certain areas of Rome, particularly along the Tiber river just across from the heart of Rome.' See also Osiek & Balch 1997: 99.

[30] Moo (2001: 36) goes on to state, 'We might infer that these separate congregations in Rome were taking quite different approaches to the issues that Paul deals with in these verses' (Rom. 14:1 – 15:13).

[31] Schreiner (1998: 798) likewise remarks, 'The presence of various churches ... may also explain the tensions between the "strong" and the "weak" in Rome.'

Thus, while some felt at liberty to eat all nature of foods (Gentile Christians), others did not enjoy such liberties (Jewish Christians) because of their adherence to the Jewish Law. These tensions caused Paul to exhort these opposing parties repeatedly to 'make every effort to do what leads to peace and to mutual edification' (14:19) and 'to stop passing judgment on one another' (14:1; my trans.). Paul reminds the believers that they are brothers and sisters in Christ with the responsibility 'to accept' (14:1; 15:7) one another because 'God has accepted' each of them (14:3).[32] It is likely that this matter of schism is still on Paul's mind in his closing salutations, where it is interesting how, immediately after addressing the divided ethnic house churches (16:5ff.), he goes on to exhort them to be vigilant and to 'watch out for those who cause *divisions* ... [and] ... Keep away from them' (16:17; my emphasis).[33] Clearly, as we shall see, Paul is sensitive to the deleterious effects of any kind of unfamilial behaviour of disunity and division that would tarnish the name and reputation of God's household.

These divisions also make sense against the prevailing historical conditions of the time, which contributed towards the ethnic hostilities in the Roman church. Katherine Grieb (2002: 7) states that an 'understanding [of] the situation in the Roman house churches' can be traced back to the time when Claudius expelled Jews from Rome in the edict of AD 49. This expulsion made the reintegration of the Jewish Christians into the remaining and predominantly Gentile church in AD 54 difficult upon their return.[34] The return of the Jewish believers 'exacerbated tensions and mutual suspicions, resulting in a fragmented community incapable of common worship' (Lane 1998: 198). What we find in Rome, then, are several satellite house churches without any 'centralized authority structure', all of which reinforced 'a tendency to fragmentation and dissension' (Witherington with Hyatt 2004: 9).[35] In the light of all of this, how does Paul counter these divided house churches?

---

[32] Note the heavy concentration of family terminology in 14:9–23, where Paul uses 'brothers' (*adelphoi*) four times and most notably in a highly contentious context.

[33] See Donfried (1991: 51–52); Black (1973: 212–213); contra, Moo (1996: 929).

[34] See the discussion in Lane (1998: 198).

[35] Lane (1998: 213) states, 'The impression conveyed by Paul's greetings in Romans 16:3–15 is of a number of small house fellowships not in close relationship with one another.'

Romans: A family letter to unite dysfunctional house churches

Paul responds to these house congregations, factionalized along ethnic lines, by crafting what is essentially 'a family letter' (Bryan 2000: 29).[36] If Paul can enable the Jews and Gentiles to see they belong to the one family of God, he will have gone some way towards achieving his goal. In this respect, Christopher Bryan has identified three main characteristics of a family letter: (1) it was written in order to uphold the good feelings of the household; (2) the recipient is identified using a family designation or term (e.g. 'brother' or 'sister'); (3) a prayer wish is offered on behalf of the recipient. Paul's letter to the Roman believers manifests all of these features. These characteristics are seen (Bryan 2000: 29–31) when ancient letters are set alongside Paul's letter to the Romans.[37]

Herakalas to Horos and Tachonis:

Heraklas to Horos and Tachonis, greetings and good health

I am worried about you. Since we have been on duty we have been sailing in the boat for eight days. With the gods' will, we shall be on board ship in three days. As for the child, watch him as you would an oil lamp, for I worry about you . . .

Paul to the Romans (as cited in Bryan 2000: 31):

Paul [. . .] to all [. . .]

First, I thank my God [. . .] for all of you [. . .] without ceasing I mention you always in my prayers, asking that by God's will I may at last succeed in coming to you. For I long to see you [. . .] I want

---

[36] Bryan (2000: 32) asserts, 'Romans is a family letter . . . [and] that Paul . . . has set his protreptic within the framework of a family letter both confirms and is confirmed by his understanding of the church.' Bryan continues, 'there are real differences within the church – Jew and gentile', but Paul is keen to bring to *mutual tolerance rival groups* within that household at Rome' (my emphasis). For more on family letters see White 1986: 196–197; Stowers 1986: 77, 177–178. See also Klein et al. (2003: 431) who also view Philippians as a 'family letter'.

[37] See Bryan (2000: 30–31) for comparisons with other family letters. Bryan (2000: 30) concludes that the same elements are also present in Romans, which, had it been totally lost apart from Rom. 1:1, 7, 8–10, 13, 'would surely have been classed as a family letter'.

163

you to know, brothers, that I have often intended to come to you, but thus far have been prevented [. . .] (Rom. 1:1, 7, 8–10, 13)

In addition to these family greetings, family letters also contained salutations to various members of the household at the end of the letter.

Appolinarius to Taesis:

Apollinarius to Taesis, his mother and lady, many greetings.

I, then, beg you, mother, look after yourself and do not worry about me, for I have come to a fine place. Please write me a letter about your welfare and that of my brothers ... I salute heartily my brothers and Apollinarius and his children, and Karalas and his children. I salute Ptolomaeus and Ptolemais and Heraclous and her children. I salute all who love you, each by name.

Paul to the Romans (Rom. 16:3, 5, 6, 7, 8, 9, 10, 21, 23) (Bryan 2000: 29–30):

Salute Prisca and Aquila ... Salute my beloved Epaenetus ... Salute Mary ... Salute Andronicus and Junia, my kin ... Salute Ampliatus my beloved ... and my beloved Stachys ... Salute my kin Herodion. The grace of our Lord Jesus Christ be with you. Timothy ... salutes you, so do Lucius and Jason and Sosipater, my kin ... Gaius, who is my host ... salutes you. Erastus ... and our brother Quartus salute you.

In addition to these features, E. Randolf Richards, in a fascinating study on first-century letter writing, concurs but goes further to argue that *all* of Paul's letters should be considered as real 'family letters' (2004: 128–129). He gives several reasons for this, chief of which is the fact that if Paul had been writing to strangers, he would have employed his family name.[38] Paul, however, does not use his family name in any of his letters, the assumption being that his recipients

---

[38] It was commonly noted that a Roman name had three parts: a first name (*praenomen*), a family name (*nomen*) and a surname (*cognomen*). Most likely Saul or Saulos was his first name and Paul or *Paulos* his surname. One other point seldom appreciated is that Paul did not change his name from Saul to Paul when he started working among the Gentiles. Paul held these two names simultaneously (cf. Acts 13:9).

knew him well. Rather, Paul uses only the one name 'Paul', which Richards states 'was the most common *when writing to family*' (my emphasis). Richards continues:

> we should expect the address to read something like 'Saulos Paulos of Tarsus'. Since his family was somewhat prominent . . . we expect him to identify himself by his family name, as was customary. Paul, however, does not.

'Rather than using his earthly household,' Richards concludes (my emphasis),

> he identifies himself as a member of a new household: . . . 'Paul a *servant* of Jesus Christ' (Rom, Phil.). Instead of identifying himself as the son of a prominent household he identifies himself as the *slave* of another.

Two other points are important to note before we move on.

First, not only does Paul employ family language to emphasize the new household of God; he also uses different family terms to highlight the fact that old tensions and divisions have been removed. In 'most of Paul's letters he is either addressing (or there is in the background) the tension between Jewish Christians and Gentile Christians' (Richards 2004: 129), and it is interesting how Paul uses this family language to signal the end of hostilities between them: you are no longer 'Jew' or 'Greek', 'for you are all one in Christ Jesus' (Gal. 3:28). The inference here is that 'When members of warring groups became *slaves in the same household*, hostilities between them had to cease' (Richards 2004: 129; my emphasis). I mention this at this stage because it could have implications for how Paul uses other family language (adoption) in Romans to overcome hostility and division.

Second, we have observed how Paul follows the format of family letters in antiquity, and it is therefore not surprising to learn that Romans itself is shot through with family terminology, with a special concentration in the eighth chapter, where the adoption metaphor is used twice (8:15, 23). The 'family imagery' in Romans 'points not to an agglomeration of individuals but to greater, corporate reality. The family is a . . . kin group, not simply a group of relatives. It is the family or clan *qua* distinct entity that Paul has in view' (Thompson 2000: 129). It is important to elaborate further on the importance of this for what follows.

Generally, Paul refers to the Roman believers by using the most intimate of family expressions, that of 'brothers' (*adelphoi*), found on nineteen occasions (e.g. 1:13; 7:1; 8:12; 10:1; 11:25; 12:1; 14:13, 15 (twice); 15:30; 16:1, 14, 23). This is a measure of how Paul expects the believers to conduct themselves towards one another, as though they are real brothers. In Romans 12:10 Paul employs the composite expression 'brotherly love' (*philadelphia*) to underscore the devotion Christians are to show to each other as members of the family of God.

More important for our theme of adoption is that the metaphor 'father is found more often in Romans than in any other of Paul's letters (e.g. 1:7, 6:4; 8:15)' (Hellerman 2001: 114).[39] Paul uses this expression in different ways in Romans, but he has a predilection for referring to God as 'Father' in the plural possessive pronoun: 'our Father' (a phrase he usually couples with 'our Lord Jesus Christ').[40] This pattern is found in the opening salutation of the letter: 'To *all* in Rome who are loved by God and called to be saints. Grace and peace to you from God *our* Father, and from the Lord Jesus Christ' (1:7; my emphasis). Paul's initial greeting affirms the inclusiveness of Jewish and Gentile believers in the one church he wishes to see being brought into existence in the community: 'to *all* in Rome ... from God *our* Father' (my emphasis). The expression 'father' is also implied and understood when the apostle describes the Christians in Rome by using other family expressions such as 'the sons of God' (*tōn huiōn tou theou*, 8:19), 'children of God' (*teknōn tou theou*, 8:21), and 'heirs' (*klēronomia*, 8:17). And of course he employs the adoption metaphor twice in Romans 8 (vv. 15, 23) and in conjunction with God as 'Father' in Romans 8:15.

A new name

All of these family terms would have struck a chord with Paul's Roman hearers. More important, though, is the fact that the heavy concentration of household terms is used by Paul to describe the ascribed honour attached to those whom God has brought into his household. It is seldom noticed how these family descriptions are skillfully used by Paul in conjunction with other related honour/ shame vocabulary, language found in every major section of the

---

[39] See Burke (2003a: 203–224) for a treatment of *philadelphia* in respect of 1 Thess. 4:9–12.

[40] I owe this thought to Thompson (2000: 118–120).

letter.[41] This heavy concentration of family language, of which adoption is an integral part, in Romans especially highlights the fact, as Philip Esler (2003: 249) insightfully observes, that it is not possible 'to conceive of a family as honourable as the one to which Paul is reminding the Christ-followers of Rome they belong'.[42]

The significance of this language and Paul's adoption term in particular also contrasts God's family with outsiders (e.g. Rom. 1:18–32) and the believers' present standing in Christ prior to their coming to faith. By so doing, their new name[43] and present position in Christ is accentuated over their old, previous name (e.g. 'slaves' [to sin], Rom. 6:17; 8:15) and way of life.[44] Paul makes similar comparisons and contrasts elsewhere in his correspondence. For instance, in his letter to the Ephesians Paul's description of believers' new name as God's 'adopted ... sons' (1:5) stands in stark contrast to the dishonourable family imagery of outsiders, '*Like the rest*, we were by nature children of wrath' (Eph. 2:3, *ēmetha tekna physei orgēs hos kai hoi loipoi*), who at one time followed the ways of this world by living as, literally, 'sons of disobedience' (Eph. 2:3, *huiois tēs apeitheias*).[45] Such language is a useful reminder to Paul's readers of their previous life in the world and the sin from which they have been delivered.

Now the problem that confronts the apostle Paul as he contemplates visiting the church at Rome, however, is that the Jewish and Gentile house churches in Rome are living dishonourably – instead of concord and unanimity, discord and division are evident, which dishonours the 'Father' or the family reputation. Paul is fully cognizant of the fact that internal strife and disunity will besmirch the reputation and honour of the household of God in the eyes of those outside the

---

[41] E.g. *timē*, 'honour' (2:7, 10; 9:21; 13:7); *doxa*, 'glory' (1:23; 2:7; 3:7; 5:2; 6:4; 8:18, 21; 9:4; 11:36; 16:27); *doxazō*, 'to glorify' (1:21; 8:30; 11:30; 15:6, 9); *epainos*, 'praise' (2:29; 13:3) etc. See Moxnes 1988a: 207–218. See especially Moxnes (1988a: 217 n. 15) for a list of such terms. See also Elliott 1994: 174–176.

[42] See also Malina 2001: 32.

[43] Williams (1999: 83 n. 137) states that 'in ... adoption, adopted sons were obligated to perpetuate the *nomen* ... and [this] duty was accomplished by taking the full name of the adoptive father ... '

[44] Interestingly, the 'slave' metaphor has a double edge to it. In Romans Paul writes that once the believers were 'slaves to sin' (Rom. 8:17), who through being justified by faith have become 'slaves to God' (Rom. 8:22) (Harris 1999: 80–86).

[45] The NIV misses the family language in its translation of both these phrases, which are rendered, 'those who are disobedient' (2:2) and 'we were by nature *objects* of wrath' (2:3). Other insulting and dishonourable terms, elsewhere in the New Testament, include for instance 'you brood of vipers' (Matt. 3:7), 'you are of your father the devil' (John 8:44) and compare the better and honourable title of 'house of David' to 'house of Herschel'.

church, since harmony and unity are the central values for natural families in the ancient world (deSilva 2000: 169). To be sure, Paul does not discuss these divisions until later in the letter (Rom. 14 – 15), but it is important to note that he introduces this family terminology and the adoption metaphor in particular (see further below) as a means of building towards and resolving these divisions, and signals the kind of united church family he wishes to see. The tensions in the churches are essentially ethnic and also centre around the consumption of certain kinds of food. Although Paul never actually identifies the 'weak' or the 'strong' apart from 14:2, where he says the 'weak' eat only vegetables, it seems that these are terms 'the Roman house churches' (presumably, the initiative coming from the 'strong') use to describe each other. The question of how Paul is going to help the Roman believers overcome these divisions and unite them is a challenge, and raises the question of where his adoption metaphor fits in and how he uses it to help them overcome their differences.

Adoption: A metaphor of inclusion for Jew and Gentile into God's family

There is little doubt that Paul has the Jewish–Gentile factions in view: evident from a close reading of the letter's contents, which shows that this issue is never far from his agenda. Indeed, 'the persistent focus on the relationship of Jews and Gentiles provides the dominant framework' (Lane 1998: 201) throughout the letter, as David deSilva (2004: 606; my emphasis) has noted:[46]

> The theme that neither Jew nor Gentile holds privileged status in God's sight and the way these diverse ethnic bodies are brought together in a single, unified community *gives coherence to the whole of Romans*, especially chapters 1–11 and 14–15.

This ethnic theme surfaces right at the beginning of the letter in 1:16–17, where Paul reminds his readers that he is not ashamed of the gospel because 'it is the power of God for the salvation of everyone who believes; *first for the Jew, then for the Gentile*' (my emphasis).[47]

---

[46] Dunn (1998: 372) also notes that the word ' "All" is one of the really key words in Romans . . . The "all" consistently means Jew as well as Gentile, Gentile as well as Jew.'

[47] See Jewett (2003: 93) for how 'honour' as an important social value is shot through the entire letter. In regard to Rom. 1:16–17 he states, 'According to the standards of the culture, he should be ashamed of proclaiming the crucified one as the redeemer of the world, including even the barbarians and the uneducated' (Jewett 1997: 253–278).

Moreover, this refrain recurs throughout the discourse of the letter (cf. 1:16; 2:9ff., 25ff.; 3:9, 29; 9 – 11; 10:12; 14:1 – 15:13), which serves the purpose of emphasizing the Jewish–Gentile divisions in the church and is Paul's means of stressing the equality of both Jew and Greek and the need to belong in one united church, the family of faith.[48] Repeatedly mentioning the Jews and Gentiles in juxtaposition to each other is Paul's way of stressing the *equality* between them; indeed, this equality is especially seen in respect of sin and justification (Chae 1997: 72).[49] As regards the former and in the first part of the letter (Rom. 1:18 – 3:20), Paul states, 'There will be trouble and distress for every human being who does evil: first for the Jew, then for the Gentile' (2:9). All without exception are indicted – Jews and Gentiles are on equal terms – and under sin, as Paul further states: '*all* who sin apart from the law will also perish apart from the law, and *all* who sin under the law will be judged by the law' (2:12; my emphasis), for 'Jews and Gentiles alike are *all* under sin' (3:9; my emphasis). Paul concludes with a statement of the universal sinfulness of humankind: '*all* have sinned and fall short of the glory of God' (3:23; my emphasis).

In the next section of the letter (3:21 – 4:25) the apostle points out that not only is there equality in respect of Jew and Gentile as sinners, but 'there is equality of Jew and Gentile in justification' (Chae 1997: 153). In this part of the letter Paul immediately sets up the question in 3:29–30: 'Is God the God of Jews only? Is he not the God of Gentiles too? . . . since there is only one God, who will justify the circumcised by faith and the uncircumcised through that same faith.' Paul then proceeds to demonstrate this through using Abraham as an example of the importance of justification by faith for Jew and Gentile alike. Abraham's faith was credited to him as righteousness prior to his being circumcised (when he resembled a Gentile), and it is only through this same faith that both Jew and Gentile can ever have Abraham as their father. Paul comments in regard to Gentiles in Romans 4:11, 'he [Abraham] is the father of all who believe but have not been circumcised, in order that righteousness might be credited to them'. In the next verse he addresses this and has his own people, the Jews, in view: 'And he is also the father of the circumcised who not only are circumcised but who also

---

[48] See Chae (1997: 6), who argues that Paul repeatedly in Romans 'affirms the *equality* of the Jew and Gentile' in presenting himself as the apostle to the Gentiles (my emphasis).

[49] I owe some of this discussion to Chae.

walk in the footsteps of the faith that our father Abraham had before he was circumcised' (4:12). Paul's interpretation of the story of Abraham 'is uniquely surprising' (Chae 1997: 203), but he makes the unmistakable soteriological point that 'Jews and Gentiles are fundamentally equal' (Chae 1997: 204). In other words, through the same faith that the patriarch exercised, Jews and Gentiles find that he 'is the father of us all ... He is *our* father' (Rom. 4:16–17; my emphasis).

If Jews and Gentiles are equal in the sight of God in terms of being sinners and in respect of justification, can we make a similar conclusion as far as their both being adopted into God's family is concerned? As far as the Jews were concerned, Paul would have been aware that the term 'sons' had long been associated with Jews in the Old Testament (e.g. Deut. 14:1–2). But Paul also understands the Israelites as having been *adopted* by God (Rom. 9:4). What about the Gentiles? Do they equally qualify as God's adopted sons and daughters? The same inclusivity and equality, I believe, are continued and developed in the next major section of the letter (Rom. 5 – 8), evident by the repeated use of the first- and second-person personal pronouns 'we' (e.g. 5:1, 11, 21; 6:23; 8:35) and 'you' (Rom. 8:15, 23) (Chae 1997: 207; Thompson 2000: 129). Indeed, in Romans 8 'the pronouns and verbs from Romans 8:1 through the end of the chapter are almost all plural' (Thompson 2000: 129) and are particularly dense in the adoption passage itself (Fee 1994: 585).

The concentration of pronouns and verbs shows that Paul wants to make a point about *both* Jews and Gentiles in relation to adoption into God's family. Within the context of the argument and set against the schismatic background of the ethnic house churches, Paul's *huiothesia* metaphor functions as part of his rhetorical strategy to bring the rival ethnic groups together into the one household in order to accomplish his goal. By so doing, there is an emphasis upon the inclusiveness Paul is eager to bring about: he takes an expression that he associates with the Israelites and applies it to Gentile Christians. He writes in Romans 8:15, 'you (pl. *elabete*) [Jewish and Gentile believers] have received the Spirit of adoption as sons' (Chae 1997: 226).[50] What is extraordinary and radical is that Paul as a Jewish convert should use the same term *huiothesia* in respect of Gentile believers as well (Rom. 8:15, 23). The fact is that both Jews and Gentiles are adopted into God's household and both are equally able

---

[50] Chae uses the general term 'sonship' and misses the uniqueness of the term *huiothesia* in vv. 15 and 23.

to call upon him as Father, as Thompson (2000: 127; my emphasis) has carefully observed:

Paul's declaration that ... those in Christ know and acknowledge God as Father does not speak only of the benefits of being in Christ but, rather, further advances the whole thrust of the argument in Romans that *in Christ God has abolished the divisions between Jew and Gentile and adopted them together into the one family.*[51]

The pervasiveness of the theme of equality between Jew and Gentile is now apparent and comes to a suitable climax with Paul's use of his adoption metaphor, which he uses to resolve the pastoral problem by enabling the Jewish and Gentile house churches to see that they belong together as members in a single household – the *familia Dei.* Moreover, when Paul comes to write chapters 9 – 11 (where he deals with the dilemma of his own unbelieving people), he does not leave any room for a triumphalist attitude by either party: the 'Gentile believers should not think that their adoption has nullified the original adoption of Israel' (Dunn 1988: 533) an adoption that is irrevocable (Walters 2003: 65), and Israel should also recognize that the Gentiles' adoption is not inferior to theirs. Both owe their adoption to the grace of God and, just as God has accepted them, they should also accept one another.

Paul's *huiothesia* expression in Romans 8 and 9 is all-encompassing and unites the factionalized house churches by underscoring that *both* have a legitimate claim to belong in the one household of God (Atkins 1991: 182). In this way, Paul's 'adoption terminology functions ... *as a metaphor of inclusion* ... [that] ... *confers equality among the* [believers in the] ... *Pauline faction*' (182; my emphasis).

Uppermost in Paul's mind, then, is that 'Unity is to be pursued so that the church worships God together in harmony. A harmonious church would bring *honour* and praise to God's name' (Schreiner 1998: 23; my emphasis). Paul is keenly aware that both the Father's and the Christian family's name and reputation are at stake and he is

[51] Thompson makes an important observation here that Rom. 4 and Rom. 8 are linked by the common theme of paternity. Thompson (2000: 131) concludes on the matter, 'the adoption of the children of God is the gospel, now expressed in language of family and inheritance. This gospel speaks of God's faithfulness to the Jews, the children of Abraham, and God's mercy to the Gentiles, also the children of Abraham. To speak of God as Father is to underscore God's faithfulness to Israel, "to whom belongs the adoption," and God's mercy towards the Gentiles who, as the heirs of God through Christ have received adoption as children and the promised inheritance.'

keen to protect it. To be sure, Paul's purpose is 'to uphold the relationships and good feelings of the household' (Bryan 2000: 31), but his aim goes above and beyond this to the need for tolerance, *acceptance* and unity (cf. Rom. 14:1; 15:7) among the Roman house churches. Specifically, the disparate and ethnically diverse house congregations in Rome need to recognize that as a result of their adoption, God has brought them together as '*a new family*, a third race, *neither Jew nor Gentile* but "in Christ"' (N. T. Wright 1992: 450; my emphasis).

The Holy Spirit: God's honourable approval of our *huiothesia*

We noted in an earlier chapter how the Spirit in Paul's conception is inseparably bound with *huiothesia*. When God justifies people, he also adopts them as his children and favourably places his own life within, the life-giving power and energy of the Holy Spirit (Rom. 8:14–15; Gal. 4:4–6). As with all of God's soteriological benefits, his giving of his Spirit to his children is an honour bestowed upon them and not something that can be earned or boasted about (Jewett 2003: 98). Certainly, prayer is one means of grace by which the affirmation of God is received (Rom. 8:16, 26–27), but we should not overlook the reception of the Spirit as God's approval and assurance that the Christian is an adopted child of God. Immediately after Paul has discussed adoption (8:15), he goes on to write that 'The Spirit himself testifies with our spirit that we are God's children' (8:16). The reception of the Holy Spirit is not only the honourable mark that God's adopted children belong in his household, but is also the indispensable proof and evidence of God's acceptance of them. God's giving of his Holy Spirit to his adopted sons legitimizes their new filial disposition and is the Father's 'approval' and witness ('*God* sent the Spirit of his Son into our hearts', Gal. 4:6; my emphasis) of our acceptance into his household. The reality and presence of the Holy Spirit is 'God's positive affirmation to the believers in the midst of unbeliever's censure' (deSilva 2000: 58). All of God's adopted children possess the Spirit (no Spirit, no adoption[52]) and are expected to obey their 'Father' and manifest the family likeness. James I. Packer's comment is a reminder of the responsibility and obligation of the believer's

[52] See chapter 6, where this viewpoint is adduced.

adoption: 'The Father impels us to act up to our position as royal children by manifesting the family likeness ... and maintaining the *family honour* (i.e., seeking God's glory)' (Packer 1988: 247; my emphasis).

What Paul writes here strikes a chord in relation to Jesus' sonship in the Gospel narratives, where immediately prior to embarking on his public ministry Christ had his sonship authenticated and approved by his Father through the Spirit at his baptism. In the Gospel of Mark the evangelist describes the double confirmation by the Father and the Spirit at the moment when Jesus came up out of the water: 'he saw heaven being torn open and the Spirit descending on him like a dove ... "You are my Son, whom I love; with you I am well pleased"' (Mark 1:10–11). The coming of the Spirit at this strategic moment – the inauguration of Jesus' earthly ministry – is important, as it is God's approval of Christ's sonship. Of no less importance is what follows: 'At once the Spirit sent him out into the desert, and he was in the desert for forty days, being tempted by Satan' (Mark 1:12–13). Although Mark does not include an account of the temptation narrative, Matthew (Matt. 4:1–11) and Luke (Luke 4:1–13) do, where both evangelists combine the notions of 'leading' (Matt. 4:1; Luke 4:1), 'sonship' (Matt. 4:3, 4; Luke 4:3, 9) and the 'Spirit' (Matt. 4:1; Luke 4:1). In particular, Matthew and Luke record how Satan's temptations of Jesus strike at the very heart of his filial relationship with his Father: 'If you are the *Son of God*, tell these stones to become bread' (Matt. 4:3; my emphasis);[53] 'If you are the *Son of God* ... throw yourself down' (Matt. 4:6; my emphasis).[54] In the face of temptation and at a time of extreme vulnerability after forty days of fasting, Jesus demonstrated allegiance and complete obedience to his Father's will.[55] With this is in view, it is interesting how Paul also combines

[53] Notice also how Luke especially stresses that the temptations of Jesus in the wilderness were not a 'one-off' but were a continual challenge during his earthly career: 'When the devil had finished all this tempting, *he left him until an opportune time*' (Luke 4:13; my emphasis).

[54] Interestingly, Matthew the evangelist (cf. also Luke 4:3, 9) employs two conditional clauses in vv. 3 and 6 by use of the Greek word *ei* (if), thereby presenting the condition as if it were so ('since'). However, Satan has more sinister motives in view; namely, to lure Jesus away from dependence upon his Father.

[55] The informed reader will have noted Jesus' deliberate citation of Old Testament Scripture; i.e. Deuteronomy in rebutting Satan's temptations. Furthermore, in the first temptation and Jesus' response there are several interesting and significant parallels centring on the common theme of the sonship of both Jesus and the nation of Israel. Both are 'sons' (Deut. 8:5; cf. Matt. 4:3, 6); both are 'led' (Deut. 8:2; cf. Matt. 4:1); both are taken to the desert/wilderness (Deut. 8:2; cf. Matt. 4:1); and both hunger (Deut. 8:3;

the three notions of 'leading', 'sonship' and the 'Spirit' in Romans 8:14: 'those who are led by the Spirit are sons of God'. Thus, just as Jesus as God's Son demonstrated obedience to his Father in the face of adversity and temptation, those whom God has made his children through an act of *huiothesia* must not show any less commitment and compliance to doing the will of their heavenly Father.[56]

This latter point is what Paul drives at in Romans 8:17, where adopted sons, who share in the sonship of Christ, also share in his sufferings (Kim 1981: 317–318; Dunn 1988: 464). Even though the Roman Christians are in possession of this most honourable status as adopted sons of God, they presently face hardship and opposition as they struggle on to glory (8:18). Paul knows full well that 'our present sufferings are not worth comparing with the glory that will be revealed in us' (Rom. 8:18ff.). The reality of being God's adopted children does not negate the fact that this will also mean sharing in the sufferings of Christ (8:17ff.).

Paul is also cognizant of the fact that there is a certain ambivalence as far as the Galatian Christians' status in the sight of God and others is concerned: within God's court of reputation (deSilva 2000: 55), the believers in Rome are adopted sons and daughters, but in the view of outsiders they are adopted sons without honour.[57] What matters most, however, is their familial (Moxnes 1988a: 216) membership in the divine household and the encouragement and support they receive from their brothers and sisters in Christ. David deSilva (2000: 211) writes in this regard, 'While the non-Christians may thus challenge the believers' honor, God himself, in the fellowship of the family of faith, continuously affirms the believers' honor as his own children.' Additionally, prayer and the encouragement of other believers in the church family are further vital stimuli to counter the strong pull and

---

cf. Matt. 4:2). The difference is that whereas God *tests* Israel as son to determine the nation's loyalty, Satan in Matthew's account *tempts* the Son of God. And, most important of all, whereas Israel as the son of God in the wilderness fails, Jesus as the Son of God prevails. The text in Deut. 8:2–5 is worth citing in full to see the parallels: 'Remember how the LORD your God led you all the way in the desert these forty years, to humble you and to test you in order to know what was in your heart, whether or not you would keep his commands. He humbled you, causing you to hunger and then feeding you with manna, which neither you nor your fathers had known, to teach you that man does not live on bread alone but on every word that comes from the mouth of the LORD. Your clothes did not wear out and your feet did not swell during these forty years. Know then in your heart that as a man disciplines his son, so the LORD your God disciplines you.'

[56] Smail (1980: 159) puts it well when he comments, 'The essence of sonship is trustful obedience . . .'

[57] New Testament scholars refer to this as 'status inconsistency' (deSilva 2000: 209).

temptations of a godless society and culture. These 'significant others' who also constitute the court of reputation have a crucial function in supporting and strengthening those whom God has adopted into his household.[58]

Summary

In the ancient world when a *paterfamilias* (head of the household) adopted a son, the latter's honour and status increased because of his new association and belonging. Against this background, we observed how Paul in his letter to the Galatian believers wastes no time in the opening salutation by registering his astonishment at his converts' desertion of God (Gal. 1:6). Paul particularly takes issue with certain agitators who are seeking kudos by foisting circumcision upon the Galatian Christians. The apostle could quite easily stress his own Jewish credentials (Gal. 1:13ff.) to emphasize his acquired honour, but chooses instead to point to the greater honour ascribed by God's call and conversion and the loyalty expected of Paul as a follower of the Son of God (cf. Gal. 1:11–12; 2:20). Paul portrays the Galatians' abandonment of God in personal and paternal terms evident by the many references to the 'Father' in the opening verses of the letter that converge in Galatians 4:6 with adoption. The Galatians have singularly failed to grasp the fact that there is no higher honour than belonging to the household of this Father God. The significance of being adopted children of the Father, the very one who initiated their salvation, is therefore set before the Galatian believers to remind them of the need to demonstrate unswerving and continued allegiance (3:1–5) to this *patēr*, who had called them by his grace.

In his letter to the Romans Paul approaches the subject of adoption from a different perspective. The apostle writes to the believers primarily to inform them of his impending missionary visit to Spain and to Rome and provides the most substantive treatment of his doctrine of justification by faith. Paul does not wish his readers to be in any doubt about his understanding of the gospel. In addition, other secondary reasons for Paul's writing this letter exist; namely, the need to address the division between Jews and Gentiles. The situation was such that separate house churches, divided along ethnic lines, were worshipping in different parts of the metropolis. While Paul does not deal with these divisions until chapters 14 and 15, the repeated

[58] Paul and Timothy, e.g., were 'significant others' for believers to imitate and follow (cf. 1 Cor. 4:14–21) (Burke 2003b: 95–113).

175

references to Jew and Gentile early in the letter and throughout, coupled with his strategic use of the adoption metaphor (Rom. 8, 9) build towards this and indicate the united household of God he is anxious to see. Fully cognizant of the consequences that a factionalized household in the ancient world would cause, Paul's adoption metaphor is a rhetorical tool he employs to stress the need for acceptance between Jews and Gentiles and the shared honour of being members of the one household of God (cf. Rom. 8:15; 9:4).

Having been adopted into God's family, God manifests and affirms his approval of believers by favourably bestowing his Holy Spirit upon them. Even though God's adopted children are honoured in his sight, they are held in contempt and dishonour by outsiders. In times of adversity and testing, however, the response of Jesus, the Son of God, serves as the example and stimulus for the Christian to emulate. According to the apostle Paul, unwavering loyalty and obedience to the Father are two of the authentic marks of the adopted child of God.

Chapter Eight

Adoption and living between the 'now' and 'not yet'

We have observed during the course of this study how Paul's adoption metaphor expresses the eschatological tension evidenced in other soteriological terms: believers on the one hand are already adopted into the family of God (Rom. 8:15), while on the other hand the full implications of their adoption still lie ahead: 'Not only so, but we ourselves, who have the first fruits of the Spirit, groan inwardly *as we wait* eagerly for our adoption as sons, the redemption of our bodies' (Rom. 8:23; my emphasis). Adoption thus spans the present as well as the future. The dialectic between the 'now' and the 'not yet' raises an important question concerning the redemptive purposes of God: What lies in the interval between this present reality of already being God's children and the full consummation of adoption? This intervening period is the subject that dominates the apostle's discussion in Romans 8:18–27, which has been rightly described as 'the most explicitly eschatological section of Romans' (Johnson 1997: 126).[1] Here eschatological expressions, with a distinctive familial flavour, abound. For example, Paul makes reference to 'sons of God' (*huioi tou theou*, v. 19), 'children of God' (*tekna tou theou*, v. 19) and 'adoption as sons' (*huiothesian*, v. 23). Indeed, regarding Paul's frequent use of these familial expressions, and *huiothesia* in particular, Marcus Loane (1968: 76; my emphasis) makes the important point:

This is the last reference in this chapter to our *adoption*, and it refers to the recognition of our status in the day of glory. St. Paul alternates between *sons* and *children* throughout the whole of this

---

[1] Esler (2003: 261) makes the point that Paul's understanding of the 'now' and the 'not yet' as an eschatological expression is very different from the timescale of twenty-first-century modern people. 'Time' in the ancient Mediterranean world was very different from the 'Swiss' time of modern people. Thus the ancients did not think of a point in time but in 'terms of a natural process occurring in the present that would produce a result in the future, unless a disaster occurred … When exactly that potentiality might be realized was not an issue as it would be for us. Rather the item at issue is the inevitability of the outcomes rather then how many and when.'

177

passage (8:14–23): his use of such terms was synonymous, but the underlying idea of *adoption* was dominant.

If Paul's overriding concern in these verses is with God's adopted sons, he particularly stresses the fact that their final adoption will not be lightly entered into because they, along with the whole cosmos (including the subhuman order), are caught up in this limbo period of suffering as everything moves inexorably towards a glorious future. In Romans 8:18–27 the final adoption of the sons of God and the cosmic renewal of all things join hands.

To understand these verses, we need to determine how they fit into the surrounding context.

Romans 8:18–27 in context

The wider context

Many scholars (e.g. Byrne, Moo, Schreiner) rightly recognize that Romans 8:18–27 is situated in the second major part of the letter that began in 5:1ff. In Romans 5:1ff. Paul discusses the fruits of the believer's justified status, which include peace with God (5:1), access into God's presence (5:2), the ability to rejoice in the hope of the glory of God (5:3), and the (unexpected) mention of rejoicing in sufferings (5:3).[2] It is hope (cf. 8:22, 24, 25) and suffering (8:18), leading to glory, that Paul picks up again in 8:17–27. Thus chapter 5:1–11 and Romans 8:18–39 function like 'two bookends' to the apostle's argument in Romans 5 – 8. The thematic link between the two chapters is clearly evident when these two chapters are set side by side:[3]

	Romans 5:1–11	Romans 8:18–39
love (of God/Christ)	5:5, 8	8:35, 39
justify	5:1, 9	8:30 (twice), 33
glory	5:2	8:18, 21, 30
hope	5:2, 4, 5	8:20, 24 (four times), 25
tribulation/suffering	5:3 (twice)	8:18, 25
save	5:9, 10	8:24
endurance/perseverance	5:3, 4	8:25

Table 8.1

[2] The latter is not a 'fruit' of the believer's justified status.
[3] This table is slightly adapted from Moo 2000: 272.

Romans 8:18–27 is part of this major section and brings Paul's argument in Romans 5 to a suitable climax. Once 'we recognize the *inclusio* that frames these chapters, we can conclude their overall purpose is *to convince the justified believers that they have assurance* for the last judgment' (Moo 2000: 272–273; my emphasis). To be sure, the present will be characterized by suffering and Paul is enough of a realist to know that although believers are part of God's family through adoption, they are not exempt from the realities and sufferings that are part of daily Christian living. Paul even views himself as intricately involved in the unfolding of this cosmic drama, evident by his repeated use of the first-person plural (e.g. '*our* struggle', v. 18; 'revealed in *us*', v. 18; '*we* know', v. 22; '*we* ourselves … groan', v. 23; '*we* were saved', v. 24; 'the Spirit helps *us*', vv. 26–27). But this struggle is only a preface to the glorious and certain future that awaits all of God's spiritual offspring.

The immediate context

Romans 8:18–27 is connected to the immediately preceding passage 8:12–17, where, after discussing adoption (8:15), Paul links this to the suffering of Jesus the Son in verse 17: 'if we are children, then we are heirs – heirs of God and co-heirs with Christ, *if indeed we share in his sufferings* in order *that we may also share in his glory*' (my emphasis). In the earlier pericope (8:12–17), adoptive sonship (8:15) and suffering (8:17) are closely woven together, and these twin ideas are repeated and further developed by Paul in 8:18–27: adoption in verse 23 and the suffering motif, depicted as 'groaning' in verses 22, 23, 26. Taken together, these verses represent an especially rich discussion of the adopted sons' place in the family of God and the tension they experience in the present era over against the future that lies ahead. In particular, the emphasis in 8:18–27 falls on the future adoption of the sons of God and our final salvation, which has anthropological and cosmological significance and effect (Peterson 2001: 164; Witherington with Hyatt 2004: 221).

Structurally, Romans 8:18–27 comprises three passages (vv. 18–22, 23–25, 27–28) and there are reasonable grounds for considering all three, since there are several recurring themes, even though there is disagreement over the relationship of the last passage to the preceding two.[4] These themes include 'groaning' (vv. 22, 23, 26), 'hope' (vv. 20, 24–25), 'expectation' (vv. 19, 23, 25), 'sonship' (vv. 19, 21), and

---

[4] I am indebted to Byrne (1979: 104) for this breakdown of the passage.

'adoption' (v. 23). Each of these themes falls within the 'subject of action': 'creation' (vv. 19–21), 'believers' (vv. 23–25) and the 'Spirit' (vv. 26–27). While there is a close parallel between the first two passages in regard to the themes of expectation and adoption or sonship, the inclusion of verses 26–27 is a little more difficult. The recurrence of the 'groaning' motif (v. 26) coupled with the connecting expression 'in the same way' (*hōsautōs de kai*, v. 26), however, 'suggest that Paul has in mind a parallel in this case too ... *so that all three elements ... would stand revealed as involving a groaning expectation of Christian sonship of God*' (Byrne 1979: 104; my emphasis). So while Paul does not mention the metaphor of adoption in verses 26–27, he does mention the Spirit and, given that some commentators view the 'inarticulate groans of believers ... are taken up by the Spirit's silent intercession on behalf of the *children of God*' (Jewett 2004: 202; my emphasis), there is sufficient merit for considering verses 26–27 as well.

One other point requires to be mentioned before we look at these verses in further detail; namely, the underlying Jewish apocalyptic currents in these verses. Scholars differ over the exact sources Paul uses here but the cataclysmic events of the end times, the mention of the first fruits of the Spirit, the influence of sin and its effects on the creation, and the renewed order are all regular motifs in apocalyptic literature in the intertestamental period (e.g. *4 Ezra* 7:11; *1 Enoch* 51:4–5; *2 Apocalypse of Baruch* 29:1–2, 5–8). Paul no doubt takes these and reworks them for his own purposes. More important, however, are the links with the Old Testament, where in Isaiah 65:17– 19, for instance, God gives the promise

> Behold, I will create
>> new heavens and a new earth.
> The former things will not be remembered,
>> nor will they come to mind ...
> the sound of weeping and of crying
>> will be heard in it no more.

Sonship, suffering and the future glory of the non-human created order (vv. 18–22)

Paul is concerned with the non-human created order in verses 19–22, but he prefaces this in verse 18 with a discussion of the believer to show the latter's involvement in the present predicament, a matter we shall consider in greater detail in verses 23–25. He does this in order to demonstrate that the rest of the created order is not only dependent upon but also looks to the sons of God for its future liberation. Put differently, the notion of sonship, not the non-material creation, is the more prominent idea in this passage. Paul writes, 'I consider that our present sufferings are not worth comparing with the glory that will be revealed in us' (v. 18). The verb 'I consider' (*logizomai*) has been understood by some commentators to be taken from the realm of accountancy (Loane 1968: 76; see also Olyott 1979: 76). Accordingly, Paul would seem to be saying that when present sufferings and future glory are balanced against each other, the scales always come down in favour of the latter. It is better, however, to take this term to be expressing 'strong assurance and not doubt . . . since Paul is making a theological declaration in light of his own faith and hope' (Newman & Nida 1973: 157). In Paul's mind there is no doubt about the glorious unveiling of the future, even though the period between the now and the not yet is characterized by present suffering that, states the apostle, continues right up to the moment of liberation.

When Paul talks of 'glory' (v. 18), he is of course referring to the final phase of redemption (cf. v. 23), when salvation will be complete (cf. 8:30). Indeed, the term 'glory' functions as an *inclusio* in this passage, beginning in verse 18 ('the glory that will be revealed in us') and finishing in verse 30 ('those . . . he also glorified'). Moreover, this glory is already in existence (and we can see it on the horizon), but it awaits the moment of full unveiling, and, says Paul, it will be revealed *in us* (*eis hēmas*, v. 18); that is, in our own bodies (v. 23, see later).[5] Paul is alluding to the future resurrection, but for the present, believers experience sufferings that are fleeting and transient and pale into insignificance when set alongside the future glory that awaits them. A similar thought is expressed elsewhere by Paul in 2 Corinthians 4:17: 'our light and momentary troubles are achieving for us an eternal glory that far outweighs them all' (cf. 2 *Apoc. Bar.* 15:8). Such sufferings, which all children of God must endure, are directly related to their union with Christ and his sufferings (8:17; cf. Phil. 1:29).[6]

[5] Morris (1988: 320) states that the 'preposition is not the one we might have expected'. He concludes that Paul 'may mean that in the coming age all that is involved in our being "sons of God" will become apparent and that this will take place in us as well as to us' (see also Witherington with Hyatt 2004: 222).

[6] According to Brendan Byrne (1986: 165) verses 19–22 are 'one of the most curious and fascinating passages in Romans. Its distinctiveness lies in the fact that here for the first time in his extant letters Paul considers human beings in relation to the non-human created world.'

Verse 19 is connected to verse 18 by the postpositive particle *gar*, 'for' (which the NIV misses) – Paul is here arguing in a logical manner and these verses are links in a chain that unfold his reasoning. The glory mentioned previously is prefaced with groaning or sufferings that Paul twins with the notion of sonship; suffering and sonship (as in the life of Christ) are not only suffused together in Paul's eschatology, but are also two sides of the same coin. The Greek word Paul employs for 'sufferings' is *pathēma*, which connotes sufferings of any kind (BDAG 2000: 747). For God's children who live on this side of eternity, sufferings may be manifested through persecution, illness, bereavement and, of course, death itself. Certainly, the nature of suffering for those who belong to the household of faith may differ, but whatever one's background, no-one is exempt, a point well stated by Loane (1968: 76; my emphasis) when he writes:

> St. Paul's basic idea was that suffering in one form or another belongs to the experience of *all who are members of God's house-hold* ... Not all are martyrs; not all are captives; not all are driven into exile for Christ's sake; not all are in fact called upon to bear insult, scorn, or assault on the open stage of the world's hostility. Many indeed are still called, just as many were called when St. Paul wrote these words, for the world is no more in love with God and his *children* now than it was before. And yet even those whose path has been most sheltered in the goodness of God will be called to endure suffering somehow, some time, in the course of this life, if they ... live as *sons of God.*

While the above examples of suffering may not be the lot of all of God's sons and daughters, in the present context the suffering and afflictions Paul has in view are more to do with their being a part of the old created order, with all its limitations, weaknesses and frustrations. In all of this, Paul is careful to show that suffering for the sons of God is not meaningless, a point he also draws out earlier in chapter 5:1ff. to demonstrate how suffering and perseverance have a divine purpose: the strengthening of hope. Just as Paul states in an earlier related passage that through suffering hope is fortified when God pours his love into our hearts through the Holy Spirit (5:4–5), similarly, in Romans 8:17ff. he says that sufferings for the child of God are not meaningless. To the contrary, they are meaning*ful*, for they too are anchored in hope (cf. vv. 24–25) and are steps along the pathway that leads towards a glorious future. Although God's people are sons already, this honourable status may be veiled to the eyes of a watching world; indeed, just as Christ was 'dishonoured' through his sufferings (Rom. 8:17) and his sonship went unrecognized, so the present is also the time when believers live as 'sons without honour' (Moxnes 1988b: 73). But there will surely come a time (Moxnes 1988b: 73), of this Paul has no doubt, when that sonship will be manifestly known to all as 'they look forward to the eschatological moment when they will be glorified with Jesus. Then the entire world will recognize their honour, when it will be openly manifest for all to see that they truly are the sons of God.'

The manner in which Paul links sonship with the term *ktisis* in verse 19 is not only striking, but demonstrates the connection between the two: 'the *ktisis* waits in eager expectation for *the sons (huioi) of God* to be revealed' (v. 19). Before we look at the linkage of these two ideas, we need to determine the meaning of the word *ktisis*. The term can refer to the activity of creating or the thing that is created.[7] J. R. Michaels pursues the latter interpretation and understands Paul as referring to human 'creatures' (Michaels 1999: 111) but it is strange for Paul to say 'the *creature* waits in eager expectation for the children of God to be revealed', which drives a wedge between 'the creature' and the 'children of God' as they are described in this passage.[8] In addition, if, as most commentators agree, Paul alludes to the Genesis account here, what does it mean to say that the 'creature' was subjected to frustration through no choice of its own? This surely was not the case with Adam. The context militates against such a reading because Paul goes on to describe how this part of creation did *not* have a role to play in bringing about the condition in which it now finds itself. It is better to understand Paul as focusing on the *subhuman* or *non-human* (Adams 2002: 28) creation (animals, shrubs, rocks), since he goes on in verse 23 to describe the suffering of the human creation. It is the subhuman order that is of immediate concern to Paul.

The link between 'children' and 'creation' is again made in verse 21, where Paul proceeds to state that the sub-human order will one day be set free to enjoy the glory of the *children (tekna) of God*. Not only does the creation 'groan', but believers, identified later as adopted sons (v. 23), also 'groan' inwardly (vv. 22–23). In these statements there is a solidarity between the created order and the children of God, in the sense that the creation's destiny is not only

---

[7] See Cranfield (1975: 411) for eight different possible readings.
[8] I owe this point to Witherington with Hyatt 2004: 224 n. 9.

dependent but is also contingent upon the children of God.[9] In all this, creation, the non-human order (see below for this view), was not itself responsible for bringing about its present predicament of bondage, but is instead a passive partner in the cosmic drama and outworking of God's future plans of restoration.

Even though Paul is talking about the created order in impersonal terms, he nevertheless personalizes it in a most graphic and unusual manner, similar to the authors in the Old Testament (e.g. Isa. 55:12)! Paul employs a forceful compound word *apokaradokia*, which comprises two Greek terms, *kara* (head) and *dekomai* (to stretch) with the prefix *apo* (away from), conveying a most vivid image of creation craning its neck as it looks forward to the day of its emancipation.[10] While Paul discusses the non-created order in these verses, the emphasis in verses 18–22 is especially on those described as 'sons of God' (v. 19) and 'children of God' (v. 22). Creation, says Schreiner (1998: 437),

> does not constitute the centre stage of Paul's vision. What creation longs for and waits for is the eschatological unveiling of the children of God. The focus is not finally on the transformation of the created world, although that is included, but the future redemption that awaits God's children.

That is to say, what creation is looking for is the disclosure of the sons of God, signalling the time of renewal for the entire cosmos.

The logic of Paul's argument is propelled forward in verse 20 with the same connecting particle as before: '*for* the creation was subjected to frustration, not by its own choice, but by the will of the one who subjected it'. On a cursory reading of this verse one cannot help being struck by the allusions the apostle makes to the creation story in Genesis. For sure, Paul does not explicitly mention the 'fall', but there are allusions to the Genesis account.[11] When he states that 'creation was subjected to frustration, not by its own choice, but by the will of the one who subjected it' (v. 20), most commentators agree that Paul is alluding to the sin of Adam where creation was implicated in Adam's action and cursed as a result. Genesis 3:17–19,

[9] My argument draws from Adams 2000: 181. For the linguistic background to *ktisis* see Adams 2000: 77–80.

[10] Delling (1991, 1: 393) writes of this expression, 'there are no instances of the term except in Christian literature'.

[11] Adams (2002: 28) states that 'Paul is reworking the Genesis story'.

for example, describes how creation was cursed and brought forth thorns and thistles. Paul states that the created order was subjected to 'futility' (*mataiotēti*, 8:20; cf. 1:21), where creation itself was unable to reach the potential for which God had originally created it (Adams 2002: 29).[12] 'The aorist tense shows the reference is to a particular event in time' (Cranfield 1974: 226). Furthermore, creation was placed in bondage to 'decay' (*phthoras*, 8:20; cf. 1:23), which is equivalent to the reign of death over the human creation. Murray J. Harris (1990: 246) has stated the ramifications of such a situation well:

> Having lost its God-ordained destiny because sinful humanity could not properly fulfil its role of exercising dominion as God's representatives on earth, creation became subject to frustrating emptiness, tantalizing imperfection, and disappointment that God's original purpose for creation remained unfulfilled.

This condition, however, is not permanent but temporary, as creation itself will be able to share in the inheritance that awaits the sons of God. Creation will one day be free from its slavery and bondage to decay; indeed, even in the present, creation can look forward with hope to its day of deliverance.

Verse 20 also raises a particularly contentious point; namely, the question of who is responsible for creation's current predicament. Given that the creation story is in view, some hold Adam responsible for subjecting creation to frustration. Scholars who take this view understand the construction *dia ton hypotaxanta* (v. 20) to have a causal meaning, '*because* of him who subjected (it)'. Others think Satan was responsible, but even though both Adam and Satan are involved in bringing about the non-human created order's present predicament, 'Scripture never assigns to Adam or to Satan the power to bring about such a far-reaching change' (Morris 1988: 321). What are we to conclude? It is better to understand the preposition *dia* in the sense of agency '*by* him who subjected (it)', which would not then refer to Adam or Satan but to God. Moreover, the context supports such a reading, since the one who subjected it did so 'in hope' (v. 20)[13] (the first of five references to 'hope' in verses 20–25), which points to God as the subject, since what has happened is not the final outcome. Rather, there will be another much more hopeful stage in this cosmic

---

[12] I am drawing from Burke (1995: 130) and Adams for this part of the argument.

[13] Paul uses 'hope' in both its verbal (vv. 24–25) and noun forms (cf. vv. 20, 24).

drama, which only God who brought about the initial frustration is able to perform.

Paul further personifies the bondage of the material creation in its present frustration by describing it as 'groaning as in the pains of *childbirth* right up to the present time' (v. 22; my emphasis). By doing so, Paul employs a highly unusual and powerful metaphor: creation is not only pregnant, but is also progressively moving towards 'full term'! 'Paul is linking the current suffering of creation with the expected outcome – a successful birth' (Esler 2003: 261). As mentioned earlier, for Paul, a male in the ancient world, to use female imagery in order to describe the future cataclysmic events is rare, but such language is found elsewhere in his letters, as Beverly Gaventa has noted. For example, Paul describes the parousia in 1 Thessalonians 5:3 and warns specifically against those who preach 'Peace and safety' when 'destruction will come on them suddenly, as labour pains on a pregnant woman, and they will not escape' (cf. 1 Thess. 2:7; Gal. 4:19). The Old Testament prophets also used the image of a mother birthing as a sign of hopefulness (Isa. 26:17; 66:7) and eschatological tribulation (Isa. 13:8; Jer. 6:24; 8:21; 13:21).[14] Although Paul most often uses male imagery in his letters, here is a good example of an instance where he breaks from the normal social expectations and uses female imagery (cf. 1 Thess. 2:7).[15]

Such terminology serves the purpose of heightening the effect of the events that will unfold. It is 'not simply a personal matter or a literary convention having to do with friendship or rebirth but reflects the anguish of the whole created order as it awaits the fulfilment of God's action in Jesus Christ' (Gaventa 1990: 194). The present pain experienced by the created order, like the birth pains experienced by a woman in labour about to deliver a child, will give way to a joyful result. Paul has in mind that such pain and hardship is temporary and transient but it is also infused with hope, as the imagery of birth pangs indicate. These sufferings cannot be compared to the eternal joys and glory that will ensue.[16] Thus the

[14] See the discussion in Tsumura 1994: 620–621.

[15] For further elaboration of 1 Thess. 2:7 see Burke 2003a: 151–154 and the literature cited there.

[16] Adams (2002: 29) remarks, 'The formulation reflects an Adamic soteriology. The "glory" to which reference is made is the pristine glory meant for Adam, eschatologically restored to redeemed humanity. When that glory is revealed, Paul implies, creation will be restored to its intended place, and God's children will be re-established in their status as stewards of the created order and enabled to exercise stewardship properly.'

pericope (v. 22) ends on a hopeful note, because the 'groaning' expresses something more than the response to suffering: it is something positive and optimistic that incorporates a yearning for liberation, and in this way becomes an expression of hope (cf. 8:24–25) (Byrne 1979: 108). Creation, one day, will indeed be liberated from its present bondage and brought into the glorious freedom of the children of God.

Adoption, suffering and future glory of believers (vv. 23–25)

There is a shift in subject matter as Paul moves from the subhuman created order (vv. 19–22, vegetation etc.) to the human created order (vv. 23–25), where the apostle again picks up the language of adoption (v. 23) mentioned earlier in verse 15. These verses are no digression; on the contrary, both 'the larger context and the nature of the argument indicate that verse 23 is the main point of everything in vv. 18–27' (Fee 1994: 572), where adoption reaches its climax. Some interpreters regard the inclusion of adoption here as problematic given that adoption has already been granted and is complete (v. 15). James Swetnam, however, seeks to resolve this dilemma by understanding the verb *apedechesthai* (8:23) to mean 'infer', where adoption is a present reality and we infer this from our present groaning (Swetnam 1967: 106). But this is not convincing, because the same verb occurring in verses 19 and 25 means 'wait' or 'long for', and the 'problem' is easily resolved once we realize that adoption here is cast in eschatological terms.

We should also take careful note here of how Paul has previously used the metaphor of *natural birth* ('creation has been groaning as in in the pains of childbirth', v. 22) to describe the *subhuman* order as it is caught in the present predicament of suffering. Now he switches to the metaphor of *adoption* (v. 23) to emphasize the eventual consummation of the *human* order described here as the believer's salvation. It is important to note this distinction in metaphorical language that Paul makes between the two orders: the first is groaning as in biological childbirth, while the second describes the groanings of believers as they wait eagerly for their final *huiothesia*. To be sure, both will be partakers of the glorious new order, but what is clear from these usages is that Paul always in his letters uses his adoption term in relation to Christians.

Adoption and the first fruits of the Spirit

The opening statement 'Not only so' in verse 23 lacks a modifier, but it is clear who the apostle has in view: believers, later identified as adopted sons of God. As part of the created order, Christians (those 'who have the first fruits of the Spirit') also groan inwardly as they await their final adoption. Being a part of creation, God's adopted sons and daughters manifest the same combination of groaning and expectation that characterize the subhuman order in verses 19–22 (Schreiner 1998: 439). Further, just as in the case of the material order, where the groaning includes a positive and hopeful outcome, Paul continues in the same positive vein in respect of believers, the adopted sons of God, the very ones upon whom the entire cosmic drama depends (vv. 23–25). The human created order has a decided advantage over the subhuman order; namely, the 'first fruits of the Spirit' (v. 23).

The expression '[those] who have the first fruits of the Spirit' has been understood in different ways. Some take the present participle 'having' (*echontes*) concessively, in which case believers groan *despite* having the Spirit; others view *echontes* causally, giving the rendering that we groan inwardly *because* we have the Spirit (Moo 2000: 267). The fact that Paul uses the phrase 'the first fruits of the Spirit' and not simply 'Spirit' is an indication that Paul is thinking of the Spirit as the one who guarantees the completion of salvation rather than as the agent of blessing. Moreover, it is the very presence of the Holy Spirit within that is the reason or cause of the tension. As believers 'we experience many tensions in our spiritual pilgrimage, *not in spite of* the fact that we are sons and have the Spirit of adoption, *but precisely because* we are sons' (Ferguson 1989: 126; my emphasis).

The term 'first fruits' (*aparchēn*) is an agricultural one that evokes three ideas: the 'first fruits' are (1) a part of the sum already present (cf. 2 Cor. 5:5); (2) an anticipation of what lies ahead; and (3) the first instalment, the pledge or guarantee of more to come. Quite possibly all three notions are present. The first fruits are the harbinger and the guarantee of the glory assured for God's adopted children. The term *aparchē* in extrabiblical Greek was often used of the first fruits of the worshipper's property dedicated as a sacrifice to a god. In the LXX the word was mainly used in connection with the cultus (e.g. Exod. 22:29, LXX v. 28]) but also in non-cultic activities (e.g. Ps. 78, LXX 77). The major difference between these usages and

Paul's in this passage, of course, is that the first fruits are not what humans have offered to God but *what has been given to humans by God*; namely, the Holy Spirit, who not only anticipates what is to come but also causes the adopted son to long for what lies ahead. As the Holy Spirit indwells and pervades the life of the adopted child of God, there is not only a renewed desire to please God but also an accompanying longing for the completion of salvation, the redemption of our bodies.

In the present context the groaning is for our final salvation, described here by Paul in terms of the consummation of adoption. Paul has earlier spoken of the fact that believers have been given the Spirit of adoption (*pneuma huiothesias*, v. 15), and the point here is that 'there is more to adoption into the heavenly family than we now experience' (Morris 1988: 324). Cranfield (1975: 419) is right when he comments, 'we have been adopted, but our adoption has yet to be publicly proclaimed'.[17] Presently, we share with the subhuman creation the limitations of being a part of the cosmos, but we are uniquely different by virtue of the fact that we also have the Spirit. The struggle with daily sin coupled with the future presence of the Spirit of adoption causes the believer to long for the future outcome. Paul elsewhere (2 Cor. 5:2–5) describes this longing:

> Meanwhile we groan, longing to be clothed with our heavenly dwelling ... For while we are in this tent, we groan and are burdened, because we do not wish to be unclothed but to be clothed with our heavenly dwelling ... Now it is God who has made us for this very purpose and has given us the Spirit as a deposit, guaranteeing what is to come.

Adoption and the redemption of the body

In the concluding part of verses 21–23 Paul in verse 23 brings together the two statements 'adoption as sons' (*huiothesian*) and 'the redemption of our bodies' (*tēn apolytrōsin tou sōmatos hēmōn*).[18] The relationship between these two statements has been a matter of debate. For example, some commentators have sought to relegate the redemption of the body under the final adoption as sons. Charles Hodge (1972: 276) asserts, 'The adoption includes far more than the redemption of the body. But the latter event is to be coincident with

---

[17] See also Dunn 1988: 470; Fitzmyer 1993: 507.
[18] I owe this point to Garner 2002: 51–53.

the former, and is included in it, as one of its most prominent parts.'[19] However, the syntactical arrangement of the two phrases 'adoption as sons' and 'the redemption of our bodies' suggests 'an epexegetical relationship of the two terms ... [where] ... Paul is fusing these two future realities, and describing them – at least in some sense – as *one*' (Garner 2002: 53; my emphasis). Cranfield (1975: 419) states thus:

> *tēn apolytrōsin tou sōmatos hēmōn* interprets *huiothesian*. The full manifestation of our adoption is identical with the final resurrection of our bodies at the Parousia, our complete and final liberation from the *mataiotēs* and *phthora*, to which we (like the subhuman creation) have been subjected.[20]

So believers await the consummation of adoption, the very climax of redemption, when through the Holy Spirit they are transformed and physically resurrected as sons. As these future events unfold, it is particularly important to note how Paul rules out any suggestion of the annhilation (Bruce 1985: 161) of the body, as he does the idea of a purely spiritual existence: 'the bodily redemption is real, bodily values will not be lost, and is not an aspect of adoption, but the very essence of it' (Garner 2002: 53). This transformation and restoration is the great 'hope' adopted sons of God have, a point Paul especially hammers home by his repeated references to 'hope' in verses 24–25.[21] God's sons and daughters wait patiently and in anticipation of this happening by placing their hope in God (v. 20; cf. 24–25), who holds the key to the unveiling of the future. Succinctly stated, 'hope holds out for this final adoption' (Stevenson-Moessner 2003: 111) and it is with one's hope firmly anchored in God that final salvation is procured. Paul's use of the aorist tense ('saved') here is striking, since generally in his writings the verb is mostly used in the future (e.g. 5:9 [twice]; 9:27; 10:9; 11:26; 13:11; 1 Cor. 3:15; 5:5; 7:16; Phil. 2:12; 1 Thess. 5:8–9). By stating that salvation is a *past* event, Paul wishes to make the point that salvation, our final adoption as sons, is secure. It will definitely come to pass (Byrne 1996: 264).

---

[19] Stibbe (1999: 170–172) also states, 'Redemption is therefore *one* aspect of our spiritual adoption' (my emphasis).

[20] Other commentators agree; e.g. Moo (1996: 521), who remarks, 'This final element in our adoption is "the redemption of our bodies".'

[21] Paul, in vv. 24–25, employs the noun 'hope' (*elpis*) three times and the verbal form (*elpizō*) twice.

Adoption and the improvisation of God's Spirit (vv. 26–27)[22]

Most commentators regard verses 26–27 as having a connection with the immediately preceding verses. The phrase 'in the same way' (v. 26) is the link and relates specifically to the continuation of the theme of 'groaning'. But what is overlooked is the fact that Paul's inclusive language begun earlier (vv. 23–25) continues in verses 26–27 and cements these verses together. More specifically, because Paul has earlier talked about adoption (vv. 23–25) there is no reason to think he has changed tack at this late stage in his logical argument. To be sure, Paul does not mention adoption in verses 26–27 but he still has these sons in view. As Robert Jewett observes, 'the ... ongoing intervention of the Spirit' is the one responsible for 'maintaining their relationship as *children of God* through the inarticulate groans they utter' (Jewett 2004: 203; my emphasis). In addition, as Paul has been describing how believers are still very much part of this present fallen world, it is not surprising he should elaborate further on their particular 'weaknesses' (spiritual in nature this time, as opposed to the physical seen earlier, vv. 23–25), especially as they await their future adoption as sons, the redemption of their bodies.

The area where this weakness is manifested is that of prayer (cf. 8:15). The difficulty is not so much with the *method* of prayer (*how* we should pray) as it is with the *content* of prayer (lit. '*for what* to pray', *to gar ti proseuxōmetha*). It is then that the Spirit intercedes for us (v. 16) with 'groanings',[23] thereby linking it to the groanings of God's adopted children (v. 23) earlier. The word Paul uses to describe such groanings is *alalētos* (v. 26), which means 'lacking speech' or 'wordless'. The Spirit groaning within the adopted sons of God does so in a way only God as the 'Spirit of adoption' (8:15) can do – in perfect harmony with his own will.[24]

Adoption and final conformity to the *eikōn* of God's Son (v. 29)

The family language with which Paul started chapter 8 by referring to God's Son (v. 3) follows through to the end of the chapter (v. 32).

---

[22] See chapter 6, where these verses have been discussed in more detail.

[23] Fee (1994: 579), who is of the opinion that Paul here refers to tongue-speaking, which does not sit easily in this context, since this is a 'weakness' that afflicts all of God's children.

[24] Contra Fee 1994: 580.

From beginning to end Paul in Romans 8 makes a number of 'strategic Christological statements' (Campbell 2002: 104)[25] and this Christological language centres on his filial description of Christ as God's Son. But it is significant that sandwiched between these twin references to the sonship of Jesus (8:3, 29) is the adoptive sonship of Christians (8:15, 23). In regard to the first Christological statement,[26] the apostle states, 'God sent his Son in the likeness of sinful flesh' (my trans.), after which he moves on to relate this to the believer's sonship by adoption in 8:15; in fact, as Hurtado recognizes, Paul 'explicitly connects ... the sending of the Son of God in Rom. 8:3 with ... both present and future consequences of divine adoption' (Hurtado 1999: 229). There can be little doubt that the order in which Paul first mentions the sonship of Jesus followed by the later mention of the adoptive sonship of believers is deliberate (Hurtado 1999: 230). In Paul's mind the two 'sonships' are not only linked but, more importantly, the adoptive sonship of believers is dependent upon the sonship of Jesus.

The second Christological connection is in 8:29, where the end point of adoption is reached, described here by Paul as being 'conformed to the likeness of his Son'.[27] The importance of Romans 8:29 to Paul's argument has been pointed out by James Scott (1992: 245) when he asserts:

> Rom. 8:29 provides a convenient point of departure for discussing the future aspect of *huiothesia*, for there the relationship between the Son and the sons of God is stressed in a way that brings the theme of sonship in Rom. 8:12–30 to a decisive climax.

Romans 8:29 contains a number of striking Old Testament nuances; for example, the believer is being conformed to the likeness of the Son of God, which immediately recalls Adam, who was created in the image of God, an image shattered as a consequence of the fall. Christ, the Son of God, is the true or second Adam (Rom. 5:12–21) into whose image the adopted sons of God will be changed. Paul's use of Adam Christology is clear here where he speaks of 'final adoption as conformity' (Peterson 2001: 171). Such conformity comes about by a

---

[25] Even though Romans is the nearest to a systematic treatise, it is often noted that the lack of Christology precludes us from thinking of Romans in this way. But while any sustained Christology may be absent from this letter, this does not mean Paul does not say anything about this subject, as Rom. 1:3–4; 8:3, 29, 32 demonstrate.

[26] There are three such statements (cf. Rom. 8:32).

[27] See chapter 5 for further treatment of this verse.

process and here again Paul may well be thinking of suffering that links back to the suffering of Christ mentioned earlier (Rom. 8:17). The role of Christ, the Son of God, is therefore vital to the overall argument in Romans 8 and is the goal towards which Paul's thesis of adoption has been driving. That is to say, while 'Christians, at the moment of justification, are adopted into God's family ... the adoption is incomplete and partial until we are finally made like *the* Son of God himself' (Moo 1996: 521).

Summary

Romans 8:18–27 has a thoroughly eschatological outlook about it, and is the locus where Paul depicts the shared experience of creation (the subhuman order) and Christians (the human order, here described as adopted sons, v. 23) as they await the future unveiling of God's cosmic plans. Pervading Paul's argument, however, is the note of hope. Creation, in the shape of the subhuman order, has been locked into the bondage of decay, a situation brought about by God. Believers too, described here as adopted sons of God and by virtue of their being a part of creation, experience suffering consistent with the suffering and sonship of Christ (Rom. 8:17). God's children, however, have an advantage over the natural created order because of the presence of the first fruits of the Spirit, the Spirit who causes them to look forward with hope to the final adoption as sons, the redemption of their bodies. In their present condition, God's adopted sons may be without honour in the eyes of the world, but one day this will give way to the honourable disclosure of who they really are when their *huiothesia* will be finally revealed. For believers this present era is also one of 'weakness', of not always knowing God's mind and will as they pray, but God the Spirit (none other than the Spirit of adoption mentioned earlier, in v. 15) assists them in determining his will.

As well as having a distinctly eschatological complexion, Romans 8 makes a number of key Christological statements. Paul consciously inserts *huiothesia* (8:15, 23) between several references to God's Son (e.g. 8:3, 29) to make the point that final adoption, coincident with the redemption of the body, will climax in the believer's conformity to the image of God's own Son.[28]

---

[28] See Eastman (2002: 263–277), who argues that full conformity to the image of the Son of God at the resurrection of Christ, when 'all Israel will be saved' and regain their sonship, neatly links the outcome of believers, Israel and all creation in Rom. 8 – 11.

Summary

As we bring this study to a close, my aim has been to show how adoption – which has long been in the shadows of other theological terms – is a related but nevertheless distinct metaphor in the Pauline corpus (chapter 1). *Huiothesia* is not only a theological but also a soteriological metaphor that underscores the subjective side of the believer's salvation (chapter 2). Found only in Paul's writings (Gal. 4:5; Rom. 8:15, 23; 9:4; Eph. 1:5), the uniqueness of the adoption metaphor lies in the fact that it brings nuances of meaning that complement and add to the apostle's rich understanding of salvation. That is, adoption is fundamentally a relational and familial metaphor, finding its origin and meaning in the household of the ancient social world of Paul's time.

The word *huiothesia* is a term Paul borrowed from the Roman sociolegal context of his day (chapter 3). Paul uses the term only in letters written to churches under Roman law and we have noted several points of contact between Paul's usage and ancient practice: adoption, for example, signals a *transfer* from one family to another, was only and always undertaken at the initiative of the *paterfamilias*, bestows a new family name upon the adoptee and is attested by witnesses. The real and spiritual implications of these aspects of adoption would have resonated with Paul's readers. On one occasion Paul employs *huiothesia* in respect of Israel (Rom. 9:4), but when we look for verification of the use of this expression in the Old Testament (LXX), we not only find it missing but also that adoption was not a Jewish practice. Much more dominant on the landscape of the Old Testament is the general notion of Israel(ites) as 'son/s', and it is here that the Old Testament background to Paul's *huiothesia* lies. More-over, if, as scholars presently argue, we cannot separate the Jewish or Graeco-Roman cultural influences that impacted the apostle Paul, then as far as his *huiothesia* expression is concerned perhaps the issue of background is not a case of 'either or' but of 'both and'.[1]

---

[1] This is the basic thesis of the volume edited by Engberg-Pedersen 2001.

In chapters 4 – 7 the theological significance of *huiothesia* is explored. Here I demonstrated how adoption is embedded in and comes about through the activity of the triune God (revealed as 'family'), where Father, Son and Holy Spirit play vital and complementary roles in bringing the believer into God's new household. Just as it was in the ancient world, so adoption for Paul is primarily and profoundly a paternal initiative (Eph. 1:1–7; Gal. 4:1–7; chapter 4). The 'Father' is always the prime mover, and while his eternal purpose is personal and individual his goal is communal – he desires to bring his adopted sons into community, a community Paul twice in the relevant letters describes as the *household* of God (Gal. 6:10; Eph. 2:19). Unlike in the ancient world, however, where no intermediary is involved in the adoption procedure, for Paul, God adopts only through his Son (chapter 5). The uniqueness of Jesus sets him apart for this role, a point highlighted by the way in which Paul distinguishes between Jesus as 'son' (*huios*, Rom. 1:3–4) and Christians as 'adopted sons' (*huiothesia*, Rom. 8:15, 23), a distinction he never blurs. Paul's use of adoption is Christologically centred in the person and work of Jesus, the Son of God (Gal. 4:4; Eph. 1:5), where the believer's adoption is not only dependent on but also impossible without God's Son. To be an adopted son of God is also synonymous with having the Spirit, evident by the meaning and use of Paul's phrase 'Spirit of adoption' (Rom. 8:15) (chapter 6). The eschatological gift of the Spirit and adoption combine in this expression to signal the fact that the law, the old epoch, has been eclipsed by the new era of the Spirit. It is the Spirit who is not only the indispensable evidence of adoption but who also brings an awareness of the Christian's new filial disposition. The presence of the Spirit in the life of the adopted son also underscores the moral dynamic and imperative for God's adopted sons and daughters to live circumspectly and in a way that honours the Father and his household.

To be called an 'adopted son' of God is to ascribe honour to the person who belongs to the most honourable of all households, and sets the believer apart from the dishonourable 'family' (Eph. 3:3) to which he had previously belonged (chapter 7). As 'proof' of our belonging to the divine family, God has given his Holy Spirit – his own mark or honourable approval of the adoptee's acceptance into his household. The twin notions of adoption and honour are vitally related in Galatians and Romans: in the former, God's adopted sons are called to demonstrate loyalty to their heavenly *patēr*, while in the latter Paul employs his *huiothesia* metaphor to unite the factionalized house churches by reminding both Jew and Gentile of their adoption into the one new household of God.

Paul's adoption term is essentially eschatological, for in keeping with other soteriological terms in his letters there is the tension between the 'now' and the 'not yet (chapter 8). The present era may be one of suffering, an aspect all adopted sons share with the suffering Son of God (Rom. 8:17), but the prospects are brighter and more glorious, for the day will dawn when the consummation of adoption – along with the whole created order – will take place. Especially prominent in Romans 8:18–27 is the future redemption of the body, the physical resurrection, which is coterminous with the final adoption (8:23), a time when believers will also be conformed to the image of God's Son (8:29).

In conclusion, one final point needs to be made. Although we have focused on theology during this study, the importance of doctrine or theology should not cause us to lose sight of the profound pastoral and practical implications a study of *huiothesia* raises.[2] This is crucial, not least because Christians sometimes lack assurance of salvation. One reason for this is that they have not properly understood the One to whom they belong. In today's world people 'crave connectedness' (Stevenson-Moessner 2003: 1), and certainly the desire to be accepted and to belong is a basic need of every human heart. Adoption is an intensely relational concept and centres upon a *relationship* with the living God. That God the Father desires to enter into a relationship with people is the essence of the Christian gospel; that this relationship is expressed in terms of familial language in general and in terms of adoption in particular *is* Pauline Christianity. The alienation and the need to be connected is where the doctrine of Christian adoption comes in because it serves the purpose of underscoring how God has dealt with the question of our estrangement by taking us from being 'children of disobedience' (Eph. 2:2) and placing us as adopted sons and daughters in his family.[3] As McGrath (2001b: 144–145; emphasis in original) put it:

---

[2] As I write this word 'practical', I am immediately taken back to Nigeria to my seminary students, who coined a much better word. Always keen to apply the text and understand how to 'live out the Word' of God, they fused two English words 'practice' and 'realize' into a most memorable neologism, 'practicalize'! 'What does it mean to "practicalize" Scripture and doctrine?' was the burning question for them.

[3] On this matter see Tournier's poignant story as recounted by Montgomery Boice 1986: 441.

Adoption is about *being wanted*. It is about *belonging*. These are deeply emotive themes, which resonate with the cares and concerns of many in our increasingly fractured society. To be adopted is to be invited into a loving and caring environment. It is about being welcomed, wanted and invited. Adoption celebrates the privilege of invitation, in which the outsider is welcomed into the fold of faith and love.

This 'celebration' and sense of belonging is perhaps best expressed in Romans 8, *the* classic New Testament passage on the subject of assurance, where Paul informs the Roman Christians that they have not received a spirit of slavery but have been given the 'loving Spirit of Adoption'[4] (Rom. 8:15). 'Verse 15 is a most important verse from the standpoint of assurance of salvation' (Lloyd-Jones 1974: 196), and the ensuing filial cry of '*Abba*, Father' (Rom. 8:15–16;[5] Gal. 4:6) is the undeniable proof that the adopted son belongs to God's new family. And, to be sure, there can be no greater privilege, responsibility or sense of belonging than having God as our adoptive Father and being related by faith to a vast network of brothers and sisters in Christ who constitute the worldwide family of believers (Gal. 6:10).[6]

[4] This is John Wesley's beautiful description of the phrase *pneuma huiothesias* in Rom. 8:15. See chapter 6 for a discussion of the meaning of this phrase.

[5] Carson (2000: 276) points out the importance of these verses for the subject of assurance: 'in many of the classic treatments on assurance there is a threefold focus: the objective work of Christ grounded in the plan of God, the demonstrable transformation of the believer ... the inner witness of the Spirit ... This third leg, tied to such passages as Romans 8:15–17 ... needs and deserves serious reflection...'

[6] As Christians our view of the church is too myopic and we need to remember and also to remind Christians that we are part of the true, universal church, the family of God.

Appendix

Some alleged cases of adoption in the Old Testament

We have noted that Paul's *huiothesia* expression does not occur in the LXX, nor is it mentioned in biblical law. This silence, however, has not prevented some scholars from advancing the view that there are cases of adoption in the Old Testament. In this appendix we shall look at some of the more pertinent examples.

Eliezer, Abraham's slave (Gen. 15:3)

The Old Testament account reveals how Abram's inability to father a child until he was eighty-six years old, when Ishmael was born, is expressed in his anguished prayer to the Lord in Genesis 15:2–3: 'O Sovereign LORD, what can you give me since I remain childless and the one who will inherit my estate is Eliezer of Damascus? ... You have given me no children; so a servant in my household will be my heir.' William Rossell, one of the first scholars to argue for cases of adoption in the Old Testament, is convinced that Abram 'adopted' Eliezer. His view is based on the similarities between this case and Mesopotamian practices of adoption in the middle of the second millennium BC. He writes (1952: 233–234):

> The adoption of the slave Eliezer is a custom well attested in the Nuzi Texts where a childless couple adopted a son to serve them as long as they lived and to bury and mourn for them at death. In return for these services the adopted son was designated an heir.[1]

[1] The Nuzi texts were unearthed in North-eastern Iraq between the years 1925 and 1931. The find comprised four thousand clay tablets in total dating back to the fifteenth century BC. The tablets contain private contracts and public records covering topics such as land, family law and order etc.

To be sure, adoption was practised in Mesopotamia (modern-day Iraq), as the Nuzi tablets confirm; however, the parallels in the Nuzi texts 'combine slavery, adoption and inheritance which strictly speaking do not occur in the account in Gen. 15' (Atkins 1991: 179). According to de Vaux (1962: 51), the noted Old Testament scholar, even if this were a case of adoption attested in Mesopotamian custom, 'it does not prove that the custom took root in Israel, and the Bible itself does not represent the act as an adoption'. Second, as Rossell himself acknowledges, the Nuzi texts make abundantly clear that 'should the adopter beget a son after the adoption, *the adopted must yield to the real son the right of being the chief heir*' (1952: 233–234; my emphasis). If we were to accept that the practice of adoption portrayed in the Nuzi texts lies behind Paul's use of his adoption metaphor, we are left with a theological problem, because, unlike in Mesopotamia, Paul's letters demonstrate that in the case of inheritance, an adopted son is no different from the naturally born son and, more importantly, could never lose his rights or forfeit his adoption privileges or inheritance. Paul himself says the adopted sons are 'co-heirs with Christ' (Rom. 8:17). This being the case, it is highly unlikely that Paul would have drawn on a background that taught otherwise.

Moses (Exod. 2:10), Ephraim and Manasseh (Gen. 48:5) and Esther (Esth. 2:7)

We shall consider the three cases of the alleged adoptions of Moses, Ephraim and Manasseh, and Esther together, since James Scott is of the view that they are interdependent because there are verbal parallels between them that might be interpreted as instances of adoption. In the case of Moses the text reads literally, 'And he was *to her for a son* (*wayĕhî lāh lĕbēn*, Exod. 2:10); in the second, we read literally, 'Ephraim and Manasseh *will be to me* as Reuben and Simeon' (*yihyû-lî*, Gen. 48:5); in the third the text states literally, 'Mordecai *took her to him* for a daughter' (*lô lĕbat*, Esth. 2:7). In addition to these verbal parallels Scott further contends that Genesis 48:5 and Esther 2:7 in particular show a linguistic dependence upon Exodus 2:10, and concludes that these 'must be taken seriously as cases of adoption' (1992: 74). In Scott's estimation we may be able to see here traces of an actual Hebrew adoption formula that is corroborated, he adds, when we realize that there is an analogy to the Old Testament marriage formula in 1 Samuel 25:42, which reads literally, 'And she was *to him for a wife*' (*watĕhî lô lĕ'iššâ*). Scott (1992: 75) concludes that these cases are analogous to each other and

> the analogy extends not only to syntax, but also to the artificial kinship relationship established. For as a woman from one family becomes a man's wife and part of his family by marriage, similarly a child from one family becomes part of another family by adoption. Hence, Exod. 2:10 contains a formulaic expression ... to describe Moses' adoption by Pharaoh.

We shall first consider the example of Jacob and Joseph's two sons, Ephraim and Manasseh. When Jacob took Joseph's two sons upon his knees, he was probably not adopting them but was more likely raising them to equal status with his own progeny. That is, the patriarch's action was simply ' "to step" up their status by one generation, treating them as his sons instead of his grandsons' (Mace 1953: 212; see also Zuck 1996: 97). In doing so, Jacob was more likely allocating rights of succession to those *already* within his family. According to G. H. Box (1908: 115), 'this is not really a case of adoption at all but one where the rights of the firstborn were transferred to a younger son'. Unlike a real case of adoption, no third party is involved.

In the case of Moses it is true he was reared in Pharaoh's household by Pharaoh's daughter, but if we look at other New Testament texts (e.g. Heb. 11:24) Moses clearly refused to consider himself an Egyptian. If Moses had indeed been adopted, why does he so forcefully dissociate himself from the Egyptians? More to the point, there is no mention of an adoption procedure in this text, and, as de Vaux (1962: 51; my emphasis) again points out in respect to the Old Testament,

> the historical books record no examples of adoption in the strict legal sense i.e., the legal acknowledgement of one born outside the family as having the rights of a child born into the family. Thus, one cannot regard as real adoptions the instances of *Moses* ... or of Genubath (1 Kgs. 11:20).

Rather than being a case of adoption, it is more likely to be an instance of fosterage (Lyall 1984: 75).

Finally, in the case of Esther the book is set within the context of exile – the people of Israel are living in a foreign land (Persia) where other laws and adoption procedures were in operation. In addition, it is unlikely Esther had been adopted, because as a woman she could not have continued the family line. We would also have to ask whether Mordecai would have used a foreign adoption procedure when there is evidence in the book of Esther itself which makes clear that the Jews were still expected to obey their own laws (which did not include adoption) even in an alien environment (cf. Esth. 3:8).

To sum up, the evidence for adoption as a legal procedure in the Old Testament is dubious to say the least. Moreover, in the event of a childless couple, other mechanisms were in place in Israelite society that obviated the need for adoption, such as the levirate marriage. Also, polygamy while permitted by God but obviously not the ideal, was another means of having an heir, as Leon Morris (1988: 314) concludes:

> Provisions such as polygamy, the giving of a concubine to provide children, and the levirate marriage took care of most situations. This probably accounts for the fact that there are no laws on adoption in the Old Testament and that even the word is lacking.

In short, 'the Old Testament laws contain no directives about adoption', and even if the notion of adoption was known in Old Testament times, it 'had little influence on daily life' (de Vaux 1962: 50–51).

Bibliography

Adams, E. (2000), *Constructing the World: A Study of Paul's Cosmological Language*, Edinburgh: T. & T. Clarke.

————(2002), 'Paul's Story of God and Creation: The Story of How God Fulfils His Purposes in Creation', in B. Longenecker (ed.), *Narrative Dynamics in Paul: A Critical Assessment*: 19–43, Louisville: Westminster John Knox.

Arde, A. van (1997), 'Side-Notes from Graeco-Roman and Hellenistic-Semitic Literature to the Notion "Adopted as God's Child"', *Acta Patristica et Byzantina* 9: 150–172.

Atkins, R. (1991), *Egalitarian Community: Ethnography and Exegesis*, Alabama: University of Alabama.

Badcock, G. D. (1997), *Light of Truth and Fire of Love: A Theology of Holy Spirit*, Grand Rapids: Eerdmans.

Balla, P. (2002), *The Child–Parent Relationship in the New Testament and its Environment*, WUNT 55, Tübingen: Mohr.

Banks, R. J. (1994), *Paul's Idea of Community: The Early House Churches in their Cultural Setting*, 2nd ed., Peabody: Hendrickson.

Barclay, J. M. G. (1997), 'Family as the Bearer of Religion in Judaism and Early Christianity', in H. Moxnes (ed.), *Constructing Early Christian Families: Family as Social Reality and Metaphor*, 66–80, London: Routledge.

Barcley, W. B. (1999), *'Christ in You': A Study of Paul's Theology and Ethics*, Lanham: University Press of America.

Barnett, P. (1999), *Jesus and the Rise of Early Christianity: A History of New Testament Times*, Downers Grove: IVP.

Barr, J. (1988a), 'Abba Father and the Familiarity of Jesus' Speech', *Theology* 91: 173–179.

————(1988b), 'Abba Isn't Daddy', *JTS* 39: 28–47.

Barrett, C. K. (1991), *The Epistle to the Romans*, 2nd ed., BNTC, London: A. & C. Black.

Barth, M. (1974), *Ephesians 1–3: A New Translation with Introduction and Commentary*, New York: Doubleday.

Barton, S. C. (1994), *Discipleship and Family Ties in Mark and Mathew*, SNTSMS, Cambridge: Cambridge University Press.

Bauer, W., F. W. Danker, W. F. Arndt and W. F. Gingrich (2000), *A Greek–English Lexicon of the New Testament and Other Early Christian Literature*, 3rd ed., Chicago: University of Chicago Press.

Beasley-Murray, G. (1987), *John*, WBC 36, Waco, TX: Word.

Berger, A. and B. Nicholas (1970), 'Adoptio and Adoption', in N. G. C. Hammond and H. H. Scullard (eds.), *The Oxford Classical Dictionary*, 8–9, Oxford: Oxford University Press.

Berger, A., B. Nicholas and S. M. Treggiari (2003), 'Adoption', in S. Hornblower and A. Spawforth (eds.), *The Oxford Classical Dictionary*, 3rd ed., 12–13, Oxford: Oxford University Press.

Berkhof, L. (1981), *Systematic Theology*, Edinburgh: Banner of Truth.

Best, E. (1998), *Ephesians*, ICC, Edinburgh: T. & T. Clarke.

Black, M. (1962), *Models and Metaphors*, Ithaca: Cornell University Press.

——— (1973), *Romans (New Century Bible)*, London: Oliphants.

Boersma, H. (2004), *Violence, Hospitality and the Cross: Reapportioning the Atonement Tradition*, Grand Rapids: Baker.

Bornkamm, G. (1970), *Paul*, London: Hodder & Stoughton.

Bowen, R. (1978), *A Guide to Romans*, London: SPCK.

Box, G. H. (1908), 'Adoption (Semitic)', in J. Hastings (ed.), *Encyclopedia of Religion and Ethics*, 114–115, Edinburgh: T. & T. Clarke.

Bruce, F. F. (1982), *Commentary on Galatians*, NIGTC, Grand Rapids: Eerdmans.

——— (1985), *The Epistle of Paul to the Romans: An Introduction and Commentary*, rev. ed., Leicester: IVP.

Bryan, C. (2000), *A Preface to Romans: Notes on its Literary and Cultural Setting*, Oxford: Oxford University Press.

Buchanan, J. (1962), *The Doctrine of Justification: An Outline of its History in the Church and of its Exposition from Scripture*, London: Banner of Truth.

——— (1966), *The Holy Spirit*, London: Banner of Truth.

Buckland, W. W. (1963), *A Textbook of Roman Law from Augustus to Justinian*, Cambridge: Cambridge University Press.

Burke, T. J. (1992), 'Adoptive-Sonship', *Foundations: An Evangelical Journal of Theology* 29: 25–29.

——— (1994), 'Adoptive Sonship (HUIOTHESIA) in the Pauline Corpus', MPhil dissertation, University College of North Wales (Bangor).

———(1995), 'The Characteristics of Paul's Adoptive (HUIO-THESIA) Motif', *IBS* 17: 62–74.

———(1998), 'Adoption and the Spirit in Romans 8', *EvQ* 70.4: 311–324.

———(2000), 'Pauline Paternity in 1 Thessalonians', *TynBul* 51.1: 59–81.

———(2001), 'Pauline Adoption: A Sociological Approach', *EvQ* 73.2: 119–134.

———(2003), *Family Matters: A Socio-historical Study of Kinship Metaphors in 1 Thessalonians*, JSNTSup 247, London: T. & T. Clarke.

———(forthcoming), 'Proclaiming Jesus in Global Mission', in T. Cornman (ed.), *Proclaiming Jesus: Essays in Honor of Joseph Stowell*, Chicago: Moody.

Burke, T. J. and J. K. Elliott (2003), *Paul and the Corinthians: Studies on a Community in Conflict. Essays in Honour of Margaret Thrall*, NovTSup 109, Leiden: Brill.

Byrne, B. (1979), *'Sons of God' – 'Seed of Abraham': A Study of the Idea of the Sonship of God of All Christians in Paul against the Jewish Background*, AnBib 83, Rome: Biblical Institute.

———(1986), *Reckoning with Romans: A Contemporary Reading of Paul's Gospel*, Wilmington: Glazier.

———(1994), 'Review of Adoption as Sons of God: An Exegetical Investigation into the Background of HUIOTHESIA in the Pauline Corpus', by J. M. Scott, *JTS* 44.1: 288–294.

———(1996), *Romans*, SP 6, Collegeville, Minn.: Glazier, Liturgical.

Caird, G. B. (1980), *The Language and Imagery of the Bible*, Philadelphia: Westminster.

Calder, W. M. (1930), 'Adoption and Inheritance in Galatia', *JTS* 31: 372–374.

Calvin, J. (1899), *Epistle of Paul to the Romans*, ed. J. Owen, Edinburgh: Calvin Translation Society.

Cameron, S. N. M. de and S. B. Ferguson (1986), *Pulpit and People: Essays in Honour of William Still on his 75th Birthday*, Edinburgh: Rutherford House.

Campbell, D. A. (2002), 'The Story of Jesus in Romans and Galatians', in B. W. Longenecker (ed.), *Narrative Dynamics in Paul: A Critical Assessment*, 97–124, Louisville: Westminster John Knox.

Candlish, R. S. (1869), *The Fatherhood of God: Being the First Course of the Cunningham Lectures Delivered before the New College, Edinburgh, in March 1864*, 5th ed., Edinburgh: A. & C. Black.

Carson, D. A. (1991), *The Gospel According to John*, Leicester: Apollos.

———(1994), 'Reading the Letters', in D. A. Carson, R. T. France, J. A. Motyer and G. J. Wenham (eds.), *New Bible Commentary 21st Century Edition*, 1108–1114, Leicester: IVP.

———(2000), 'Reflections on Assurance', in T. R. Schreiner and B. A. Ware (eds.), *Still Sovereign: Contemporary Perspectives on Election, Foreknowledge and Grace*, 147–176, Grand Rapids: Baker.

Carson, D. A. and D. Moo (2005), *An Introduction to the New Testament*, 2nd ed., Grand Rapids: Zondervan; Leicester: Apollos.

Carson, D. A., P. T. O'Brien and M. A. Seifrid (2001), *Justification and Variegated Nomism: The Complexities of Second Temple Judaism*, vol. 1, Tübingen: Mohr Siebeck; Grand Rapids: Baker Academic.

Carson, D. A., P. T. O'Brien and M. A. Seifrid (2004), *Justification and Variegated Nomism: The Paradoxes of Paul*, Mohr Siebeck: Tübingen; Grand Rapids: Baker Academic.

Castelli, E. A. (1991), *Imitating Paul: A Discourse of Power*, Literary Currents in Biblical Interpretation, Louisville: Westminster John Knox.

———(1994) 'Romans', in E. S. Fiorenza (ed.), *Search the Scriptures: A Feminist Commentary*, 272–300, Crossroad: New York.

Chae, D. J.-S. (1997), *Paul as Apostle to the Gentiles: His Apostolic Self-Awareness and its Influence on the Soteriological Argument in Romans*, Carlisle: Paternoster.

Christianen, E. J. (1997), *The Covenant in Judaism and Paul: A Study of Ritual Boundary Markers as Identity Markers*, AGJU, Leiden: Brill.

Coetzer, W. C. (1981), 'The Holy Spirit and the Eschatological View of Paul', *Neot* 15: 180–198.

Cohen, S. J. D. (1993), *The Jewish Family in Antiquity*, BJS 289, Atlanta: Scholars Press.

Combes, I. A. H. (1998), *The Metaphor of Slavery in the Writings of the Ancient Church*, JSNTSup 156, Sheffield: Sheffield Academic Press.

Cook, J. I. (1978), 'The Concept of Adoption in the Theology of Paul', in J. I. Cook (ed.), *Saved by Hope: Essays in honour of Richard C. Ouderslusy*, 133–144, Grand Rapids: Eerdmans.

Cosgrove, C. H. (1988), *The Cross and the Spirit: A Study in the Argument and Theology of Galatians*, Macon, GA: Mercer.

Cotterell, P. and M. Turner (1989), *Linguistics and Biblical Inter-pretation*, London: SPCK.

Cranfield, C. E. B. (1975), *Romans*, vol. 1, ICC, Edinburgh: T. & T. Clarke.

Crook, J. (1967), *Law and Life in Rome*, London: Thames & Hudson.

——— (1984), *Law and Life of Rome 90 BC–AD 120*, New York: Cornell University Press.

Cullman, O. (1995), *What the New Testament Says about Prayer*, London: SCM.

D'Angelo, M. (1992), 'Abba and Father Imperial Theology and the Jesus Tradition', *JBL* 111: 611–630.

Dabney, R. L. (1996), *Syllabus and Notes of the Course of Systematic and Polemic Theology*, Edinburgh: Banner of Truth.

Davids, P. H. (2001), 'Adoption', in W. Elwell (ed.), *The Evangelical Dictionary of Theology*, 13, London: Pickering.

Davidson, D. (1978), 'What Metaphors Mean', in S. Sacks (ed.), *On Metaphor*, 29–46, Chicago: University of Chicago Press.

De Boer, P. A. H. (1974), *Fatherhood and Motherhood in Israelite and Judean Piety*, Leiden: Brill.

Delling, G. (1991), 'apokaradokia', *TDNT* 1: 393.

deSilva, D. A. (2000), *Honor, Patronage, Kinship and Purity: Unlocking New Testament Culture*, Downers Grove: IVP.

——— (2001), *New Testament Themes*, St. Louis: Chalice.

——— (2004), *An Introduction to the New Testament: Contexts, Methods & Ministry*, Downers Grove: IVP; Leicester: Apollos.

Dillon, R. J. (1998), 'The Spirit as Taskmaster and Troublemaker in Romans 8', *CBQ* 68: 682–702.

Dixon, S. (1992), *The Roman Family*, Baltimore: Johns Hopkins University Press.

Donfried, K. P. (1991), *The Romans Debate: Revised and Expanded Edition*, Edinburgh: T. & T. Clarke.

Donfried, K. P. and P. Richardson (1998), *Judaism and Christianity in First-Century Rome*, Grand Rapids: Eerdmans.

Duling, D. C. (2003), ' "Whatever Gain I Had . . . ": Ethnicity and Paul's Self-Identification in Philippians 3:5–6', in D. B. Gowler, L. G. Bloomquist and D. F. Watson (eds.), *Fabrics of Discourse: Essays in Honor of Vernon K. Robbins*, 222–241, Harrisburg: Trinity Press International.

Dunn, J. D. G. (1970), *Baptism and the Holy Spirit: A Re-Examination of the New Testament Teaching on the Gift of the Spirit in Relation to Pentecostalism Today*, London: SCM.

————(1975), *Jesus and the Spirit: A Study of the Religious and Charismatic Experience of Jesus and the First Christians as Reflected in the New Testament*, London: SCM.

————(1983), 'The New Perspective in Paul', *BJRL* 65: 95–122.

————(1985), 'Works of the Law and the Curse of the Law (Gal. 3:10–14)', *NTS* 31: 523–542.

————(1988), *Romans*, vol. 1, WBC 38a, Waco, TX: Word.

————(1992), 'Prayer', in J. B. Green, S. McKnight and I. H. Marshall (eds.), *Dictionary of Jesus and the Gospels*, 617–625, Downers Grove: IVP; Leicester: IVP.

————(1993), *A Commentary on the Epistle to the Galatians*, BNTC, London: A. & C. Black.

————(1996), 'Spirit Speech: Reflections on Romans 8:12–27', in S. K. Soderlund and N. T. Wright (eds.), *Romans and the People of God: Essays in Honor of Gordon D. Fee on the Occasion of His 65th Birthday*, 82–91, Grand Rapids: Eerdmans.

————(1998), *The Theology of Paul the Apostle*, London: T. & T. Clarke.

Eastman, S. (2002), 'Whose Apocalypse? The Identity of the Sons of God in Rom. 8:19', *JBL*: 263–277.

Elliott, J. H. (1991), *A Home for the Homeless: A Sociological Exegesis of 1 Peter, Its Situation and Strategy*, Philadelphia: Fortress.

————(1994), 'Disgraced Yet Graced: The Gospel according to 1 Peter in the Key of Honor and Shame', *BTB* 24: 166–178.

————(2002), 'Jesus was not an Egalitarian: A Critique of an Anachronistic and Idealistic Theory', *BTB* 32: 75–91.

Engberg-Pedersen, T. (2001), *Paul Beyond the Judaism/Hellenism Divide*, Louisville: Westminster John Knox.

Esler, P. F. (1995), *Modelling Early Christianity: Social-Scientific Studies of the New Testament and its Context*, London: Routledge.

————(1997), 'Family Imagery and Christian Identity in Gal. 5:13–6:10', in H. Moxnes (ed.), *Constructing Early Christian Families: Family as Social Reality and Metaphor*, 121–149, London: Routledge.

————(2000), 'Keeping it in the Family: Culture, Kinship and Identity in 1 Thessalonians and Galatians', in J. W. van Henten and A. Bremer (eds.), Familia *and Family Relations as Represented in Early Judaisms and Early Christianities: Texts and Fictions*, 145–184, Leiden: Deo.

——— (2003), *Conflict and Identity in Romans: The Social Setting of Paul's Letter*, Philadelphia: Fortress.

Eyben, E. (1991), 'Fathers and Sons', in B. Rawson (ed.), *Marriage, Divorce and Children in Ancient Rome*, 114–143, Oxford: Clarendon.

Fatehi, M. (2000), *The Spirit's Relation to the Risen Lord in Paul: An Examination of its Christological Implications*, WUNT 128, Tübingen: Mohr Siebeck.

Fee, G. D. (1994), *God's Empowering Presence: The Holy Spirit in the Letters of Paul*, Peabody: Hendrickson.

——— (1997), 'Paul's Conversion as Key to His Understanding of the Spirit', in R. N. Longenecker (ed.), *The Road from Damascus: The Impact of Paul's Conversion on His Life, Thought and Ministry*, 166–183, Grand Rapids: Eerdmans.

Ferguson, S. B. (1981), *The Christian Life: A Doctrinal Introduction*, London: Hodder & Stoughton.

——— (1986) 'The Reformed Doctrine of Sonship', in N. de S. Cameron and S. B. Ferguson (eds.), *Pulpit and People: Essays in Honour of William Still on his 75th Birthday*, 81–88, Edinburgh: Rutherford House.

——— (1989), *Children of the Living God*, Edinburgh: Banner of Truth.

——— (1996), *The Holy Spirit*, Downers Grove: IVP; Leicester: IVP.

Finger, R. H. (1993), *Paul and the Roman House Churches*, Pennsylvania: Herald.

Fitzmyer, J. A (1992), 'Abba and Jesus' Relation to God', in J. Mélanges (ed.), *À Cause de l'Evangilo: Etudes sur les Synoptiques et les Actes: Offertes au P. Jacques Dupont, OSB à l'Occasion de son 70e Anniversaire*, 15–38, Dupont: LD 123; Paris: Cerf.

——— (1993), *Romans: A New Translation with Introduction and Commentary*, AB 33, New York: Doubleday.

Foerster, W. (1991), 'klēronomos', *TDNT* 3:768–785.

Fowl, S. (1990), 'A Metaphor in Distress: A Reading of NĒPIOI in 1 Thessalonians 2.7', *NTS* 36: 469–473.

Frilingos, C. (2000), 'For My Child Onesimus: Paul and Domestic Power in Philemon', *JBL* 119: 91–114.

Fung, R. Y. K (1988), *The Epistle to the Galatians*, NICNT, Grand Rapids: Eerdmans.

Furnish, V. P. (1978), *Theology and Ethics in Paul*, Nashville: Abingdon.

Gaffin, R. B. (1978), *The Centrality of the Resurrection: A Study in Paul's Soteriology*, BBMS, Grand Rapids: Baker.

Gardner, J. F. (1998), *Family and* Familia *in Roman Life*, Oxford: Clarendon.

Gardner, J. F. and T. Wiedemann (1991), *The Roman Household: A Sourcebook*, London: Routledge.

Garner, D. B. (2002), 'Adoption in Christ', PhD dissertation, Westminster Theological Seminary.

Gaventa, B. R. (1990), 'The Maternity of Paul: An Exegetical Study of Galatians 4:19', in R. Fortuna and B. R. Gaventa (eds.), *The Conversation Continues: Essays in Honor of J. Louis Martyn*, 189–201, Nashville: Abingdon.

————(1996), 'Our Mother St. Paul: Toward the Recovery of a Neglected Theme', *PSB* 17: 29–44.

George, T. (1994), *Galatians, New American Commentary*, Nashville: Broadman & Holman.

Gerrish, B. A. (1993), *Grace and Gratitude: The Eucharistic Theology of John Calvin*, Edinburgh: T. & T. Clarke.

Girardeau, J. L. (1986), *Discussions of Theological Questions*, Harisonburg, Va: Sprinkle.

Godet, F. L. (1977), *Commentary on Romans*, Grand Rapids: Kregel.

Goody, J. (1969), 'Adoption in Cross-Cultural Perspective', *Comparative Studies in Society and History* 11: 55–78.

Green, J. B. and M. D. Baker (2000), *Rediscovering the Scandal of the Cross: The Atonement in the New Testament and Contemporary Contexts*, Downers Grove: IVP.

Grieb, A. K. (2002), *The Story of Romans: A Narrative Defense of God's Righteousness*, Louisville: Westminster John Knox.

Griffith, H. (2001), ' "The First Title of the Spirit": Adoption in Calvin's Soteriology', *EvQ* 73.2: 135–154.

Gundry, R. (1985), 'Grace, Works and Staying Saved in Paul', *Bib* 60: 1–38.

Guthrie, D. (1981), *New Testament Theology*, Leicester: IVP.

Haacker, K. (2003), *The Theology of Paul's Letter to the Romans*, Cambridge: Cambridge University Press.

Hafemann, S. J. (1993), 'Paul and His Interpreters', in G. F. Hawthorne, R. P. Martin and D. G. Reid (eds.), *Dictionary of Paul and His Letters*, 666–679, Downers Grove: IVP; Leicester: IVP.

Hamilton, N. Q. (1957), *The Holy Spirit and Eschatology in Paul*, SJTOP 6, London: Oliver & Boyd.

Hansen, G. W. (1989), *Abraham in Galatians – Epistolary and Rhetorical Contexts*, JSNTSup 29, Sheffield: JSOT Press.

———(1994), *Galatians*, IVP New Testament Commentary, Downers Grove: IVP; Leicester: IVP.

Harris, M. J. (1990), *From Grave to Glory: Resurrection in the New Testament. Including a Response to Norman Geisler*, Grand Rapids: Zondervan.

———(1999), *Slave of Christ: A New Testament Metaphor for Total Devotion to Christ*, NSBT 9, Leicester: Apollos.

Hellerman, J. H. (2001), *The Ancient Church as Family*, Minneapolis: Fortress.

Hendriksen, W. (1981), *Exposition of Paul's Epistle to the Romans*, 2 vols., Grand Rapids: Baker.

Hengel, M. (1977), *Hellenism and Judaism*, 2 vols., Philadelphia: Fortress.

———(1991), *The Pre-Christian Paul*, Philadelphia: Trinity Press International.

Hengel, M. and A. M. Schwemer (1997), *Paul between Damascus and Antioch: The Unknown Years*, London: SCM.

Hester, J. D. (1968), *Paul's Concept of Inheritance: A Contribution to the Understanding of Heilsgeschichte*, SJTOP 4, Edinburgh: Oliver & Boyd.

Hodge, C. H. (1972), *A Commentary on Romans*, London: Banner of Truth.

———(1979), *Systematic Theology*, 3 vols., Grand Rapids: Eerdmans.

Hoehner, H. W. (2002), *Ephesians: An Exegetical Commentary*, Grand Rapids: Baker.

Hoekema, A. (1994), *Saved by Grace*, Grand Rapids: Eerdmans.

Hollingshead, J. M. (1998), *The Household of Caesar and the Body of Christ: A Political Interpretation of the Letters from Paul*, Lanham: University Press of America.

Hopkins, K. (1999), *A World Full of Gods: Pagans, Jews and Christians in the Roman Empire*, London: Phoenix.

Horrell, D. G. (2001), 'From *adelphoi* to *oikos theou*: Social Transformation in Pauline Christianity', *JBL* 120: 293–311.

Hurtado, L. W. (1993), 'Son of God', in G. F. Hawthorne, R. P. Martin and D. G. Reid (eds.), *Dictionary of Paul and His Letters*, 900–906, Downers Grove: IVP; Leicester: IVP.

———(1999), 'Jesus' Divine Sonship in Paul's Epistle to the Romans', in S. K. Soderlund and N. T. Wright (eds.), *Romans and the People of God: Essays in Honor of Gordon D. Fee on the Occasion of his 65th Birthday*, 217–233, Grand Rapids: Eerdmans.

———(2003), 'Paul's Christology', in J. D. G. Dunn (ed.), *The Cambridge Companion to St. Paul*, 185–198, Cambridge: Cambridge University Press.

Irenaeus (1995), 'Against Heresies', trans. A. Roberts and W. H. Rambaut, in A. Roberts and J. Donaldson (eds.), *Ante-Nicene Fathers*, vol. 1, 315–567, Peabody: Hendrickson.

Jeffers, J. S. (1991), *Conflict at Rome: Social Order and Hierarchy in Early Christianity*, Minneapolis: Fortress.

———(1999), *The Greco-Roman World of the New Testament Era: Exploring the Background of Early Christianity*, Downers Grove: IVP.

Jeremias, J. (1967), *Prayers of Jesus*, London: SCM.

———(1971a), *New Testament Theology*, vol. 1, London: SCM.

———(1971b), *New Testament Theology: The Proclamation of Jesus*, New York: Scribner's.

Jewett, R. (1997), 'Honor and Shame in the Argument of Romans', in V. Wiles, A. Brown and G. F. Snyder (eds.), *Putting Body and Soul Together: Essays in Honor of Robin Scroggs*, 253–278, Valley Forge, PA: Trinity Press International.

———(2003), 'Romans', in J. D. G. Dunn (ed.), *The Cambridge Companion to St. Paul*, 91–105, Cambridge: Cambridge University Press.

———(2004), 'The Question of the "Apportioned Spirit" in Paul's Letters: Romans as a Case Study', in G. N. Stanton, B. W. Longenecker and S. C. Barton (eds.), *The Holy Spirit and Christian Origins: Essays in Honor of James D. Dunn*, 193–206, Grand Rapids: Eerdmans.

Johnson, L. T. (2001), *Reading Romans: A Literary and Theological Commentary*, Macon, GA: Smyth & Helwys.

Joubert, S. J. (1995), 'Managing the Household: Paul as *paterfamilias* of the Christian Household Group in Corinth', in P. F. Esler (ed.), *Modelling Early Christianity: Social-Scientific Studies of the New Testament and its Context*, 213–223, London: Routledge.

Judge, E. A. (1960), *The Social Pattern of Christian Groups in the First Century*, London: Tyndale.

Käsemann, E. (1980), *Commentary on Romans*, trans. and ed. G. W. Bromiley, Grand Rapids: Eerdmans.

Kim, S. (1981), *The Origin of Paul's Gospel*, WUNT 4, Tübingen: Mohr Siebeck.

———— (2002), *Paul and the New Perspective: Second Thoughts on the Origins of Paul's Gospel*, Grand Rapids: Eerdmans.

Kittay, E. F. (1987), *Metaphor: Its Cognitive and Linguistic Structure*, Oxford: Oxford University Press.

Klein, W. W. (1990), *The New Chosen People: A Corporate View of Election*, Grand Rapids: Zondervan.

Klein, W. W., C. L. Blomberg and R. Hubbard (2003), *Introduction to Biblical Interpretation*, rev. ed., Nashville: Nelson.

Knight, G. A. F. (1998), *A Christian Theology of the Old Testament*, BTCL 21, Carlisle: Paternoster.

Kreitzer, L. J. (1994), 'Eschatology', in G. F. Hawthorne, R. P. Martin and D. G. Reid (eds.), *Dictionary of Paul and His Letters*, 253–269, Downers Grove: IVP; Leicester: IVP.

Kruse, C. G. (1996), *Paul, the Law and Justification*, Leicester: IVP.

Lagrange, M.-J. (1908), 'La Paternité de Dieu dans l'Ancien Testament', *RB* 5: 482–483.

Lakoff, G. and M. Johnson (1980), *Metaphors We Live By*, Chicago: University of Chicago Press.

Lampe, P. (1991), 'The Roman Christians of Romans 16', in K. P. Donfried (ed.), *The Romans Debate*, 216–230, Edinburgh: T. & T. Clarke.

———— (2003), *Christians at Rome in the First Two Centuries: From Paul to Valentinus*, Minneapolis: Fortress.

Lane, W. L. (1998), 'Roman Christianity during the Formative Years from Nero to Nerva', in K. P. Donfried and P. Richardson (eds.), *Judaism and Christianity in First-Century Rome*, 196–244, Grand Rapids: Eerdmans.

Lassen, E. M. (1997), 'The Roman Family: Ideal and Metaphor', in H. Moxnes (ed.), *Constructing Early Christian Families: Family as Social Reality and Metaphor*, 103–120, London: Routledge.

Leenhardt, F. J. (1961), *The Epistle to the Romans: A Commentary*, London: Lutterworth.

Leith, J. H. (1973), *Assembly at Westminster: Reformed Theology in the Making*, Atlanta: John Knox.

Liefeld, W. (1997), *Ephesians*, IVP New Testament Commentary, Downers Grove: IVP; Leicester: IVP.

Lightfoot, J. B. (1975), *The Epistle of St. Paul to the Galatians with Introductions, Notes and Dissertations*, Grand Rapids: Zondervan.

———— (1976), *Saint Paul's Epistle to the Philippians*, Grand Rapids: Zondervan.

Lincoln, A. T. (1990), *Ephesians*, WBC 42, Waco, TX: Word.

———(2002), 'The Stories of Predecessors and Inheritors in Galatians and Romans', in B. W. Longenecker (ed.), *Narrative Dynamics in Paul: A Critical Assessment*, 172–203, Louisville: Westminster John Knox.

Lloyd-Jones, D. M. (1974), *Romans: The Sons of God. An Exposition of Chapter 8:5–17*, Edinburgh: Banner of Truth.

Loane, M. L. (1968), *The Hope of Glory: An Exposition of the Eighth Chapter of the Epistle to the Romans*, London: Hodder & Stoughton.

Longenecker, R. N. (1990), *Galatians*, WBC 41, Waco, TX: Word.

Lull, D. J. (1980), *The Spirit in Galatia: Paul's Interpretation of Pneuma as Divine Power*, SBLDS 49, Chicago: Scholars Press.

Lyall, F. (1969), 'Roman Law in the Writings of Paul – Adoption', *JBL* 87: 456–468.

———(1984), *Slaves, Citizens, Sons: Legal Metaphors in the Epistles*, Grand Rapids: Zondervan.

Mace, D. R. (1953), *Hebrew Marriage: A Sociological Study*, London: Epworth.

Malherbe, A. J. (1995), 'God's New Family in Thessalonica', in L. M. White and O. L. Yarbrough (eds.), *The Social World of the First Christians: Essays in Honour of Wayne A. Meeks*, 53–66, Minneapolis: Fortress.

Malina, B. J. (1993), *The New Testament World: Insights from Cultural Anthropology*, rev. ed., Louisville: Westminster John Knox.

———(1996), *The Social World of Jesus and the Gospels*, London: Routledge.

———(2001), *The New Testament World: Insights from Cultural Anthropology*, 3rd ed., Louisville: Westminster John Knox.

Malina, B. J. and Neyrey, J. M. (1996), *Portraits of Paul: An Archaeology of Ancient Personality*, Louisville: Westminster John Knox.

Malina, B. J. and R. L. Rohrbaugh (1998), *Social-Science Commentary on the Gospel of John*, Minneapolis: Fortress.

Marshall, I. H. (1967), 'The Divine Sonship of Jesus', *Int* 21: 85–103.

———(1976), *The Origins of New Testament Christology*, rev. ed., Leicester: IVP.

Marshall, L. H. (1960), *The Ethics of the New Testament*, London: Macmillan.

Martin, D. B. (1996), 'The Construction of the Ancient Family: Methodological Considerations', *JRS* 86: 40–60.

Martin, R. P. (1990), *Reconciliation: A Study of Paul's Theology*, rev. ed., Grand Rapids: Zondervan.

Martyn, J. L. (1997), *Galatians: A New Translation with Introduction and Commentary*, New York: Doubleday.

Mawhinney, A. (1982), '*Huiothesia* in the Pauline Epistles: Its Background, Use, and Implications', PhD dissertation, Baylor University.

―――(1987), 'Baptism, Servanthood and Sonship', *WTJ* 49: 35–64.

―――(1988), 'God as Father: Two Popular Theories Reconsidered', *JETS* 31: 181–189.

―――(1992) 'Huiothesia in the Pauline Epistles: Its Background, Use and Implications', PhD dissertation, Baylor University.

―――(1993), 'The Family of God: One Model for the Church of the 90s', *Presbyterion: Covenant Seminary Review* 19: 77–96.

McFague, S. (1987), *Models for God: Theology for an Ecological Age*, London: SCM.

McGrath, A. (1988), *Justification by Faith: What it Means to us Today*, London: Marshall Pickering.

―――(2001a), *Christian Theology: An Introduction*, Oxford: Blackwell Press.

―――(2001b), *Knowing Christ*, London: Hodder & Stoughton.

McIntyre, J. (1992), *The Shape of Soteriology*, Edinburgh: T. & T. Clarke.

McKnight, S. (1995), *Galatians*, NIVAC, Grand Rapids: Zondervan.

McKnight, S. and I. H. Marshall (eds.), *Dictionary of Jesus and the Gospels*, 617–625, Downers Grove: IVP; Leicester: IVP.

Meeks, W. A. (1983), *The First Urban Christians: The Social World of the Apostle Paul*, New Haven: Yale University Press.

―――(1986), *The Moral World of the First Christians*, LEC 6, Philadelphia: Westminster.

―――(1993), *The Origins of Christian Morality: The First Two Centuries*, New Haven: Yale University Press.

Michaels, R. J. (1999), 'The Redemption of Our Body: The Riddle of Romans 8:19–22', in S. K. Soderlund and N. T. Wright (eds.), *Romans and the People of God: Essays in Honor of Gordon D. Fee on the Occasion of His 65th Birthday*, 92–114, Grand Rapids: Eerdmans.

Michel, O. (1975), *Der Brief an die Hebräer*, 7th ed., Göttingen: Vandenhoeck & Ruprecht.

Miller, J. C. (2001), 'The Romans Debate: 1991–2001', *CR:BS* 9: 306–349.

Montgomery Boice, J. (1986), *Foundations of the Christian Faith: A Comprehensive and Readable Theology*, Downers Grove: IVP; Leicester: IVP.

Moo, D. J. (1983), '"Works of the Law" and Legalism in Paul', *WTJ* 45: 73–100.

——— (1987), 'Paul and the Law in the Last Ten Years', *SJT* 40: 287–307.

——— (1991), *Romans 1 – 8*, WEC, Chicago: Moody.

——— (1996), *The Epistle to the Romans*, NICNT, Grand Rapids: Eerdmans.

——— (2000), *Romans*, NIVAC, Grand Rapids: Zondervan.

——— (2001), *Encountering the Book of Romans*, Grand Rapids: Baker Academic.

Moore-Crispin, D. R. (1989), 'Galatians 4:1–7: The Use and Abuse of Parallels', *EvQ* 60: 201–223.

Morris, L. (1960), *Spirit of the Living God*, London: InterVarsity Fellowship.

——— (1983), *The Atonement: Its Meaning and Significance*, Leicester: IVP.

——— (1988), *The Epistle to the Romans*, Grand Rapids: Eerdmans; Leicester: IVP.

Mounce, R. H. (1995), *Romans*, NAC 27, Nashville: Broadman & Holman.

Moxnes, H. (1988a), 'Honor, Shame, and the Outside World in Paul's Letter to the Romans', in J. Neusner et al. (eds.), *Essays in Tribute to Howard Clark Kee: The Social World of Formative Christianity and Judaism*, 207–218, Philadelphia: Fortress.

——— (1988b), 'Honour and Righteousness in Romans', *JSNT* 32: 61–77.

——— (1993), 'Honour and Shame', *BTB* 23: 167–172.

——— (1997), *Constructing Early Christian Families: Family as Social Reality and Metaphor*, London: Routledge.

Murray, J. (1960), *The Epistle to the Romans*, 2 vols., Grand Rapids: Eerdmans.

——— (1961) *Redemption Accomplished and Applied*, Edinburgh: Banner of Truth.

——— (1976), *Collected Works*, vol. 2, 223–234, Edinburgh: Banner of Truth.

Newman, B. M. and Nida, E. A. (1973), *A Translator's Handbook on Paul's Letter to the Romans*, Stuttgart: UBS.

Neyrey, J. N. (2004) *Render to God: New: Testament Understanding of the Divine*, Minneapolis: Fortress.

Ninan, I. (1994), 'Jesus as the Son of God: An Examination of the Background and Meaning of "Son of God" in Paul's Christology with Particular Reference to Romans 8', PhD dissertation, Coventry University.

O'Brien, P. T. (1994), 'Benediction, Blessing, Doxology, Thanksgiving', in G. F. Hawthorne, R. P. Martin and D. G. Reid (eds.), *Dictionary of Paul and His Letters*, 68–71, Downers Grove: IVP; Leicester: IVP.

———(1999), *The Letter to the Ephesians*, Pillar New Testament Commentary, Leicester: Apollos.

Obeng, E. A. (1986), 'The Origin of the Spirit Intercession Motif in Romans 8:26', *NTS* 32: 621–632.

———(1988), 'Abba, Father: The Prayer of the Sons of God', *ExpTim* 99: 363–366.

Olyott, S. (1979), *The Gospel as it Really Is: Paul's Epistle to the Romans Simply Explained*, Welwyn: Evangelical Press.

Orr, D. G. (1978), 'Roman Domestic Religion: The Evidence of the Household Shrines', *ANRW* 16.2, 1557–1591, Berlin: de Gruyer.

Osiek, C. and D. L. Balch (1997), *Families in the World of the New Testament: Households and House Churches*, Louisville: Westminster John Knox.

Packer, J. I. (1988), *Knowing God*, London: Hodder & Stoughton.

Palmer, H. E. (1958), *The Holy Spirit*, Grand Rapids: Baker.

Patzia, A. G. (1995), *Ephesians, Colossians, Philemon*, NIBCNT, Peabody: Hendrickson; Carlisle: Paternoster.

Perdue, L. G. (1997), 'The Household, Old Testament Theology, and Contemporary Hermeneutics', in D. S. Browning and I. S. Evison (eds.), *Families in Ancient Israel*, 223–258, Louisville: Westminster John Knox.

Petersen, N. R. (1985), *Rediscovering Paul: Philemon and the Sociology of Paul's Narrative Thought World*, Philadelphia: Fortress.

Peterson, D. (1995), *Possessed by God: A New Testament Theology of Sanctification and Holiness*, NSBT 1, Leicester: Apollos.

Peterson, R. A. (2001), *Adopted by God: From Wayward Sinners to Cherished Children*, Phillipsburg, NJ: Presbyterian & Reformed.

Porter, S. E. (2003), 'Family in the Epistles', in R. S. Hess and M. D. R. Carroll (eds.), *Family in the Bible: Exploring Customs, Culture, and Context*, 162–165, Grand Rapids: Baker Academic.

Räisänen, H. (1983), *Paul and the Law*, Tübingen: Mohr.

Rawson, B. (1986), 'The Roman Family', in B. Rawson (ed.), *The Family in Ancient Rome: New Perspectives*, 1–57, Ithaca: Cornell University Press.

——— (1991), *Marriage, Divorce and Children in Ancient Rome*, Oxford: Clarendon.

Rees, T. (1977), 'Adoption', in G. W. Bromiley (ed.), *International Standard Bible Encylopedia*, vol. 1, A–D, 53–55, Grand Rapids: Eerdmans.

Richards, R. E. (2004), *Paul and First-Century Letter Writing: Secretaries, Composition and Collection*, Downers Grove: IVP; Leicester: Apollos.

Ridderbos, H. (1977), *Paul: An Outline of his Theology*, London: SPCK.

Rogers, C. L., Jr and C. L. Rogers III (1998), *The New Linguistic and Exegetical Key to the Greek New Testament*, Grand Rapids: Zondervan.

Rollins, W. G. (1987), 'Greco-Roman Slave Terminology and Pauline Metaphors for Salvation', in K. Richard (ed.), *Society of Biblical Literature 1987 Seminar Papers*, 100–110, Atlanta: Scholars Press.

Roon, A. van (1992), *The Authenticity of Ephesians*, NovTSup 39, Leiden: Brill.

Rossell, W. (1952), 'New Testament Adoption: Greco-Roman, or Semitic?', *JBL*: 233–234.

Rowdon, H. H. (1978), 'Adoptionism', in J. D. Douglas (ed.), *The New International Dictionary of the Christian Church*, 2nd ed., 13–14, Exeter: Paternoster.

Russell, W. B. (1997), *The Flesh/Spirit Conflict in Galatians*, Lanham: University Press of America.

Ryken, L., J. C. Wilhoit and T. Longman III (1998), *Dictionary of Biblical Imagery*, Downers Grove: IVP; Leicester: IVP.

Sacks, S. (ed.) (1978), *On Metaphor*, Chicago: University of Chicago Press.

Saller, R. P. (1984), '*Familia, Domus* and the Roman Conception of the Family', *Phoenix* 28: 336–355.

——— (1994), *Patriarchy, Property and Death in the Roman Family*, Cambridge: Cambridge University Press.

Sampley, J. P. (1995) 'Romans in a Different Light: A Response to Robert Jewett', in D. M. Hay and E. E. Johnston (eds.), *Pauline Theology*, vol. 3: *Romans*, 109–129, Minneapolis: Fortress.

——— (ed.) (2003), *Paul and the Greco-Roman World: A Handbook*, Harrisburg: Trinity Press International.

Sanders, E. P. (1977), *Paul and Palestinian Judaism: A Comparison of Patterns of Religion*, Philadelphia: Fortress.

Sandnes, K. O. (1994), *A New Family: Conversion and Ecclesiology in the Early Church with Cross-Cultural Comparisons*, Studies in the Intercultural History of Christianity 91, Bern: Lang.

Schlatter, A. (1995), *Romans: The Righteousness of God*, Peabody: Hendrickson.

Schmidt, K. L. (1992), 'Horidzō', *TDNT* 5: 452–453.

Schnackenburg, R. (1991), *The Epistle to the Ephesians: A Commentary*, Edinburgh: T. & T. Clarke.

Schreiner, T. R. (1998), *Romans*, BECNT 6, Grand Rapids: Baker Academic.

——— (2001), *Paul, Apostle of God's Glory in Christ: A Pauline Theology*, Downers Grove: IVP.

Schweizer, E. (1993), '*Huiothesia*', *TDNT* 8: 397–399.

Scott, C. A. A. (1961), *Christianity According to St. Paul*, Cambridge: Cambridge University Press.

Scott, J. M. (1992), *Adoption as Sons of God: An Investigation into the Background of HUIOTHESIA*, WUNT 52.48, Tübingen: Mohr.

——— (1993) 'Adoption, Sonship', in G. F. Hawthorne, R. P. Martin and D. G. Reid (eds.), *Dictionary of Paul and His Letters*, 15–18, Downers Grove: IVP.

Seifrid, M. A. (1993), *Justification by Faith: The Origin and Development of a Central Pauline Theme*, NovTSup 68, Leiden: Brill.

——— (1994), 'Blind Alleys in the Controversy over the Paul of History', *TynBul* 45: 73–95.

——— (2000), *Christ, our Righteousness: Paul's Theology of Justification*, NSBT 9, Leicester: Apollos.

Sherwin-White, A. N. (1978), *Roman Society and Roman Law in the New Testament*, Grand Rapids: Baker.

Smail, T. (1980), *The Forgotten Father: Rediscovering the Heart of the Christian Gospel*, London: Hodder & Stoughton.

Smith, M. S. (1970), 'Adoption, Greek', in N. G. C. Hammond and H. H. Scullard (eds.), *The Oxford Classical Dictionary*, 9, Oxford: Oxford University Press.

Snodgrass, K. (1996), *Ephesians*, NIVAC, Grand Rapids: Zondervan.

Soskice, J. (1985), *Metaphor and Religious Language*, Oxford: Clarendon.

Spanje, T E. van (1999), *Inconsistency in Paul? A Critique of the Work of Heikki Räisänen*, WUNT 110, Tübingen: Mohr Siebeck.

Spencer, S. F. (2003), *What Did Jesus Do? Gospel Profiles of Jesus' Personal Conduct*, Harrisburg: Trinity Press International.

Stacey, W. D. (1956), *The Pauline View of Man*, London: Macmillan.

Stanton, G. N. (2002), *The Gospels and Jesus*, 2nd ed., Oxford: Oxford University Press.

———(2003), 'Paul's Gospel', in J. D. G. Dunn (ed.), *Cambridge Companion to St Paul*, 173–184, Cambridge: Cambridge University Press.

Stegemann, W. (1978), 'War der Apostel ein Römischer Bürger?', *ZNW* 78: 200–229.

Stendahl, K. (1976), *Paul Among Jews and Gentiles*, Philadelphia: Fortress.

Stevenson-Moessner, J. (2003), *The Spirit of Adoption: At Home in God's Family*, Louisville: Westminster John Knox.

Stibbe, M. (1991), *John as Storyteller*, Cambridge: Cambridge University Press.

———(1999), *From Orphans to Heirs: Celebrating our Spiritual Adoption*, Oxford: Bible Reading Fellowship.

Stott, J. R. W. (1968), *The Message of Galatians*, BST, Leicester: IVP.

———(1979), *God's New Society: The Message of Ephesians*, BST, Leicester: IVP.

———(1994), *The Message of Romans*, BST, Leicester: IVP.

Stowers, S. K. (1986), *Letter Writing in Greco-Roman Antiquity*, Philadelphia: Westminster.

Strange, W. A. (1996), *Children in the Early Church: Children in the Ancient World, the New Testament and the Early Church*, Carlisle: Paternoster.

Strom, M. (2000), *Reframing Paul: Conversations in Grace and Community*, Downers Grove: IVP.

Stuhlmacher, P. (1994), *Paul's Letter to the Romans: A Commentary*, Louisville: Westminster John Knox.

Swete, H. B. (1931), *The Holy Spirit in the New Testament*, London: Macmillan.

Swetnam, J. (1967), 'On Romans 8:23 and the "Expectation of Sonship"', *Bib* 48: 102–108.

Talbert, C. H. (2002), *Romans*, Macon, GA: Smyth & Helwys.

Theron, D. J. (1956), '"Adoption" in the Pauline Corpus', *EvQ* 28: 6–14.

Thielman, F. (1993), 'Law', in G. F. Hawthorne, R. P. Martin and D. G. Reid (eds.), *Dictionary of Paul and His Letters*, 529–542, Downers Grove: IVP; Leicester: IVP.

Thompson, M. M. (2000), *The Promise of the Father: Jesus and God in the New Testament*, Louisville: Westminster John Knox.

Towner, P. H. (1993), 'Households and Household Codes', in G. F. Hawthorne, R. P. Martin and D. G. Reid (eds.), *Dictionary of Paul and His Letters*, 417–419, Downers Grove: IVP; Leicester: IVP.

Trueman, C. (2002), 'The Marcions Have Landed!', *Them* 28.1: 1–4.

Trumper, T. J. R. (1997), 'The Metaphorical Import of Adoption: A Plea for Realisation. II: The Adoption Metaphor in Theological Usage', *SBET* 15: 98–115.

———(2002), 'An Historical Study of Adoption in the Calvinist Tradition', PhD dissertation, University of Edinburgh.

———(2005), 'A Fresh Exposition of Adoption: I. An Outline', *SBET* 23: 60–80.

Tsumura, D. T. (1994), 'An OT Background to Rom. 8:22', *NTS* 40: 620–621.

Turner, M. (1996), *The Holy Spirit and Spiritual Gifts: Then and Now*, Carlisle: Paternoster.

Turner, N. (1980), *Christian Words*, Nashville: Nelson.

Vaux, R. de (1962), *Ancient Israel: Its Life and Institutions*, London: Darton, Longman & Todd.

Vèrmes, G. (1973), *Jesus the Jew: A Historian's Reading of the Gospels*, London: Collins.

Wallace, D. B. (1996), *Greek Grammar Beyond the Basics: An Exegetical Syntax of the New Testament*, Grand Rapids: Zondervan.

Walters, J. C. (2003), 'Paul, Adoption and Inheritance', in J. P. Sampley (ed.), *Paul in the Greco-Roman World: A Handbook*, 42–76, Harrisburg: Trinity Press International.

Wanamaker, C. A. (1980), 'The Son and the Sons of God: A Study in Elements of Paul's Christological and Soteriological Thought', PhD dissertation, University of Durham.

Wansink, C. S. (2000), 'Roman Law and Legal Systems', in C. A. Evans and S. E. Porter (eds.), *Dictionary of New Testament Background*, 984–991, Downers Grove: IVP; Leicester: IVP.

Watson, A. (1975), *Rome and the XII Tables: Persons and Property*, Princeton, NJ: Princeton University Press.

Watson, F. (1991), 'The Two Roman Congregations: Romans 14:1 – 15:13', in K. P. Donfried (ed.), *The Romans Debate*, 201–215, Edinburgh: T. & T. Clarke.

———(1986) *Paul, Judaism and the Gentiles: A Sociological Approach*, SNTSMS 56, Cambridge: Cambridge University Press.

Watt, J. G. van der (1999), *Family of the King: Dynamics of Metaphor in the Gospel according to John*, Leiden: Brill.

Wedderburn, A. J. M. (1988), *The Reasons for Romans*, Edinburgh: T. & T. Clarke.

Weima, J. A. D. (1990), 'The Function of the Law in Relation to Sin: An Evaluation of H. Räisänen', *NovT* 32: 219–235.

——— (1994), *Neglected Endings: The Significance of the Pauline Letter Closings*, JSNTSup 101, Sheffield: JSOT Press.

Wenham, D. (1995), *Paul: Follower of Jesus or Founder of Christianity?* Grand Rapids: Eerdmans.

Westerholm, S. (1997), *Preface to the Study of Paul*, Grand Rapids: Eerdmans.

Westhead, N. (1995), 'Adoption in the Thought of John Calvin', *SBET* 13: 102–115.

Whaling, T. (1923), 'Adoption', *Princeton Theological Review* 21: 223–235.

White, J. L. (1986), *Light from Ancient Letters*, Philadelphia: Fortress.

——— (1992a), 'God's Paternity as Root Metaphor in Paul's Conception of Community', *Foundations and Facets Forum* 8.3–4: 271–295.

——— (1992b), *Light from Ancient Letters*, Philadelphia: Fortress.

Williams, D. J. (1999), *Paul's Metaphors: Their Character and Context*, Peabody: Hendrickson.

Witherington, B., III (1990), *The Christology of Jesus*, Minneapolis: Fortress.

——— (1997), *Grace in Galatia: A Commentary on Paul's Letter to the Galatians*, Grand Rapids: Eerdmans.

——— (1998), *The Paul Quest: The Renewed Search for the Jew of Tarsus*, Downers Grove: IVP; Leicester: IVP.

Witherington, B., III with D. Hyatt (2004), *Paul's Letter to the Romans: A Socio-Rhetorical Commentary*, Grand Rapids: Eerdmans.

Witherington, B., III and L. M. Ice (2002), *The Shadow of the Almighty: Father, Son and Holy Spirit in Biblical Perspective*, Grand Rapids: Eerdmans.

Woodhouse, W. J. (1908), 'Adoption, Roman', in J. Hastings (ed.), *Encyclopaedia of Religion and Ethics*, vol. 1, 111–114, Edinburgh: T. & T. Clarke.

Wright, C. J. H. (1990), *God's People in God's Land: Family, Land and Property in the Old Testament*, Grand Rapids: Eerdmans.

————(1992), *Knowing Jesus through the Old Testament*, Downers Grove: IVP.

————(1997), *God's People in God's Land: Family, Land and Property in the Old Testament*, BTCL 14, Carlisle: Paternoster.

————(2001), *The Message of Ezekiel*, BST, Leicester: IVP.

Wright, N.T. (1991), *The Climax of the Covenant*, Edinburgh: T. & T. Clarke.

————(1992), *The New Testament and the People of God*, London: SPCK.

Yarbrough, L. O. (1995), 'Parents and Children in the Letters of Paul', in L. M. White and O. L. Yarbrough (eds.), *The Social World of the First Christians: Essays in Honor of Wayne A. Meeks*, 126–141, Minneapolis: Fortress.

Ziesler, J. (1992), *The Epistle to the Galatians*, London: Epworth.

Zuck, R. B. (1996), *Precious in His Sight: Childhood and Children in the Bible*, Grand Rapids: Baker.

Index of authors

223

Index of Scripture references

Index of extrabiblical and classical references